ADVANCE PRAISE FOR

The Lowrider Studies Reader

"This groundbreaking book presents a wide overview of lowrider (counter)culture which combines identity politics with systemic activism. Particularly, contributors articulate and illustrate how lowriding is more than a hobby–more than just cars and even bikes–but a cultural expression and mode of healing that is multidimensional and multinational."

> —Nathan Poirier, Assistant Editor of Journal for Critical Animal Studies

"This edited collection is as innovative as it is timely. The growing field of Lowrider Studies–and scholars of social justice more broadly–will undeniably benefit from the contributors' diverse array of theories and stories."

> —Dr. S. Marek Muller, Assistant Professor of Rhetorical Studies
> Florida Atlantic University

"The Lowrider Studies Reader perfectly captures, articulates and speaks-to the power and potential of Lowrider culture as a liberatory conception. In doing so the book makes an original and extremely timely contribution to the literature, and should be an "essential read" for many critical scholars and activist communities alike."

> —Dr. Richard J. White, Reader in Human Geography,
> Sheffield Hallam University, UK

"As an individual of Mexican descent who grew up adjacent to the Lowrider culture and not fully immersed in it, this book takes an interesting ride. Now that Anthony J. Nocella II, the co-founder of lowrider studies has decided to cruise his ranfla through the barrios of the mind, let us hope that this tentative car show just broadens the newly developed field."

> —Victor Mendoza, McNair Scholar, Texas Southern University

"Poetry in ese form, both of us blackened by the system this low ridin cry for freedom sheds light on the urgent need for solidarity."

> —Reece Graham-Bey, Director of Environmental Justice, Save the Kids

"The Lowrider Studies Reader ushers in an original subfield that intersects with many dominant disciplines--sociology, communication studies, performance studies, rhetoric, criminal justice and criminology, Lantinx and Chicana/o Studies, Cultural Studies, and so on. Full of thought provoking themes, the book views lowrider phenomena through wide-ranging issues of identity, power, culture, spirituality, resistance, and social justice. Get a copy and enjoy!"
—Dr. Jason Del Gandio, author of Rhetoric for Radicals:
A Handbook for 21st Century Activists

"The Lowrider Studies Reader provides priceless depth in understanding the cultural significance of lowriders, both in their Chicanx/Cholx/Latinx communities of origin, and by extension, globally. Revealing their role as an expression of resistance, aesthetics, cultural reconnection and reclamation, community healing, and solidarity amongst the world's colonized and oppressed, Lowrider Studies is a powerful collection of voices speaking up for the value of this subculture–and about the critical need to protect it from corporate co-optation/exploitation and other forms of violence and erasure under globalized neo-colonial Capitalism."
—Laura Schleifer, Co-founder of Plant the Land

"The Lowrider Studies Reader is a great introduction to the global, cultural, and political impact of lowriders. This inaugural book of the field shows how lowrider culture has both a liberatory effect for cholx, latinx, and chicanx communities while simultaneously being co-opted by oppressive cultures. This is a must read for anyone interested in the socio-political dynamics of lowrider culture."
—Dr. Lauralea Banks Edwards, Assistant Vice President for Institutional
Effectiveness, SUNY Delhi

"The Lowrider Studies Reader illustrates the history of youth and justice, with the development of a brilliant culture. It is a great primer for introducing the lowrider culture to students, as well as a needed compendium of contemporary literature."
—Lucas Alan Dietsche, Adjunct Professor, Adams State University

"The book is a beautiful ride of healing through culture, values, and liberation with Cholx, Latinx, and Chicanx empowerment in the driver's seat."
—Brock M. Smith, Co-founder, FourLifers Incorporated

"At last a book that holistically illuminates the evolution of a vital facet of Chicanx and Mexican-Indigenous culture that has too long been ignored."
—Isabella La Rocca González, artist and activist

The Lowrider Studies Reader

Lowrider Studies

Anthony J. Nocella II, William A. Calvo-Quirós,
and Elizabeth Gaeta Ramos
Series Editors

Vol. 1

The Lowrider
Studies Reader

Culture, Resistance, Liberation, and Familia

Edited by
Anthony J. Nocella II

PETER LANG

New York · Berlin · Bruxelles · Chennai · Lausanne · Oxford

Library of Congress Cataloging-in-Publication Control Number: 2023017973

Bibliographic information published by the Deutsche Nationalbibliothek.
The German National Library lists this publication in the German
National Bibliography; detailed bibliographic data is available
on the Internet at http://dnb.d-nb.de.

Photography of car by Chis Cano Photography LLCCar

Cover image: The owner of the car featured on the front cover is Mel Garcia with Firme
Image Car Club, Salt Lake, Utah. The car's name is Firme 48.

Cover art by Ricardo Cortez, Lowrider Fever LLC, lowriderartist@gmail.com

ISSN 2831-4468 (print) ISSN 2831-4476 (online)
ISBN 9781433197482 (paperback)
ISBN 9781433197475 (hardback)
ISBN 9781433197260 (ebook)
ISBN 9781433197277 (epub)
DOI 10.3726/b20708

© 2024 Peter Lang Group AG, Lausanne
Published by Peter Lang Publishing Inc., New York, USA
info@peterlang.com - www.peterlang.com

This publication has been peer reviewed.

Table of Contents

Acknowledgments

I would like to thank all the contributors of this book Frank Hernandez, Selinda Guerrero, William A. Calvo-Quiros, John Ulloa, Ben Chappell, Daniel Osorio, Xris Macias, Lea Lani Kinikini & Marlena Wolfgramm, Dionicio Miguel Garcia, David Escobar, Juan Roman Medina, Martín Morales Ramírez, Elizabeth G. Ramos, Guillermo Avilés-Rodríguez, Estella Inda, Kathryn Blackmer Reyes, Julia Curry Rodriguez, and Luis Alvarez. I would also like to thank Jackie, Dani and everyone at Peter Lang Publishing who have been kind, respectful, and dedicated to scholarship, inclusive, equitable, and just. I would like to thank my family too—Kris, Chris, Rick, Nicky, Angelina, Journey, Connor, Logan, Mom (Ruth), Dad (Tony), Kim, Si, Emma, Lucy, Delano, Vaughn, Rachel, Beth, Sara-Katherine, Gloria, the Johnson family, Dwight, Anthony, Gwen, Manny, Tyler, Mckenzie, Arva, and Brianna. I would like to thank my friends Ben, Jay, Emily, David R., Julia, Antonette, Kate, Katie, Eden, Danielle, Nelson, Ryan, Jeff, Gina, Rita, Gloria, Mike Hanseen, Brad, Chris, Rob, Mark, Joey, Amber George, Laura, Lucas, Reece, Alisha, Lou, Daphne Jackson, Moneka Stevens, Selinda, Mecke Nagel, Mark Seis, Jason Del Gandio, Sean Parson, Frank Hernandez, John Ulloa, Xris, Wes Wesson, Mac Allred, Chelsie, Christina, Elke, Emily, Rocio, Zane, Matt Sparks, Isabella, Nathan, Sarah, Sara, Josh, Brock, Lauralea, Marek, David B., Roderic, Ahmad Washington, Chandra, Brenda from the Dream Center at SLCC, Idolina at the West Valley Campus, Luke Reynolds, Pierre, Dallas, Erik J., Jeni Haines, Daniel White Hodge, Richard White, Will, Marisol, Tony Q., Brian, Jeremy, Brett, Cecile, Amy, Chris, Stephanie, Ricardo, Liz, William, Patrick, Alma, Hailey, Dani, Noel, Lucas, Cindy, Caleb, James, Nick, Juone, Peter, and Lauren. I would also like to thank the many supportive and kind reviewers of this book—Nathan Poirier, S. Marek Muller, Richard J. White, Victor Mendoza, Reece Graham-Bey, Scott Hurley,

Jason Del Gandio, Ken Tay, Laura Schleifer, Lauralea Banks Edwards, Lucas Alan Dietsche, Brock M. Smith, and Isabella La Rocca González. I would like to thank the many organizations and those involved in those organization I am involved with too—Save the Kids, Wisdom Behind the Walls, Poetry Behind the Walls, Institute for Critical Animal Studies, Society for Critical Animal Studies, Total Liberation Campaigns, Ecoability Collective, Peace Studies Journal, Peace Studies Conference, Academy for Peace Education, Peace and Justice Garden at SLCC, SLCC FDAR Senate Committee, SLCC JEDI Senate Committee, SLCC Department of Criminal Justice, Students for Peace Education, American Friends Service Committee, Alternatives to Violence Project, HIPP, Houston Animal Right Team, SLCC LGBT+ Steering Committee, Waterside Village HOA Board, Green Theory and Praxis Journal, Transformative Justice Journal, Salt Peace and Justice Center, Revolt bookstore, Arissa Media Group, Peace Studies Journal, Journal for Critical Animal Studies, Journal of Hip Hop Studies, Lowrider Studies Journal, and PARC and Social Science Program at Syracuse University.

Dedication

This book is dedicated to all of those that have been repressed or oppressed by colonialism, ICE, and borders because they were Cholx, Latinx, or Chicanx.

Foreword

Frank Hernandez

Lowrider and custom-designed cars have been a part of my life as far back as I can remember. I grew up during the late 1970s and early 1980s in West Dallas in the Elmer Scott Housing Projects. At that time, the projects were the greatest concentration of low-rise family public housing in the United States. We were all poor, our parents were young, and almost all families living there relied on government assistance. My grandparents lived in Ledbetter, a small barrio about as far west as one could go in Dallas. There, we had the Jaycee Center, where we learned to do ceramics, play ping pong, and swim. We had *tíos* and *tías* and cousins who lived in Oak Cliff, another isolated community in Dallas where mostly Black Mexican American families lived. Oak Cliff has changed over time and now serves as a hub for the area's Mexican American community. My formative years revolved around those three communities. It was there that I learned to appreciate *pan dulce*, the importance of a *quinceañera*, and the extent to which the design and accessories of one's car could shape one's identity.

When my immediate family and I visited my grandparents in Ledbetter, I grew quite personally familiar with lowriders and the lowriding community. It was not unusual to see four to five lowrider cars on the lawn of my grandparents' house. The hoods and the doors on the cars would be open, and more than likely, *Tejano* music would be playing. My *tíos* and their male friends would walk around each car, talking in detail about their vehicular work while taking sips from cans of Schlitz beer. They would start an engine to rev it up and show how loud and powerful it was. Other times, the gentlemen would bounce their cars, which was fascinating for me as a child to see. Then, my *tíos* and their friends were off to Oak Cliff to cruise Jefferson Street along with other lowriders across the city. Whether it was the best rims on the streets, a paint job like no other, the flashiest hydraulics, or beautiful chrome—all played a role in lowrider culture.

As a scholar today, I now have a much deeper understanding of the role of the lowrider and custom cars that my *tíos* and their friends worked on and shared with the community. The men loved these cars not just for their intrinsic beauty and uniqueness but also for their representativeness of Mexican American culture. The men were proud of this culture and used the cars to express, in a political way, their own identities. The cars were works of art that brought immediate and extended family members together. An important point is that lowrider culture often served to combat stereotypes about lowlifes and gangsters in the Mexican American community. In this regard, lowriding was a family-oriented culture passed down from one generation to the next. Younger family members would often start out with "lowrider" bicycles, designed in imitation of lowrider cars.

Even with all of the expressions of culture and family that stem from the lowriding community, some people still try to silence and obstruct this beautiful element of Mexican American culture. Cities like Dallas and Fort Worth continue to create new ordinances that affect where lowrider cars can be parked and where they can cruise.

This ground-breaking critical well-organized book edited by Anthony J. Nocella II, which is important for the academic world and for social justice movements, highlights lowriding and its relationship to culture, resistance, liberation, and *familia*. *The Lowrider Studies Reader: Culture, Resistance, Liberation, and Familia*, a collective of diverse lowrider scholars provides personal reminiscences from members of and witnesses to the lowriding communities in the United States and around the world. From a general perspective, the information herein can assist readers in thinking critically about spaces, communities, and the symbols that define culture and its connection to identity. Anthony J. Nocella II an outstanding intersectional scholar-activist and lowrider puts together a pivotal book that will lay the groundwork for the development the emerging new scholarly field, lowrider studies.

Preface

SELINDA GUERRERO

In May of 2021, Albuquerque Police Department, one of the deadliest police forces per capita in the United States, revealed they had spent $35,000 in tax dollars and an additional $60,000.00 of in-kind donations to build and display to the community a police lowrider car. This is a police department who has experienced all eight of the recommended reforms and still today remains under the Department of Justice oversight as one the most harmful cops in the entire U.S.

I bring this spectacle of cultural appropriation up as a deliberate example of the power of lowriding as a culture. Oppressive power structures of colonialism steal everything, even our swag! This structure of state violence recognized the power of our lowrider culture. They have attempted to infiltrate our communities by attempting to assimilate into our culture. There is a long history of this practice from confidential informants being on cops payroll, such as setting up community members to be arrested and even recently a string of Black and Brown folks being introduced as Police Ambassadors. Law enforcement continue to create tactics of assimilation to infiltrate and oppress our people. Last year during the debut of the police lowrider car we organized a protest and drove through the police car show with a megaphone playing political Hip Hop! We encouraged all true lowriding communities to rally against this so-called police lowrider car and continue to encourage them to run the police off the block every time they try to show up, even if it is in a lowrider.

You see, lowriding is a sacred culture of unity and pride. As long as I can remember one of my best memories was the feeling of sitting in the "ranfla" while hitting switches. There is nothing like that feeling in the entire world! If you could capture the essence of self determination and liberation in a moment in time that would be it. It is the pride of a badass ride, bouncing in freedom, music playing loud in the background with all the homies applauding and celebrating with you! It is a moment of feeling in total control and in full power of your own self, literally liberating. The unity of our people in true solidarity that nobody can mess with, it cannot be broken, we ride for each other, in the most literal sense of this phrase.

I was just a child when my cousin took me lowriding in his 1975 Impala hardtop with the bubble window in the back. I thought I was big shot cruising with the older cousins. Riding slowly and waving at our people in the neighborhood as we rolled by. That's when I recognized the unity that lowriding was all about. My cousin Bertha and I would walk to the back of the lowrider park San Gabriel Park in the 80's and 90's and car hop with all the homies to cruise on the weekends. We lived for that energy and joy. Seeing all our friends bragging about each other's cars, having spontaneous bounce contests and hitting three wheel motion. This was also the era of mini trucks, we had entire car clubs of mini trucks, some of the homies would put "juice" on the truck beds and make the beds dance while we cruised up and down Route 66, Central Ave in Albuquerque, NM. This was 2 miles of two lanes up and two lanes down bumper to bumper cruising on the weekends. After Hip-Hop concerts they would come out and cruise with us. I had the privilege to cruise Central with Kid Frost, Lighter Shade of Brown and DJ Quick. The Albuquerque Police have criminalized cruising on Central Avenue and continue harassing and criminalizing lowriders in all their hypocrisy.

New Mexico is also the home of Espanola, the lowrider capital of the world! In the 80's and 90's there was no cruising better than in Espa. Some of the most beautiful cars in the world are here in rural New Mexico. Most of these cars were featured in Lowrider Magazine, you knew you were the shit when you were featured in Lowrider Magazine. I had the honor of being a lowrider car model in the magazine in my younger years at the car shows. Lowriding culture has always been part of my life and lives deep in my soul. I told my kids they could not make me a grandma until I got my lowrider, so my grandbabies could hit switches with me as we cruise through our neighborhoods.

It is the essence of Chicano, Black, and Asian Cultures. This is a worldwide phenomenon for the reasons of power and unity. This is a culture that unites across race and ethnicity with a deep respect of solidarity. This is why lowrider culture is targeted by state violence, they fear our power and unity. When Chicano, Black, and Asian folks come together in power we can accomplish anything. That is the biggest fear of global imperialism, is when communities come together in unity and resistance.

In my work as a community organizer, I often talk about why we floss so much, why our swag is so important. When people experience oppression, sometimes all we have is HOPE and these pockets of liberation. We like to shine because they told us we couldn't, these are the experiences that give us the confidence to resist. Our people have always resisted and have always fought back since the colonization through genocide and enslavement of our people and we are still strong today standing on the shoulders of our ancestors and the old school values.

So, for all the snitches and police collaborators, our message is clear this is a culture so deep and so solid it cannot be shaken. During the 2020 uprisings, police believed they would have an advantage of pushing the uprising into downtown Albuquerque where the lowriders cruise in Albuquerque on Sunday evenings. Instead of an advantage, the lowrider community was ignited to join the uprising and went into an all night stand off with riot police. This is the night I was shot by a rubber bullet while resisting with the youth who were downtown for lowriding. This night was one of the most powerful and profound nights of uprising I supported in my work as an organizer against state violence because I witnessed young people who were not even at the protest be ignited and they were with the shit! They have felt the pressure state violence profoundly from restrictions on cruising, window tint, volume of music, too many people standing together, driving past the same location too many times, etc. They took to the streets in powerful unity and resistance and that is the power of the lowriding community!

As someone who grew up in Hip-Hop, lowriding is like an underlying element of Hip-Hop or maybe the 10th element. Lowriding holds the essence of the elements of Hip Hop from the cars dancing on their switches in the spirit of breakdancing; the woofers blast the beat of bass in your ear in true DJ fashion; most cars are designed with some of the most profound graffiti art that exists on the planet; you must be an entrepreneur to have the privilege of the investment of a lowrider; the swag because you must be dressed to impressed if your taking your car out for a cruise, and most of all we have the power of street knowledge.

This is a story that is so big and so deep and why this book is so important. I am so grateful for our stories to finally be told because we are a mighty people with deep culture. That is why we cannot be infiltrated and will protect and hold sacred forever our lowrider culture.

Introduction: The Rise of Lowrider Studies

GUILLERMO AVILES-RODRIGUEZ, WILLIAM A. CALVO-QUIROS,
ANTHONY J. NOCELLA II, AND ELIZABETH G. RAMOS

For over three decades lowriders have been written about by scholars, specifically, from social, historical, and anthropological perspectives (Bright, 1994; Chappell, 2012; Plascencia, 1983; Sanchez, 2017; Sandoval, 2003; Tatum, 2011; Rivera, 2014; & Usner, 2016). This book is a collective of original articles that emerged prior to and from the 1st Annual International Lowrider Studies Conference that was free, open to the public, recorded, online, and hosted by Save the Kids. The conference was chaired by John Ulloa, Xris Macias, and Anthony J. Nocella II, with no budget and while advertised for months, was put together in about three weeks. The conference was a hit with great energy, synergy, and a location for the development of collaboration and friendships. Two projects that emerged from this conference were the *Lowrider Studies Journal* that is online and being edited by Elizabeth G. Ramos and the *Lowrider Studies book series* with Peter Lang Publishing being edited by us, Guillermo Aviles Rodriguez, William A. Calvo-Quiros, Anthony J. Nocella II, and Elizabeth G. Ramos.

It is without doubt that lowrider culture has legitimacy, meaning that it is valid and a highly complex and established identity and culture. Lowrider studies is a recent development in the last two years, with this book being the first book dedicated to the field. Lowrider studies aims to articulate and archive the lowrider culture, while also giving creditability to its knowledge, ethics, philosophy, and behaviors. Lowrider culture is a liberatory conception, from a place of racial oppression. Lowrider studies is grounded in critical pedagogy, critical race theory, intersectionality, anti-colonialism, anti-imperialism, liberation, art, resistance, and self-determination (Bell 1993; Crenshaw, 1989; Fanon, 1961; & Freire, 1970).

The lowrider culture emerged in the early 1940s with fashion, style, and attitude rooted from the Cholx, Chicanx, and Latinx culture (Penland, 2003; Tatum, 2011). It was about no fear, confidence, and being present, therefore leaving and coming slow, low, and chill (i.e., relaxed as one could be). Lowriders would also commonly say in English they were, "just chillin." This attitude developed bright, chromed, gold, elaborate, candy-colored cars, bicycles, and an art that today has gone global (Kercher, 2015; Lopez Pulido, 2015) and with museums dedicated to the lowrider culture (Boyle, 2016). The culture is rooted in traditional Chicanx family values and the restoration of things that are old into new. Similar to the Hip Hop culture, lowrider culture instead of being founded by Black youth, was founded by Brown youth. Lowrider culture was a way to be involved in art from cars, clothes, bicycles, and tattoos, similar to rapping, dancing, graffiti, and DJ'ing within the Hip Hop culture. The lowrider culture and Hip Hop culture have become an outlet for marginalized, oppressed communities to express themselves, while avoiding violence, drugs, domestic violence, and suicide.

Book Outline

Chapter 1, "Cruising into the Classroom: Lowriding as a Pedagogical Practice," by John Ulloa treats the reader to an introduction to the possibilities of how lowriding can be used as an effective teaching tool to reach students of color. Further, he argues that lowrider pedagogy is a viable culturally relevant and culturally sustaining pedagogical framework. Drawing from his positionality as a lifelong lowrider and nearly twenty years of teaching in the California community college system, Ulloa leans into his intersectionality. By relying upon a critical ethnographical approach coupled with portraiture, Ulloa's central argument is that equitable education is fully-customizable education.

Chapter 2, "Aesthetics and the Battle for the Eastside: Google's Lowrider, Chicano Park, and the Performance of Space," by Ben Chappell discusses lowriding's ability to be both a tool of resistance to normative culture, when deployed by subaltern subjects and a tool for gentrification when mobilized by multinational corporations. Though the primary focus is lowriding in East Austin, Texas, the chapter has resonances with many other communities of color who are dealing with the consequences of gentrification and realizing the way money can co-opt cultural signifiers for their own benefit and profit— with no concern for the bodies of color that created the tradition, community, and culture revolving around lowriders. Through its examination of space this chapter illustrates how confrontations over space have at their core a tension between real lives versus real estate.

Chapter 3, "East Side Hero," by Daniel Osorio catalogues the injustices perpetrated on people of color in the recent past and points out the recent escalation of antagonistic behavior against primarily subaltern subjects. Osorio outlines some of the ways that Chicano/Latinx youth are systematically attacked and torn asunder with the help of mainstream media. In colloquial language he relates personal experiences where his life was endangered by a type of systematic warfare on his identity—a warfare in which lowriders and their beautiful lowriding culture became a chariot and shield.

Chapter 4, "Our Existence is Resistance," by Xris Macias scrutinizes lowrider culture for its ability to aid in the resistance to oppression, education of the next generation and as a means to reclaim one's lost heritage and connecting to a rich pre-conquest history and tradition all as a way of *rebrowning America*, or reasserting this continent's indigenous roots. In this way lowriders cars and enthusiasts create a safe and unique cultural space that in many cases exists as an alternative to mainstream exclusionary and white spaces. Part of the chapter is dedicated to the mobilization of lowrider art as a form of both protest and education, Macias scrutinizes murals and their ability to narrate stories, and make strong political statements. For him, lowriders are artistic, poetic and cultural manifestations of sacred stories of survival that in turn allow them to become a connection and an acknowledgement of lost heritage, knowledge, and lands.

Chapter 5, "Maui the Lowrider: Healing the House of Trouble," by Lea Lani Kinikini and Marlena Wolfgramm, explores the legacies of Kita Lealao, founder and member of The Uso Family Car Club in California, and its network of over 38 club chapters located around the world. In particular, they analyze the healing practices that emerged by the intersection of Polynesian Samoan alofa (love), ainga (kinship), and Chicano ethics and cultural values of love, care, and mutual recognition within the case of the Uso Family Lowrider community. As they explain, healing tends to be overlooked in many lowrider studies because of the predominant position of lowrider's visual elements in the definition of the field. The authors demonstrate that lowrider culture is not only about restoring cars, but about deconstructing laws and norms, while creating a new self within the individuals engaging in lowriding. As Kinikini and Wolfgramm explain, both the car(s) and the person(s) are the manifestations of broader community values.

Chapter 6, "Car Clubs to Cohorts" by Dionicio Miguel Garcia, explores lowriders' processes of car modifications and customizations as physical manifestations of a broader project of self-crafting and care that defines the

Latina/o community. Presented as a beautiful self-reflective account of his own experience growing up within a lowrider family, Garcia explores the struggles created by the stereotypes (and rejection practices) imposed on his lowrider community by school officials, academics, and the mass media. He explains how solidarity within a divided community because of oppression is essential. Furthermore, Garcia describes how the lowrider culture has provided him with a new transformative pedagogy, a repertoire of support practices, for students to engage with their own histories and cultures related to liberation and oppression. For Garcia, self-crafting and car customizations are intimately connected by the desire for a collective better future for all. For Garcia the personal is collective.

Chapter 7, "Lowrider Healing," by David Escobar, examines the use of color within lowriding both as an act of defiance and auto-definition. As he explains, the predominant use of bright colors in lowrider cars works not only as a disruptive mechanism against artistic normalcy that has been imposed (and expected) by society on Latinx communities, but they are "part of a healing methodology." Moreover, it manifests "a long trajectory of exercises in self-acknowledgment, a barrier against alienation [...and] a type of political resistance." For Escobar, healing within the lowrider community embraces not only colors but also "clothing, oldies music, Calo language, mural art tattoos, tortillas and a whole host of other elements, they all mix into medicine." A type of *cultura que cura*, that is "dynamic and always adjusting itself to fit the present" and its "contradictions."

Chapter 8, "It's Not a Hobby, It's My Culture," by Juan Roman-Medina, engages in a critical analysis of the disjunctions between the academic interpretations, definitions, and emphasis given to lowriders cars over the collective elements of the slow 'n low culture. As Roman-Medina explains, lowrider cars cannot be disassociated from the vast network of cultural artifacts and practices that surround them. This is why, according to Roman-Medina, cruising (more than driving) and lowrider music are so profoundly interrelated. For him, lowrider music and the emergence of particular songs, styles, and genres must be understood as historical markets of social change and cultural pride that are directly tied to political and social forces within and outside the lowrider community. As Roman-Medina shows, it is impossible to embrace the material culture manifested by lowrider cars without the society that produces and sustains them. Both are interconnected and codependent as expressions of the multidimensionality slow 'n low world.

Chapter 9, "El Campesino Project: *Conciencia y las Raices de Tu Causa*," by Martín Morales Ramírez, emphasizes the importance of knowing and understanding one's history as inspiration and motivation to keep the vision of those before us alive—*La Causa*. Martín Morales Ramírez shares his journey of struggle, discovery, and empowerment—for himself, his community, and generations to come. His lowrider and the El Campesino Project, provide him a means of demonstrating resistance, remembering history, and creating positive change by encouraging others to think and open their minds to greater possibilities beyond the agricultural fields and gang life. The expression of self and others through art is something passed along by our ancestors and something we can continue using constructively to elevate our communities.

Chapter 10, "Raza's Membership in Lowrider Car Clubs," by Elizabeth G. Ramos, focuses on how the lowrider culture burgeoned out of a time of conflict and oppression and evolved into a culture, a community, and a lifestyle that is rooted in Mexican American values, customs, and aspirations. It explores how a desire to be seen, respected, and accepted during a time when rasquachismo was the foundation of most efforts at survival or even progress evolved to an internationally distinguished culture. It explores the lived experiences of lowrider car club members—their values, the impact of lowriding on their identity, and the motivations they share. It aims at highlighting the positive aspects of lowriding and demystifying negative stereotypes. It demonstrates how being part of a lowrider car club serves as a support system, surrogate family, and trusted network of individuals that share the same passions in life—familia, cultura, pride, and classic cars.

Chapter 11, "Lowriding Murals: Freeways, Automobiles and Mobility," by Guillermo Aviles-Rodriguez, explores how the changes in aesthetic and mechanical ingenuity speak to the continuous movement, progress and evolution of Chicano Culture. It examines the many ways automobiles have been used by Mexican Americans as platforms for positive self-expression, evidence of achieving the American Dream, and resistance in response to sociopolitical pressures. Lowriders, in their design and purpose, have been deliberate, meaningful, and iconic both within Chicano communities across the United States and internationally—among enclaves that emulate the lowrider style, values, and customs. The chapter also speaks to the way lowriders have mobilized murals much in the same way that their ancestors did in ancient times. In this way a connection between the Mayans, Mexica, Incas and contemporary lowriders revels itself atop of lowriders and delivers messages, captures space and time, and in many cases memorializes loved ones.

Chapter 12, "Exploring San José's Lowrider Industries," by Estella Inda, Kathryn Blackmer Reyes, and Julia Curry Rodriguez, go beyond highlighting the positive aspects of lowriding as a culture to reflect the contributions made by individuals in the Mexican American / Chicano community in San

José's east side. It demonstrates that despite sociopolitical or economic hardships, the community of San Jose became a model of resilience and prosperity for other lowrider communities. Community members identified gaps in their resources and pioneered new avenues to better meet the needs of their increasingly segregated community. Lowrider culture goes beyond the cars and includes a variety of different industries and trades that work together (as networks and familia) to mobilize, empower, and facilitate growth within communities, like San José, California.

This collection edited over two years by Anthony J. Nocella II, is a gathering of diverse scholarly voices studying many different topics within the global lowrider culture. This book does not assume to be the be all and end all of lowrider studies, rather, it hopes to be a one of thousands of books within the field, movement, and culture of lowrider studies. This book will hopefully grow with more editions, edits, and more contributions. We hope you engage and enjoy this book as you immerse yourself into the lowrider studies essential elements—culture, resistance, liberation, and familia.

References

Bell, D. (1993). *Faces at the bottom of the well: The permanence of racism.* Basic Books.

Boyle, M. (2016). Take a little trip: A cruise through lowrider history in New Mexico. *The New Mexican's Weekly Magazine of Arts, Entertainment & Culture.* http://www.santafenewmexican.com/pasatiempo/art/museum_shows/take-a-little-trip-a-cruise-through-lowrider-history-in/article_484e1da9-103d-5c93-877a-8b15747aa721.html

Bright, B. J. (1994). *Mexican American low riders: An anthropological approach to popular culture* (Publication No. 9514155) [Doctoral dissertation, Rice University]. ProQuest Dissertations & Theses Global database.

Chappell, B. (2012). *Lowrider space: Aesthetics and politics of Mexican American custom cars.* University of Texas Press.

Crenshaw, K. (1989). "Demarginalizing the intersection of race and sex: A black feminist critique of antidiscrimination doctrine, feminist theory and antiracist policies." *University of Chicago Legal Forum,* no. 1, 139–167.

Fanon, F. (1961). *The wretched of the Earth.* Grove Press.

Freire, P. (1970). *Pedagogy of the oppressed.* Continuum.

Kercher, S. (2015). Lowriding culture goes global. *New York Times,* p. 12. https://www.nytimes.com/2015/12/06/fashion/lowriding-culture-goes-global.html

López Pulido, A. (2015). San Diego lowriders go global. http ://laprensa-sandiego.org/featured/san-diego-lowriders-go-global/

Penland, Paige R. (2003). *Lowrider: History, Pride, Culture.* Minneapolis, MN.

Plascencia, L. F. B. (1983). Low riding in the Southwest: Cultural symbols in the Mexican community. In M. T. Garcia, F. Lomeli, M. Barrera, E. Escobar, & J. Garcia (Eds.), *History, culture, and society: Chicano Studies in the 1980s*. Bilingual Press/Editorial Bilingüe.

Rivera, S. J. (2014). *Lowriting: Shots, rides & stories from the Chicano soul*. Broken Sword Publications.

Sanchez, S. N. (2017). *Rooster tails, ranflas, and rags: The language and literacy practices of latin@ lowriders in San Antonio, TX* (Publication No. 10279011) [Doctoral dissertation, University of Texas-San Antonio]. ProQuest Dissertations & Theses Global database.

Sandoval, D. (2003). *Bajito y suavecito/Low and slow: Cruising through Lowrider culture* (Publication No. 3086760) [Doctoral dissertation, Claremont Graduate University]. ProQuest Dissertations & Theses Global database.

Tatum, C. M. (2011). *Lowriders in Chicano culture: From low to slow to show*. Greenwood.

Usner, D. J. (2016). *¡Órale! Lowrider: Custom made in New Mexico*. Museum of New Mexico Press.

1. Cruising into the Classroom: Lowriding as a Pedagogical Practice

John Ulloa

Introduction

Lowriding has been a huge part of my life ever since I can remember. My earliest childhood memories are sitting in front of the small television in our living room every week waiting to see the opening credits of Freddie Prinze's show, "Chico and the Man." In that opening sequence, real video footage showed everyday lives of real people in East Los Angeles. For me, the jewel in the crown was seeing lowriders on television, especially Jesse Valadez's *Gypsy Rose*. It was very familiar to me, and it looked—and felt—like being across town in South Modesto at my grandparents' house. I knew then at the age of 4 years old that lowriding was much bigger than being limited to the confines of the Mexican American barrio experience, the context in which I understood it in real life.

Although lowriding has transcended the confines of the barrio experience in the United States, and it is now global phenomenon, there is an opportunity to use lowriding as a pedagogical tool. The work is in forging a new space for lowriding in various teaching and learning spaces. Hip-hop pedagogy has been in existence for decades as an attempt to reach Black, Indigenous, People of Color (BIPOC) students through culturally relevant pedagogy. I am extending that ladder by placing more rungs to continue to elevate possibilities for engaging those same students through development of lowrider pedagogy.

Lowriding as Pedagogy

Lowriding as an artform, lifestyle, cultural practice, and more originated from the Mexican American barrio experience in the southwestern United

States. Largely considered "A Mexican Thing," lowriding has grown over the past 50 years into a global phenomenon (Williams, 2020). Global reach in various media formats has helped to propel lowriding to transcend beyond the confines of the barrios to the rest of the world. As it has grown, lowriding has also become more commonplace in educational spaces and academic institutions. However, the way lowriding has been used to date does not fully use the essence and special elements that have made it so popular. Therefore, there is a need to explore how the cultural elements of lowriding can be better incorporated into the teaching practices of educators working with BIPOC students. Although lowrider studies is a new and emerging field of study, my intent is to integrate and formally institutionalize lowrider studies into educational contexts. It is important to distinguish lowrider studies and lowrider pedagogy. Lowrider studies is the meta, or umbrella, under which lowrider pedagogy falls. In short, if lowrider studies is the hub of the wheel, lowrider pedagogy would represent the wheel's spokes. Lowrider pedagogy is the utilization and implementation of lowriding in any iteration, in any teaching and learning context as the centralized theme, topic, or approach.

Historically, lowriding has been criminalized and media depictions have contributed significantly to this trend. The Pachucos or Zoot Suiters in the 1940s were criminalized due to the Sleepy Lagoon murder, and the media helped to fan the flames of public beatings and humiliation of Pachucos (Gerber, 2018). Moving forward into the 1970s and 1980s, lowriding was associated with Cholos and gang culture (Cowan, 2004). Motion pictures in the 1970s and 1980s cosigned and perpetuated this narrative. However, the image of lowriding has changed in the contemporary period. Lowrider Magazine has a "Roll Models" series on YouTube, which features more coverage of global lowriding; this series has improved the image of lowriders. Lowriding is also used more on television in commercials and shows. The presence and use of lowriders in Gangsta Rap videos in the early 1990s was the first punctuated cultural diffusion of lowriders, followed by the rapid and nearly vertical ascendence of social media. Although the narrative has not completely flipped lowriding to a saintly image, it has certainly improved. Nonetheless, the history of lowriding the sum of the cultural parts and various facets of the lowriding diamond have presented possibilities to formulate and integrate it into educational spaces.

For the last 2 years in a row, the National Football League featured lowriding during the Super Bowl. In 2021, Modelo Beer released a commercial featuring Mark Machado aka "Mr. Cartoon," a prominent tattoo artist, graphic designer, graffiti artist, and all-around street culture icon. The 30 second commercial cost the beer manufacturer $5.5 million dollars, and four lowriders were included in the footage. Mr. Cartoon was depicted airbrushing a mural on one of the cars, tattooing, and seemingly enjoying time with friends drinking beer. Although these depictions are realistic and not over sensationalized, the focus was alcohol consumption and branding. The 2022 Super Bowl showcased lowriders during the halftime show, featuring Dr. Dre, Snoop Dogg, 50 Cent, Mary J. Blige, and Eminem. The show was nostalgic and greatly anticipated, featuring classic hip-hop artists. It is also notable that it took place in Los Angeles, the birthplace of Gangsta Rap and arguably lowriding, and three cars were used as stage props with dancers performing on the hoods of the cars. Within my own lowrider community, I observed controversy on the decisions regarding the limited number of cars and people dancing on them. The fact that the performers were largely of African descent immediately sparked criticism of the spectacle by those who claimed "real raza" would have never allowed this kind of performance. Therefore, the performance sparked racialization, an ongoing tension in lowriding culture.

Despite any criticism of the Super Bowl performance, the current popularity, intrigue, and captivating nature of lowriding culture provides an opportunity to use it as a viable classroom tool. There is an opportunity to take the sum of lowriding and its human complexities and develop it into a pedagogical framework. Although a body of academic lowrider literature exists, and some educators use lowriding as pedagogy, there is an absence of theoretical foundation or framework to effectively root and sustain lowrider studies as a field. Historically, lowriding has been negatively depicted in the media as a criminal element; yet, it is a culture of creativity and resistance against dominant paradigms through social, cultural, or artistic means. Lowriding offers multiple entry points to discuss, analyze, interpret, and bridge time periods on a myriad of issues affecting BIPOC communities. This work is an exploration of how a new pedagogical model can be created to recruit and retain historically minoritized students. As the state of California is making a push toward teaching ethnic studies, this initiative fits within that curricular reform.

Although there has been some acknowledgement of lowriding in educational spaces, the scope has been limited. Lowriding broke through to educational institutions largely through curated museum exhibits and installations. Exhibits and shows dedicated to lowriding culture have been featured across the country, including at the Smithsonian Institute (Parsons et al., 1999), San Diego Automotive Museum, Mission Cultural Center for Latino Arts, and even college campuses such as California State University, San Marcos. I have also contributed to this recognition of culture by curating an exhibit at Skyline College in San Bruno, CA. I have observed faculty over the last10 years in a range of disciplines using lowriding as pedagogy in ethnic studies, art, anthropology, history, and counseling. Although inclusion of lowriding history in educational spaces has been increasing, to date, it has been limited almost exclusively to teaching content. However, the rising popularity of lowriding and its rich cultural elements have suggested the need to move beyond teaching lowriding as content, and instead develop a formal pedagogical framework.

Engaging students, particularly Latina/o/x students, with the intention of improving their success and retention is necessary because the established (i.e., traditional) models are failing. Using lowriding as pedagogy in framing the teaching and learning experiences for students who identify with lowriding will help mitigate high attrition rates and aid in student centeredness, student engagement, and ultimately, student success. By examining Garcia's (2021) critical car culture narrative, rooted in Yosso's (2006) counternarrative work, lowrider pedagogy is an opportunity to synthesize critical race theory (Ladson-Billings & Tate, 1995) and Paris's (2012) culturally sustaining pedagogy. As the state of California is making ethnic studies an academic requirement, all teachers could use lowrider studies to reach students with a new and fresh pedagogical framework, whether they are lowriders or not.

Theoretical Frameworks: Building Upon Funds of Knowledge

All lowriders have six elements in common: individuality, creativity, community, family, history, and culture. These six elements are drawn from my lifelong involvement in lowriding and derived from the last 15 years of my participant observation fieldwork documenting the globalization of lowriding culture. This initial assessment has demonstrated a connection to other asset-based theories and pedagogical strategies to help determine the potential of a lowriding pedagogical framework. By grounding lowrider pedagogy in these universal elements, educators have access to an asset-based framework to draw upon. In my teaching, I have successfully used these elements, and these patterns are echoed in Garcia's (2021) work. The six universal elements of lowriding provide a valuable lens to center the student's experience in their educational journey.

Moll et al. (1992) created a groundbreaking asset-based educational framework, funds of knowledge (FoK), which recognizes, celebrates, and incorporates a student's knowledge acquired in their social and cultural contexts outside of the classroom. Garcia's (2021) critical car narratives build on this general approach by specifically using lowriding counternarratives to have students better understand Los Angeles history, centering themselves to make connections between their contemporary lived experiences and situating themselves to challenge historical narratives. My work extends and builds on Garcia's work by developing lowrider pedagogy from my perspective as an educator and life-long lowrider.

In summation, the six universal elements of lowriding serve as crucial components in which lowrider pedagogy can be established as a framework and built on, interpreted, and used based on the teaching style and subject matter of the educator. This framework provides a blueprint to make a relatable and coherent set of materials and instruction approach based on lowriding. These elements are shared by all lowriders and can be applied to all students regardless of background, although the intent of lowrider pedagogy is to foster and improve the teaching and learning experiences for BIPOC students, primarily Latina/o/x students.

Leadership Implications

The leadership style that most connects to lowrider pedagogy is transformative leadership. According to Shields (2010):

> The focus on the moral purposes or ends of leadership has led to both transformational and transformative concepts. It is patently obvious that both theories of leadership – transformational and transformative – have at their heart the notion of transforming or changing something. (p. 564)

Lowrider pedagogy is designed with change at the forefront. Therefore, my attempt to offer a new paradigm to reach students is a cornerstone and motivating factor for creating this pedagogy. As such, it makes sense that transformative leadership would support a new way of reaching students.

Shields (2010) was correct in saying transformative leadership has a goal to "create learning contexts or communities in which social, political, and cultural capital is enhanced in such a way as to provide equity of opportunity for students as they take their place as contributing members of society" (p. 572). The implications of developing and implementing lowrider pedagogy though transformative leadership set the stage for a completely customizable educational experience for students and the opportunity for creating a more dynamic and holistically equitable teaching and learning environment. Transformative leadership would be the ideal support to allow lowrider studies and lowrider pedagogy to come to fruition to be institutionally sustainable over the long-term trajectory.

The Empirical Literature

Overview of the Related Literature

Lowrider studies and lowrider pedagogy are brand new to the educational field, and as such, my work seeks to ground and solidify lowriding as a pedagogical framework in the grand scheme of using lowriding in education. There has been ample work in the social science and humanities on lowriding history, culture, and lifestyle using various methodologies, such as ethnography, historical inquiry, oral history, and gender studies. Bright (1998) did groundbreaking anthropological fieldwork in the 1980s with her ethnographies on lowriding. Sandoval (2003) carried the torch for Bright with her historical work in the early 2000s, and she has remained the main academic voice for lowriding. Chappell's (2010) work moved the needle somewhat by adding to the cannon of publication on lowriding in the social sciences; however, he stayed in the hyper localized, myopia of his predecessors. All three of these academics wrote from an outsider's point of view, and each of them focused on local lowrider communities, and so their views of the broader scene and its authentic impacts were limited. Indeed, lowriding has always been bigger than how it has been presented in academia. As such, my work is a shift to reframe the discussion and viability of lowriding as a pedagogy, with the distinct purpose to formulate a theoretical framework that will apply lowriding as a teaching tool. Given that the state of California is making ethnic studies required curriculum, an opportunity now exists to develop and implement lowriding into academic programs. The larger goal is to develop a pedagogical framework applicable to the educational pipeline from early childhood through higher education and inclusive of community-based educational contexts. Due to limitations of space, this review is limited to focus on applications of FoK in secondary and higher education contexts. The discussion is organized to begin with an examination of FoK with Moll et al. (1992), set in an Arizona high school. In the tradition of Moll, I discuss Duncan-Andrade's (2007) seminal work in critical hip-hop pedagogy, which is also set in a high school context. I then trace the work of Garcia's critical car narratives (2021), as it is specific to lowrider culture and the most current in the field. I conclude the review by briefly discussing the work of Daddow (2016) who applies FoK in higher education educational settings. Daddow and Garcia both ground their research in an extensive body of work of Kiyama, who has published widely on FoK in higher education (with Ramos & Judy, 2021; Kiyama & Rios, 2017; Kiyama, 2010, 2011) Overall, this review demonstrates FoK is an appropriate baseline upon which to develop lowrider pedagogy.

Key Selected Studies

Moll's et al. (1992) "Funds of Knowledge for Teaching" set the stage for FoK as a theoretical approach in education. The goal of FoK is to incorporate an asset-based framework where the student's social and cultural contexts outside of the classroom function as contributors to their learning inside the institutional learning context or the classroom. Through ethnographic analysis of household dynamics, examination of classroom practices, and after school study groups with teachers, Moll et al. demonstrated that this approach accounted for the totality of the students' learning acquisition outside of school, informing how they approach learning in school, largely by the questions they ask rather than material taught by adults. Moll et al.'s findings showed FoK was (and still is) a key theoretical framework in connecting with Latina/o/x students, in this case, students of Mexican descent in Arizona. Having teachers as coresearchers was paramount in this groundbreaking qualitative study, and FoK sought to mitigate stereotyping of students by not only understanding their social and familial contexts, but also by incorporating that knowledge in the classroom as a new method of teaching and learning. Moll et al.'s work was key in asset-based pedagogy.

Duncan-Andrade's (2007) work challenged those educators who do not walk the talk. "Gangstas, Wankstas, and Ridas" by Duncan-Andrade (2007) is a necessary read for any educator working with urban youth as it contains gems for all educators to sharpen and refine their toolkits. The study highlighted five indicators for effective teaching over a 3-year program in Los Angeles. The author challenged the notion of equality in exchange for equity-practicing education, which is determined by context, or in his words, "specific needs." (ibid). Like Moll et al. (1992), Duncan-Andrade's methods for data collection were done through an ethnographic lens, including classroom visits, field notes, interviews with teachers, and artifact collection in the form of lesson plans and student assignments. The crux of the article was Duncan-Andrade's critique of the Gangsta educators, or the educators in power who are absolutist and punitive in their approach with students; Wankstas, who do not walk their talk, playing it safe; and Ridas, the educators who will go to great lengths for their students' success with total commitment. He continued to highlight and present his five pillars of effective practice: (a) critically conscious purpose, (b) duty, (c) preparation, (d) Socratic sensibility, and (e) trust. Duncan-Andrade's findings showed educators who possessed and engaged students with these five pillars were successful. As equity–practitioners and educators who are socially just in their orientation, this practice is educational heavy lifting. Duncan-Andrade (2007) concluded, "It is hard out there, and there are no shortcuts." (p. 636). Duncan-Andrade's work heavily informs lowrider pedagogy as it was designed to offer the Ridas an alternative pedagogical framework, and the Wankstas a new direction as emerging Ridas.

Currently, FoK is used as a viable asset-based, social justice framework, extending it beyond its original focus. Garcia (2021) represented the most current iteration and application of FoK in his critical car narrative approach in the discipline of art. Drawing on Kiyama and Rios's (2018) work on FoK, which is an extension of Ladson-Billings et al.'s (1995) culturally responsive pedagogy, Garcia used FoK to critically examine history through a social justice lens using art as the communicative component. Garcia's work also echoed Duncan-Andrade's (2007) critical hip-hop pedagogy. However, all roads seem to point to Freire and Ramos (1970). FoK is the fruit born from the deep social justice roots of Freire and the trunk of Ladson-Billings. My goal with this current work is to build on Garcia's critical car narrative approach, not only in depth, but also in breadth to continue the work he has done. The challenge is to apply FoK in a way that would work in all disciplines in addition to art, which Garcia has already developed.

Two major common themes run throughout the literature I reviewed thus far: (a) Western/Eurocentric pedagogical practices, or what might be considered colonial or colonizing pedagogy; and (b) educational inequities in education that need to be rectified. Garcia's (2021) work sought to challenge these narratives, thus connecting to Duncan-Andrade's (2007) work and building upon the call to flip or tell history as it is. As such, I have turned to Daddow's (2016) work in Australia, which argued that applying FoK in a university setting to historically marginalized students to level the playing field.

Thus far the work in this literature review focused on Latina/o/x and Mexican students, however considerations must be extended to students outside of these groups. Looking at non-traditional university students in Social work, she explored how using critical literacy through a FoK lens helped students achieve success Daddow (2016). Daddow's work is valuable, because it uses FoK with a very different population. However, the body of work by y Kiyama (Cite) can be used fruitfully in higher education. Limitation of space prohibit the discussion of Kiyama here. A choice I have made here, because Kiyama' work focuses on Latina/o/x students. Garcia (2021) was correct by reminding readers that if FoK is the accumulated home-based knowledge acquired by students, then all students' experiences provide assets for educators to draw upon, despite existing inequities.

In conclusion, from my review of the literature, I have determined more empirical research is needed to further explore how to ground lowrider pedagogy in education. The FoK framework provides a solid foundation to develop lowrider pedagogy because it is an asset-based approach. As such, I plan to integrate FoK into my work, providing a case study or further ethnographic research to afford me the opportunity to contribute to the field, thus extending the work in another rung on the FoK ladder.

My rationale for selecting these articles was that they represented a sampling of the evolutionary trajectory in the literature, including the most current and highly relevant published work in the field (Garcia, 2021). My problem of practice underscores a need to connect and engage with students in culturally relevant and sustaining ways that give students a voice by recognizing, honoring, and uplifting their voices in the processes of teaching and learning. This selection of literature does so in a collective harmonization of scholarly voices, which, together, identify the needs of relevant curriculum and pedagogy for students, particularly students of color, and real ways to implement strategies providing educational pivots that better serve BIPOC students.

Summary on the Empirical Literature

Moll et al.'s (1992) study of FoK was bookended nicely with Garcia's (2021) cultural car narratives as these studies are respective chronological bookends in the literature. Duncan-Andrade's (2007) work provided a more contemporary iteration of asset-based pedagogy, in a time where educators needed an explanation of how they might connect with students in a way that honored their cultural backgrounds and framed their experiences as assets coming into the classrooms. Daddow (2016) drew upon Moll et al.'s work, and later Kiyama and Rios's (2012) work, to demonstrate how FoK is useful and effective in Australia by working with international students.

In summation, these studies were asset-based coupled with the notion that students do better in educational contexts when they recognize they are represented in the curriculum and the process. In short, students do better when there is a direct connection to the process of teaching and learning. I am still trying to reconcile the reflexive question of, "How can the pedagogical processes be more enriching for all stakeholders and more importantly, more holistic in approach and design?"

Shifting Gears: The Qualitative Emic Perspective

I have drawn from (a) my lived experience, (b) my constant connection to the global lowriding community beginning with the local shop where I am building my latest car, (c) social media, (d) my travels, and (e) connecting with lowriders from other states and geographical locations. The deep dive into my work involves analysis and synthesis of the data. At this point, my corpus of qualitative data has grown, but it is still a work in progress. It is continuing to evolve, especially as I conduct more interviews and collect more data. In my research and data focus thus far, I employed narrative inquiry, portraiture, and autoethnography.

I have chosen three collaborators as portraiture to compliment my autoethnography. They are Ruben Diaz, Jr., Elton, and Shunsuke Ohsawa. My rationale for choosing these people as my portraits is rooted in core/periphery theory. Core/periphery is a subset of world systems theory, and it is early diffusionist theory which maps the way culture flows from ground zero, or the core to the periphery. So, I begin with Ruben "RJ" Diaz, Jr. from Newark, CA, who is the son of a Bay Area pioneer in lowriding since the late 1960s/early 1970s. RJ grew up in and around lowriding and he is the proprietor of RJ Hydraulics, a suspension modification shop, and much more!

The second portrait is Elton; he is the lead mechanic for the Hawaiian lowriding scene. He has been very active since the 1990s. Elton is the go-to mechanic, taking pride in the fact that he serves his lowriding community by keeping them going. He explained to me that seeing the "little girl's face" after he got her father's car going makes it "all worth it." I have presented him second because he is still in the United States, but farther from the core.

Shunsuke Ohsawa is third; I had an opportunity to cruise with him and interview him on my trip to Japan. The largest lowriding scene outside of the United States is in Japan; and Shun's club, Primera Car Club, sets a very high standard for lowriding. I should point out here that as of this writing, Shun is no longer the President of the Club. This was recently communicated to me via through Instagram direct messaging by the then Vice-President, Ken, as he is now the President of the club.

I am very emic in my perspective. I have been involved in lowriding my whole life. I am currently building my seventh car. I have had the opportunity to visit Japan to attend lowrider functions in Nagoya, and I have made multiple trips to Sao Paulo, Brazil. I have been the keynote speaker at lowrider events in educational institutions. I have an Instagram page with nearly 11,000 followers. I have a brand titled "Lowride Worldwide" and a podcast under the same name with episodes consisting of interviews with lowriders within and outside of the United States and people connected to lowriding. Although I am well-connected to the global lowriding community, I am finding it a challenge to shift gears into educational research. There is no shortage of sources in the social sciences. However, making this problem of practice fit theoretically into an educational context is more of a challenge.

Anderson (2006) stated autoethnography "demands enhanced textual visibility of the researcher's self" (p. 384). I have found this to be particularly true in my work thus far. I find it disingenuous to pretend there is a wall between myself and my research. Instead, I have made a concerted effort for these worlds to meld, and hopefully vulcanize. They are symbiotic as two hands washing the same face. I argue against Anderson's (2006) contention that, "the autoethnographer must not allow herself or himself to be drawn into participating heavily in activities in the field at the expense of writing field notes" (p. 389). Why not? The researcher could be missing an opportunity to bond, connect, and further cement relationships with collaborators, and they would potentially sacrifice an opportunity to become further emic in the research process. The note taking can wait, for sure.

Milner's (2007) article on positionality is a great anchor for researchers as he offers much to be considered. His call for the researcher to research "the self" and the self "in relationship to others" (Milner, 2007) is essentially what cultural anthropologists refer to as the comparative approach. Although I am very cognizant of race in the field, cultural differences in Japan and Brazil have posed challenges. Race is always at the forefront of my consciousness; however, Milner's argument is applied and filtered through the lens of class when it comes to my work. I find this true when dealing with blue collar car builders. It is often tricky to negotiate spaces and be authentically nonacademic when necessary. Chavez's (2012) work is a reminder to take all the background experience I have and incorporate it into my research, as they are inseparable.

With the portraits, I have leaned heavily on Benham's (2007) perspective for storytelling from an indigenous perspective. All three of my portrait collaborators, RJ, Elton, and Shun, have stories to tell. The sacred whole that Benham referred to is the entirety of lowriding culture. I see this as independent of time, space, or place. The challenge of indigenizing the narrative is tricky, as lowriding culture has what I call the creation myth, or the birthplace. As Los Angelinos have a very legitimate claim, other geographical locations also claim ground zero for lowriding. There are many sites and scenes for lowriding that extend throughout the world, and my portraits highlight that. The fact that I am trying to come from the emic or insider's perspective is an attempt to tell the story from within. As such, the complexities of these relationships echo Benham's call to tell the truth by using indigenous narrative.

Conclusion

Establishing and formalizing lowrider pedagogy and lowrider studies is a viable option to reach BIPOC students through transformative and community-based epistemologies. Educators who are lowriders and non-lowriding educators are using the resurgence in lowriding popularity as a teaching tool in various ways. As such, lowriding is a powerful pedagogical tool in classrooms, counseling sessions, community workshops, museum panel discussions, or informal teaching and learning contexts. It is an effective tool to use as an entry point to connect to deeper and more broadly reaching topics and themes such as cultural diffusion, identity, class, institutionalized racism, racial profiling, criminalization of aesthetics, police brutality, race and racism, patriarchy, machismo, sexism, transgenerational knowledge sharing, and/or consumption.

References

Anderson, L. (2006). Analytic autoethnography. *Journal of Contemporary Ethnography*, *35*(4), 373–395. https://doi.org/10.1177/0891241605280449

Aguilar, Cecilia Rios, and Judy Marquez Kiyama, eds. *Funds of Knowledge in Higher Education: Honoring Students' Cultural Experiences and Resources as Strengths*. New York: Routledge, 2018. Web.

Benham, M. (2007). Moʻōlelo: On culturally relevant story making from an indigenous higher education: Students' funds of knowledge as a bridge to disciplinary learning. *Teaching in Higher Education, 21*(7), 741–758.perspective. In D. Clandinin (Ed.), *Handbook of Narrative Inquiry: Mapping a Methodology* (pp. 512–534). SAGE Publications. https://doi.org/10.4135/9781452226552

Bright, B. (1998). 'Heart Like a Car': Hispano/Chicano Culture in Northern New Mexico. *American Ethnologist, 25*(4), 583–609. Web.

Chappell, B. (2010). Custom Contestations: Lowriders and Urban Space. *City & Society, 22*, 25–47. https://doi.org/10.1111/j.1548-744X.2010.01029.x

Chavez, M. S. (2012). Autoethnography, a Chicana's methodological research tool: The role of storytelling for those who have no choice but to do critical race theory. *Equity & Excellence in Education, 45*(2), 334–348. https://doi.org/10.1080/10665 684.2012.669196

Cowan, P. (2004). Devils or angels: Literacy and discourse in lowrider culture. In J. Mahiri (Ed.), *What They Don't Learn in School: Literacy in the Lives of Urban Youth* (pp. 47–74). Peter Lang.

Creswell, J. W., & Creswell, J. D. (2018). *Research design: Qualitative, quantitative, and mixed methods approaches* (5th ed.). SAGE Publications.

Daddow, A. (2016). Curricula and pedagogic potentials when educating diverse students in higher education: Students' Funds of Knowledge as a bridge to disciplinary learning. *Teaching in Higher Education, 21*(7), 741–758. https://doi.org/10.1080/13562 517.2016.1183619

Duncan-Andrade, J. M. R. (2007). Gangstas, wankstas, and ridas: Defining, developing, and supporting effective teachers in urban schools. *International Journal of Qualitative Studies in Education, 20*(6), 617–638. https://doi.org/10.1080/09518390701630767

Freire, P., & Ramos, M. B. (1970). *Pedagogy of the oppressed*. Herder and Herder.

Garcia, L. (2021). Cruising LA's political landscape: Critical car-culture narrative in art education, *Art Education, 74*(5), 38–43. https://doi.org/10.1080/00043125.2021.1928473

Gerber, M. (2018, June). Zoot Suit riots: After 75 years, L.A. looks back on a violent summer. *Los Angeles Times*. https://www.latimes.com/local/lanow/la-me-ln-zoot-suit-riots-anniversary-20180604-story.html

Kiyama, J. M. (2010). College aspirations and limitations: The Role of educational ideologies and funds of knowledge in Mexican American families. *American Educational Research Journal, 47*(2), 330–356.

Kiyama. J. M. (2011). Family Lessons and funds of knowledge: College-going paths in Mexican American families. *Journal of Latinos and Education, 10*(1), 23–42. https://doi.org/10.1080/15348431.2011.531656

Kiyama, J. M., & Rios-Aguilar, C. (Eds.). (2012). Funds of Knowledge: *An Approach to Studying Latina(o) Students' Transition to College. Journal of Latinos & Education,* 11(1), 2–16.

Kiyama, J. M., & Rios-Aguilar, C. (Eds.). (2017). *Funds of knowledge in higher education: Honoring students' cultural experiences and resources as strengths* (1st ed.). Routledge. https://doi.org/10.4324/9781315447322

Ladson-Billings, G., & Tate, W. F. (1995). Toward a Critical Race Theory of Education. *Teachers College Record, 97*(1), 47–68. https://doi.org/10.1177/016146819509700104

Milner, R. H. (2007). Race, culture, and researcher positionality: Working through dangers seen, unseen, and unforeseen. *Educational Researcher, 36*(7), 388–400. https://doi.org/10.3102/0013189X07309471

Moll, L. C., Amanti, C., Neff, D., & Gonzalez, N. (1992). Funds of knowledge for teaching: Using a qualitative approach to connect homes and classrooms. *Theory Into Practice, 31*(2), 132–141. https://doi.org/10.1080/00405849209543534

Paris, D. (2012). Culturally sustaining pedagogy: A needed change in stance, terminology, and practice. *Educational Researcher, 41*(3), 93–97. https://doi.org/10.3102/0013189X12441244

Parsons, Jack, Carmella. Padilla, and Juan Estevan. Arellano. *Low 'n Slow: Lowriding in New Mexico*. Santa Fe: Museum of New Mexico Press, 1999.

Ramos, D., & Judy, M. K. (2021). Tying It All Together: Defining the Core Tenets of Funds of Knowledge. *Educational Studies (Ames), 57*(4), 429–449.

Saldaña, J. (2021). *The coding manual for qualitative researchers* (4th ed.). SAGE Publications.

Sandoval, D. M. (2003). *Bajito y Suavecito/Low and slow: Cruising through lowrider culture*. The Claremont Graduate University.

Shields, C. (2010). Transformative leadership: Working for equity in diverse contexts. *Educational Administration Quarterly, 46*(4), 558–589. https://doi.org/10.1177/0013161X10375609

Williams, A. (2020, October). Cruising around the world: How California lowrider culture spread across the globe. *Local News Matters.* https://localnewsmatters.org/2020/10/14/cruising-around-the-world-how-california-lowrider-culture-spread-across-the-globe/

Yosso, T. J. (2006). *Critical race counterstories along the Chicana/ Chicano educational pipeline.* Routledge.

2. *Aesthetics and the Battle for the Eastside: Google's Lowrider, Chicano Park, and the Performance of Space*

BEN CHAPPELL

Introduction

In March, 2018, the massive South by Southwest (SXSW) multi-media festival descended as usual on Austin, Texas. The company Google took its trade-show exhibition game to the next level to introduce Google Assistant technology, by inviting conference attendees to a "smart house" on Austin's Eastside. The house had been equipped with 12 rooms of "activations," showing off automation and voice recognition such as a robotic spice rack, a beer delivery system, and other amenities. Parked in front of the house was a 1964 Chevy Impala lowrider, restored to pristine condition and equipped with a hydraulic suspension. In publicity for the exhibit, amid hashtags like "brand activation" and "property takeover," Google's marketing partner firm promised visitors a chance to sample barrio street culture:

> Ever wonder what it's like to experience a lowrider with hydraulics? At The Google Assistant SXSW Fun House, ... command "Hey Google, Bounce" to cue the vintage car to bounce or go on three wheels for an experience only found at SXSW. (Sparks, n.d.)

In an op-ed piece for the *Austin American-Statesman,* Michael Ramos-Lynch (2018) suggested that Google "Bounce your SXSW lowrider out of East Austin!" Ramos-Lynch noted that Google had mounted its PR campaign in a historically minority-white neighborhood where bouncing lowriders could certainly be found on occasions other than a marketing event for Google. It also was an area subjected to some of the most intensive gentrification of any city in the United States, in the most economically segregated large metro area in the USA (Ramos-Lynch, 2018).

It was ironic then, or you might say perverse, that Google went to pains to achieve aesthetic competence in decorating its SXSW smart house with "local color," and offering a way for visiting conventioneers to come to the barrio and enjoy the low lows without necessarily needing to deal with the people who build and drive them. To the marketers' credit, the lowrider on display conformed to lowrider aesthetic requirements: the royal blue Impala had immaculate chrome and sat on Dayton spoke wheels. The high-quality ride gave a sheen of hipster cool to the trade-show exhibition, emphasizing Southwest flair in much the same way that media industry hordes who have flocked to SXSW over the years savor Texas breakfast tacos as part of the conference experience.

But because automation was ultimately the product on display, there was no need for the presence of the people who build lowriders—Google alone could make this ride hop on command. When I read the news story, I could not avoid flashing back to my fieldwork with lowriders, and critical conversations about those who buy their way into the scene by purchasing a ride already built and customized. On cruising strips, such would-be lowriders might show themselves by clumsily controlling the hydraulic setup they know only as a product of consumption, not a project they were involved in assembling, or that they hold familiar after years of watching others work them, leading up to the moment when a father, uncle, or older brother might let you "hit the switches" for the first time. No, the wonder of technology in this case was that the precise calibration of the Google Assistant controls let the lowrider car show off its capabilities itself. Human error was eliminated, and at in the same move, human agency. High tech nullified the learning curve necessary for a novice lowrider and let its customers step directly into the fantasy of street culture figured as both alluring and dangerous. A minoritized aesthetic was there to be consumed without minoritized people. It was a spatial, material form of what bell hooks (1992) decades ago called "eating the other."

The neighborhoods of East Austin were designated for Mexican American and African American residence in a 1928 master plan for the city, formalizing and organizing segregation for maximum containment and efficiency (Chappell, 2012, pp. 44–45). As University of Texas scholars Tang and Falola (2018) recently documented, Austin's rapid growth, driven partly by the high-tech sector, has kicked gentrification into high gear in the formerly cordoned-off areas of East Austin, displacing many long-time residents, some of whom have organized around the political cause of a "right to stay." The 78702 ZIP code, which roughly covers the Eastside, is one of the most intensely gentrifying neighborhoods in the United States. Austin has grown

2–3 times its size since I studied and conducted fieldwork there in the late 1990s and early 2000s. The Eastside, a pleasant neighborhood very close to downtown, has been particularly targeted. and the people who have made their home there for generations since they were pushed there for segregation beginning in the 1920s now are being pushed out. A decade ago, Eastside homes were still valued at less than half the median for the Austin area, at a little over $100,000. Today the median sale price in the former barrio pushes $800,000 (Holley, 2021).

Google's lowrider and the fun house were not the first time that SXSW event planners ventured into East Austin. In 2015, a business on César Chavez Street, the heart of the Eastside, was demolished without warning even though the business owner held a lease for two more years. The shop, called "Jumpoline," dealt in piñatas, "jump houses" and other party supplies, and was a colorful and familiar landmark in the neighborhood. As the story unfolded, it became clear that Jumpoline had been demolished by its landlords because SXSW event planners had their eyes on an adjacent property and needed parking space to meet city codes. The traumatic event sparked outcry, expressed perfectly in an enduring hiphop track "What Happened to Austin?" by Lench Martinez, but the rapid destruction of Jumpoline demonstrated the power of property and capital to blast through community space and answer questions later, if at all (see Chappell, 2020).

Clashes between Eastside residents and the overwhelming but temporary presence of SXSW are a small part of the long-term, historical struggle over the Eastside. I moved to the neighborhood in 1999 in order to begin my fieldwork with lowriders, and already then I spotted an activist's sticker on a stop sign, reading "Warning: This Neighborhood is Being Gentrified." From activist friends in the community and colleagues across the highway at the University of Texas, I heard different accounts about the "peaceful" or "dangerous" Holly Street neighborhood on the south end of the Eastside, a residential area abutting parkland that runs along the stretch of the Colorado River that is dammed into a series of lakes.

Each Sunday as part of my fieldwork, I made my way to Martin Middle School in the Holly Street area, and a parking lot on the edge of land that everyone who in the lowrider scene called Chicano Park, which today is officially designated as Edward Rendon, Sr. Park at Festival Beach, named after a well-known late Eastside activist. The Sunday cruises were an impromptu gathering for car clubs and lowrider appreciators to gather, appreciate the rides, and kick it with family and friends at the end of a weekend. Sometimes curious Anglo frisbee players or dog walkers would pass through, and usually there were a couple of police cars parked at a conspicuous distance, leaving the cruising scene alone until dusk, when they would flash their strobelights or take a slow turn through the parking lot to let people know it was time to head home.

In August 2020, Greystar Real Estate Partners out of Charleston, South Carolina, opened The Weaver, a luxury apartment complex adjacent to the park. A selling point of the complex was the opportunity for residents to live in a "community that is rich in history and tradition" (Holley, 2021). The next spring, cruising was vibrant at Chicano Park—the scene has always waxed and waned along with a complex of factors including weather and gas prices, but perhaps a year of pandemic isolation spurred more custom car enthusiasts to join the open-air meetup. Not only lowriders but other genres of custom car, including Houston-derived "slabs," filled the Martin parking lot, which offers a circular route for low and slow cruising circuits, where drivers show off their finished rides or works in progress. Deep vibrations of multiple sound systems ripple through a space like this when lowriders post up and make the park temporarily their own. The dense sound and clustered traffic brought the ire of some tenants of The Weaver in a confrontation that drew national attention after the magazine *Texas Monthly* reported on it and other outlets followed suit.

When *Texas Monthly* reported on the contested space of Chicano Park, a handful of residents of The Weaver were on hand to express their discontent with the impromptu car show that the Sunday cruising scene occasioned. Some of the complaints were speculative—that the tire smoke produced by occasional burnouts would kill trees, or that emergency vehicles would not have access to the area because of clogged streets; while others were more general: that the collective display of urban street style amounted to a public concentration of toxic masculinity. One particularly agitated resident, filming the proceedings on her phone, told a reporter "You can't tell me drugs aren't being distributed over there... The brazenness of it all just kills me!" (Holley, 2021). The speaker's sensitivity to imagined, brazen substance use suggested that she had not spent time around the Greek houses a few miles away on the edge of the University of Texas campus, or perhaps that no one had tried to tell her that drugs were not being distributed in the student quarter. In any case, the mood conveyed by news reports was one of moral panic from the new residents of the Eastside.

This was not uniform, as some residents showed their appreciation with signs or thumbs-up. The week after the *Texas Monthly* story, lowriders converged for a much larger rally to claim their long-standing connection to the park. Mayor Steve Adler and other city officials joined the rally, some taking an abbreviated cruise in a passenger seat. With the community reaction amplifying to a national scale via social media shares of the *Texas Monthly* piece along with videos shot from within the cruising scene, the apartment complex owners issued a statement that read in part:

> The Weaver community understands and respects the importance of the weekly car club tradition in the East Austin community. As such, no one ever speaking on behalf of the property or property management has ever asked the car clubs to move or end their Sunday gatherings. (KXAN, 2021)

The statement refers to efforts to "reach out" to car clubs and community leaders to facilitate understanding and solutions, and also to claim The Weaver's bona-fides for its connection to the development of affordable housing for senior citizens. The Weaver's representatives emphasized that it was a vocal minority that had complained to the police, and noted that it was not uncommon for such complaints to follow any "large, festive gatherings" (KXAN, 2021). Nothing to see here, the statement seemed to suggest. Just neighbors who can learn to get along.

Speakers at the rally on March 28 recognized the reality if not the inevitability of neighborhood change, without relinquishing their right to claim access to the park, or the barrio as their home. One said, "I know we have a lot of newcomers and we need to welcome them, but we have to remember we cannot let them take over" (Martinez, 2021). Edward Castillo, a regular at Chicano Park cruise nights said to a television news reporter, "We fought for this park. . . I challenge everyone to look at the history of Chicano Park and see what black and brown people did in the city, why we were pushed here, and why we're so protective of it" (Lehmkuhl, 2021).

Although the Eastside was designed as a segregated sector through the coercive processes urban historians call "barrioization," people who had little choice but to make the barrio their home also have had to struggle throughout the near-century since the Master Plan to wrest some control over spatial matters in their neighborhood, whether it was protesting chemical spills and environmental contamination attributed to the Holly Street Power Plant or demanding relocation of the Aqua Fest which brought thousands of spectators to the Eastside to watch speed boat races on the part of the Colorado River then called Town Lake. In 1978 at a demonstration against the Aqua Fest that also involved locals driving strategically slowly around Chicano Park to slow the visitors down, one protestor held a sign that got to the point: "Rich People Go Home" (Bingamon, 2020). The Aqua Fest protestors were met with police violence that members of the community recall all too well.

As both the scene and the object of this history of struggle, Chicano Park has accumulated historical value, a meaning- and memory-rich home for the community. Castillo characterized it this way to another reporter in the midst of The Weaver confrontation, "It's a place I've always known to be a comfort place where I know every Sunday I can come here and be around my people" (Bontke, 2021). Bertha Rendón Delgado, the granddaughter of the official namesake of the park, who now chairs its planning committee succinctly broke down why The Weaver residents' concerns may seem tenuous to Eastside residents: "It's just really, really confusing they could be upset when (the car clubs) were here way before y'all were here" (Bontke, 2021). Sabino "Pio" Rentería, a city council member who has lived in the barrio for forty years, concurred with a possibly unconscious double entendre about the custom car gatherings that have gone on as long as he has been around, "we've got customs here that have been going on for decades and they're going to continue" (Holley, 2021). Rentería also noted that long-time residents were not immune to calling in a noise complaint when car owners were reluctant to disperse by the traditional time of dusk, but counseled patience over panic to the newcomers, "it's just a few hours out of the week."

In the politics of space and the business of real estate, people often use a generalized discourse of aesthetics, talking about a "nice area" or a "bad neighborhood," but far from being an absolute scale, this comes down to who is asking. The production of space (Lefebvre, 1992) engages aesthetics, not only in the built environment, but through the effects of style and form in varying ways of inhabiting space. I've argued elsewhere (Chappell, 2020) that gentrification has an aesthetic dimension, as the local color of rich history may be a selling point, as it was for The Weaver, but that in practice, the commerce in real estate tends to treat urban land as a blank slate, mirroring in small scale the "terra nullius" of settler colonialism, a land without people that presents itself as a resource to be taken and put to use (Dunbar-Ortíz, 2014, pp. 230–231). This lends affective power to Chicano Park as a lowrider gathering point, the site of a politics of presence that registers the specificity of Chicano experience and the relationship of a community to the specific land they are on. On the scale of a park, the confrontation over space distilled a fundamental conflict in the process of gentrification: real estate as an investment and object of commerce vs. a place to live.

In her recent work, Jennifer Ponce de Leon (2021) argues that aesthetics is a medium for street-level politics as social movements confront dominant structures, in part over ways of "feeling and seeing reality" (p. 6). Thus aesthetics is the matter of a "socially forged sensory composition of a world" (p. 4). When people struggle for a different world, they also make the world different, through art, through graffiti and music and ways of speaking and dressing and again, style and form. On the Eastside of Austin, as in many barrios, this struggle was first to make a home in barrio space that people had been pushed into for containment. The current phase, however, after generations of community life made the barrio homespace commercially desirable to outsiders, is when the struggle is to hold onto places that residents have layered with meaning from years of presence and use. The aesthetics of barrio space can certainly take durable form, as in the A. B. Cantú Pan American Recreation Center nearby, a public facility bearing an individual's Spanish surname to mark the central role it has played in the community that has rapidly gentrified around it. These forms themselves are the means and objects of struggle, as in the recently restored Chicano Park mural on the wall of a public pool building near Martin school. But space is also fluid and takes shape in time. This is why it is contested, and why identity adheres forcefully to mobile and plastic forms like a custom car.

In my book *Lowrider Space* (2012), I presented the argument that lowrider style, as a vernacular aesthetic asserted in public, "works on the sensorium of specific sites" (p. 23), in what I call a "performance of space" (p. 205), exactly the kind of aesthetic action and production that Ponce de Leon writes about in the context of social movements. Through such aesthetic performances in vernacular contexts, evaluated collectively by viewer-participants according to specific formal conventions but also in terms of the capacity to make an audience "trip out," lowrider car style forms an aesthetic that creates zones of social space recognizable as tied to Mexican American barrio histories. It does not only reflect or reference barrio space, but is iconic with that landscape of power, feeling, and memory. Thus the appearance of lowrider style, and the assertiveness of lowriders cruising, posting up, or gathering in public enact and produce areas of significance, intervening in the "affective politics of space" (Chappell, 2012, p. 22) that precipitate in the overlapping structures of presence, material force, and feeling that make up a stratified and segregated urban landscape in the U.S.A.

My argument is partly that the lowrider performance of space accounts for many of the strong investments lowriders have in their aesthetics, and also for the strong repressive responses they meet when asserting themselves in places not identified as barrios, or where that identity is contested. In other words, the affective power of lowrider aesthetics prompts reaction from those invested in figuring space as the anti-barrio, as much as it may create a home-effect for others. As an early scholar of lowriding, Brenda Jo Bright (1995), observed in her multi-sited fieldwork, cars adorned with barrio aesthetics provided mobility against the history of barrioization and containment, thus asserting repressed Mexican American identities across neighborhood boundaries.

Google's lowrider forced a caveat to my argument that popular, material aesthetics make and mark space, because the Google Assistant 64 Impala made plain the fact that aesthetic forms do not operate alone, or in a vacuum. The performance of space and the affective politics of style take place in intersections of territory, form, and people. Google's lowrider shows that popular aesthetics can be reproduced in ways that may ring true to an area, while simultaneously fueling the commercial desires that drive property values up and long-time residents out. Whether it is for a temporary weekend installation, or a more permanent settlement, though, aesthetic practices can be severed or extracted from the social life and history of a neighborhood in which they have been embedded.

But add people to the mix of form and land, and what emerges is vernacular space, space in use, space layered with specific sensations and memory to make up what Alex Chávez (2017) describes as a "palimpsest dense with meanings" (p. 297). Such space is not only made of blocks and buildings, but what Chávez calls "moments," formed out of "places, feelings, people thrown together" (p. 297). Aesthetic material forms like a custom car are what draw people together and generate the feelings that fuel these significant moments.

Two weeks after the confrontation in Chicano Park covered by *Texas Monthly*, and one week after the rally to support the lowrider cruising scene, I spotted outraged social media posts from Austin lowriders I remain in touch with, from a distance. "Now the laws are going to shut down Chicano Park for sure" was the general tenor, "Fools ruin it for everybody." Easter Sunday had drawn the traditional crowds as Eastside residents and car clubs gathered in the park. An altercation among three men led to one of them pulling a knife and another a gun. A bystander was injured by shots fired. Car clubs rallied again after the event, publicly condemning the fight and shooting. News coverage noticed that there had been one arrest in the matter but police reported at least fifteen calls from picnickers reporting the shots. (Powell, 2021).

Delgado spoke passionately to the local newspaper about the tradition of spending Easter in the park:

> We want to continue the tradition here in Chicano Park with everything that we do, and we don't want any violence here. We ask the public to understand this: Do not bring your guns to Chicano Park! Do not bring your violence to Chicano Park. That will not be accepted at all, and we will take the safety measures we have to get you fined or arrested. We are not playing. (Morales, 2021).

It is hardly surprising that a fight might lead to shots in gun-rich Texas, a state currently considering legislation to allow permitless carry of handguns.

But some in the public were quick to deploy tropes of violent Mexicans to characterize the event. The online discussion board AR15.com, which bills itself as "the world's largest firearm community" hosts a discussion board on which one participant referred to the shooting as "cultural homicide," apparently tying the violence to the recent high-profile presence of lowriders and their supporters. The poster shared a photo of the mayor riding in a lowrider at the support rally the week before, under the title "Austin's mayor approves of cultural homicide," and added comments tying the shooting to car-club gatherings. Another comment reads,

> Saw that coming a mile away when he started defending the idiocy a couple weeks ago. There is no "Chicano Park" BTW, it's the parking lots near the elementary school. The entire area is known as Fiesta Gardens. (ar15.com, 2021)

These posts work to identify violence with car clubs even while they perform cultural erasure by denying the place-identity that has accrued from decades of community social practice. Delgado expressed the frustration of community members who do not see respect for the importance of their park reflected either in the street fight itself or in public priorities. She told a television reporter, "I've asked for lighting. I've asked for patrols on Sunday. . . These are the demands and the recommendations that have been brought already to the Parks Department" (Powell, 2021).

The fight ruptured an aura of resistance and celebration that had formed through the community response to confrontation with wealthy newcomers. This trauma no doubt reminded some Eastsiders, including lowriders, of "the Easterday shootout," an infamous event in the 1980s that I heard recounted numerous times while posting up with lowriders in fieldwork, including in Chicano Park. In that event, rival cliques brought their turf battle to the Easter celebrations, disrupting the peaceful Sunday afternoon and driving families away. Lowriders bemoaned the event as a loss of their space to gather, and maintained an ethos disapproving of "troublemakers" who bring danger and unwanted police pressure to cruising scenes. The gang wars of the 1980s eased off when a local politician brokered a truce between sets, gathering their representatives on the Pan American Center Hillside Stage, a site residents identify with free summer concerts, surrounded by murals depicting images of community and cultural pride (Chappell, 2020).

In fieldwork over a decade later, I learned about that Easterday shootout as part of the adversity that had been overcome as car clubs had resumed their tradition of spending the holiday at the park. I was cruising with a club the night before Easter in the early 2000s when cell phone reports came in that families and clubs were already staking out their areas for the day's festivities.

The largest shelter houses were claimed already before midnight, but there were some shaded picnic tables near the water. The club I was with decided to spend the night at one of these spots in order to take full advantage of the holiday. With a few members monitoring brisket on a slow smoke at home, the rest of us assembled in a corner of the park, in the quiet cool of a spring-time Texas night. It felt more like a backyard of someone's home than the public space of a "bad neighborhood," as members set up chairs and one rigged a VCR to his car's sound system to watch a movie (Chappell, 2012).

This was a barrio homespace, a lowrider space that Google's technology couldn't begin to replicate, and that might not even occur to marketers as the meaning or identity of that place. The peace of the quiet night was not a simple contrast with the boom of systems and engines that would flood the same area the next day. One was not the absence of the other, but they formed a continuity, knit together by memory, relationship, and on-going practice. This presence, marked and identified by specific aesthetics and rhythms of daily life, was threatened by outsiders expecting or suggesting that it should just disappear. But what they didn't understand is how the practices and aesthetics of barrio space make up a tradition in the sense that folklorist Dorothy Noyes (2009) ties to the Roman concept of "traditio," "the hand-to-hand transfer of—something. A practice, a body of knowledge, a genre, a song, anything sufficiently framed and internally structured to be … a cultural object" (p. 248). Lowrider style and barrio space are handed from generation to generation as cultural material to be maintained. By summoning the resources and the resiliency to "represent," to perform their style in public and remake their barrio space as they do it, lowriders are not just indulging in an idiosyncratic interest or trafficking in a freeform exchange of signs. They are accepting responsibility to make a barrio presence continue, a responsibility they may feel they owe to their predecessors, their community, and their park.

References

AR15.com. (2021, April 5). "Austin's mayor approves of cultural homicide." https://www.ar15.com/forums/General/Austin-s-mayor-approves-of-cultural-homicide/5-2441251/#i92019597

Bingamon, B. (2020, November 20). "A long activist legacy survives on the Eastside: Holding on to El Barrio." *The Austin Chronicle.* https://www.austinchronicle.com/news/2020-11-20/a-long-activist-legacy-survives-on-the-eastside

Bontke, J. (2021, March 24). "East Austin community responds to 'car culture' complaints from new residents." CBS Austin. https://cbsaustin.com/news/local/east-austin-community-responds-to-car-culture-complaints-from-new-residents

Bright, B. J. (1995). "Remappings: Los Angeles low riders." In B. J. Bright & L. Blackwell (Eds.), *Looking high and low: Art and cultural identity* (pp. 89–123). University of Arizona Press.

Chappell, B. (2012). *Lowrider Space: Aesthetics and Politics of Mexican American Custom Cars.* University of Texas Press.

–––. (2020). "Traditions of the oppressed: Popular aesthetics and layered barrio space against the erasure of gentrification in Austin." In A. D. Storey, M. Sheehan, & J. Bodoh-Creed (Eds.), *The everyday life of urban inequality: Ethnographic case studies of global cities* (pp. 87–104). Lexington Books.

Chávez, A. E. (2017). *Sounds of crossing: Music, migration, and the aural poetics of huapango arribeño.* Duke University Press.

Dunbar-Ortíz, R. (2014). *An indigenous peoples' history of the United States.* Beacon Press.

Holley, P. (2021, March 23). "They just moved into an Austin neighborhood. Now they want to end one of its traditions." *Texas Monthly.* https://www.texasmonthly.com/news-politics/austin-car-clubs-gentrification/

hooks, b. (1992). *Black looks: Race and representation.* South End Press.

KXAN. (2021, March 28). "Community leaders stand by decades-old car club tradition at east Austin's Chicano Park." https://www.kxan.com/news/local/austin/community-leaders-stand-by-decades-old-car-club-tradition-at-east-austins-chicano-park/

Lefebvre, H. (1992). *The production of space.* Wiley/Blackwell.

Lehmkuhl, C. (2021, March 28). "East Austin car club members rally in support of Sunday tradition." Fox 7 News. https://www.fox7austin.com/news/east-austin-car-club-members-rally-in-support-of-sunday-tradition

Martinez, K. (2021, March 29). "This Texas lowrider club won't stop gathering despite complaints from luxury apartment residents." *Remezcla.* https://remezcla.com/culture/lowrider-club-wont-stop-gathering-despite-complaints-luxury-apartment-residents

Morales, L. (2021, April 11). "Car club community denounces violence that broke out near East Austin neighborhood car shows." *Austin American-Statesman.* https://www.statesman.com/story/news/local/2021/04/11/east-austin-car-shows-texas-clubs-denounce-violence/7149856002

Noyes, D. (2009). "Tradition: Three traditions." *Journal of Folklore Research, 46*(3), 233–268.

Ponce de Leon, J. (2021). *Another aesthetics is possible: Arts of rebellion in the Fourth World War.* Duke University Press.

Powell, J. (2021, April 5). "Man arrested after shooting at Chicano Park Easter celebration, police looking for 2 others." KXAN News. https://www.kxan.com/news/
crime/man-arrested-after-shooting-at-chicano-park-easter-celebration-police-look
ing-for-2-others

Ramos-Lynch, M. (2018, March 15). "Commentary: Hey, Google! Bounce your SXSW
lowrider out of East Austin!" *Austin American Statesman.* https ://www.states
man.com/news/20180315/commentary-hey-google-bounce-your-sxsw-lowrider-
-out-of-east-austin

Sparks. (n.d.). *Google Assistant SXSW.* https ://wearesparks.com/work_experiential/
google-assistant-sxsw

Tang, E. & Falola, B. (2018). *Those who stayed: The impact of gentrification on longstand-
ing residents of East Austin.* Austin: University of Texas Institute for Urban Policy
and Analysis.

3. East Side Hero

Daniel Osorio

This is Our America

It's 2021, and Chicano/Latinx are being attacked on all levels like never before. Street vendors are being beaten, robbed and killed (Chavez, 2020) for internet likes. Police are killing our innocent youth in broad daylight with no repercussions (Myers, 2021). Our people in the fields continue to feed our nation through a pandemic in slave like working conditions (Jordan, 2020). Immigration and Customs Enforcement (I.C.E.) are separating families and has our kids suffering unjustly in cages at the border (RAICES, 2020). Gentrification and the destruction of our art and history within our schools and communities in California is rampant (Castaneda, 2018), where prisons are being built at a faster rate than college institutions (Palma, 2021) continuing the imprisonment of our Raza with no end in sight.

The system is specifically attacking and tearing apart our Chicano/Latinx youth systemically in the vast majority of underserved neighborhoods. Hollywood, no matter if its online, TV, or film, vastly underrepresents Chicano/Latinx (Wolf, 2020) and highlights the negative stereotypes within our communities, such as gangs, drug abuse and violence, along with casting characters either as immigrants or those with low status occupations like field workers, janitors, or housekeeping (Arrellano, n.d.), aligning those teachings alongside an educational system that gentrifies and washes away our language, history, and culture. The overall picture in the U.S. of our traditions and plentiful contributions to our collective humanity are hidden, the facts distorted for the masses to consume daily, leading to many misperceptions and confusion of who we really are as a Chicano/Latinx society. This is our America, welcome to the front lines.

Oppression on Identity

Growing up in the East Side of San Jose, California, a pre-dominantly lower class, blue collar Chicano neighborhood, on Gittle Ct. (off Jackson and Dobern Ave.), like a lot of fellow friends in the neighborhood, I slept in a garage. Where the carbon monoxide in the water heater was a constant reminder that any day could be the death of me. My dad moved it outside, but the hating ass neighbors reported it as illegal, thus being placed back in the garage. Let alone everything waiting to hurt me outside such as the gangs, drugs, police, violence. . .great times lol.

But ever since I can remember, the mental, physical, and spiritual warfare is what I fought every day to conquer. From the moment I would wake up and step outside into the world until the moment I would go to sleep, in order to continue to survive in my neighborhood, I had to struggle with finding my true identity, not the pre-destined one that I'm being told to become.

The big movies that came out during my youth were "American Me" (Olmos, 1992) and "Blood In, Blood Out" (Hackford, 1993), two epic gang themed movies that were heavily advertised on billboards to youth in my neighborhood. Alongside the "Joe Cool" Camel cigarette displays (Broder, 1997) on bus stops and liquor stores prominently in business on every corner, the image was painted very clearly of what I, as well as what everyone else in the neighborhood, should strive to be like. The subconscious attack and warfare on one's identity was very real, even though I didn't know how deep it truly was at the time.

And don't get me wrong I enjoyed both films, just like everyone else in the neighborhood did. I mean, we as Raza didn't really have anything else that portrayed or showcased us in mainstream Hollywood on such a large scale. Quotes like "Life's a Risk Carnal" (Hackford, 1993) and "Don't look at Me!" (Olmos, 1992) are a part of my dialogue 'til this day because of those films. And everyone's group pictures, whether at the Quincenera, the backyard family carne asada, or at the school dance, were comparable to that of "La Eme" (Olmos, 1992) and "La Onda" (Hackford, 1993).

Now, I wasn't even close to ever repping a gang physically, but mentally, I was being guided on how a young Chicano in the hood should think and act by the media around me. It just goes to show how powerful these representations are, not only within Chicano/Latinx communities, but of our overall existence to the masses. And though these two films are only a mere fraction of our stories and what we represent in our collective Raza, it's crazy that from that time until now, we are still mostly only shown by Hollywood and perceived in the same way through popular media with damaging stereotypes that effect our Raza as a whole (Google, n.d.).

I came to realize that the game hasn't changed, only the players. And this trend of systematic degradation towards Chicano/Latinx is nothing new, as this oppression on identity has been around since way before my time. It's continually being pushed upon us, no matter where you are from, feeling very overwhelming and insurmountable to overcome (Arrellano, n.d.).

The big question is then how do we collectively break free from these oppressive identity chains, that seem inevitable, unbearable and unbreakable, and thus bringing to light the amazing realization of what it really means to be Chicano/Latinx individually and as a whole? I believe I have found the answer, not only for myself, but for our collective Raza throughout Aztlan by digging deeper and rediscovering ourselves through our beautiful lowriding culture.

Lowriding in Aztlan

I've always believed that in order to understand how to create change, you must immerse yourself into the very topic or environment you try to create the change in. So rather than pursuing a masters degree in filmmaking, I decided to create my own film, a documentary on lowriding, with all my own resources and pursue a better knowledge of self and understanding of Chicano/Latinx culture through this pursuit. And it was a great place to start as San Jose was the birthplace of Lowrider Magazine (Pineda, 2019) and Story & King, the cruise capitol of the world (Pizarro, 2019) which was literally thriving in my backyard as a youth.

I can remember all those hot summer nights cruising on various packed streets of San Jose, California, everything from Cinco De Mayo to Boulevard Nights and every weekend in between, the cruise strip was really the place to be. "No cruising zone" signs were posted everywhere (and still are to this day) but that never stopped anyone from cruising and participating in what I believe is our cultural birth right. I learned so much about myself by simply indulging in the culture and found everything one could ever want in life: great friends, the vigor to live life, and profound love. My foundation as a person as well as my first film was "Lowriding in Aztlan" (Code Black Films, 2005) documenting the lowriding experience in Northern California.

The message was simple: address the stereotypes that have been imposed on the art and culture of lowriding for decades. Which in essence, was my attempt to address the very same thing from the perspective of our people in general, while using lowriding as the literal vehicle to address the current state of our issues at hand. And after an amazing 5-year journey, from inception of idea, to national distribution deal (Netflix, Wal-Mart, Best Buy, just to name a few ways the film was accessible at the time), the film opened the conversation across the country on the very state of lowriding, the false perception imposed on our culture, and the awesome impact lowriding has had around the world as well (Osorio, 2005).

It was a journey that made a big difference, as the lowriding community now had the proper voice through film, a piece of moving art on screen, to speak on a respected societal platform, that represented the reality of the lowriding community with dignity and with respect, as the voice of our gente was heard directly from the source (Osorio, 2005).

The success of "Lowriding in Aztlan" (Osorio, 2005) was an amazing, enriching and life changing experience. But the question still remained, where is lowriding, as well as our Chicano/Latinx people in general, going into the future? How is my personal identity, as well as the lowriding culture going to make that next giant leap in society to solidify the identity of our Chicano/Latinx as a people in our nation as a whole? I knew that my documentary was not enough as there was a lot more work to be done moving forward in my lowriding journey. But it wasn't clear until only a few years ago on how to exactly do it.

The Vision Is the Mission

In 2017, I had a vision, an awakening on my mission atop the glorious mountains of Gilroy, CA. Something so deep, so cosmic, I was not able to comprehend the depth of the message consciously until after my deep interdimensional experience was complete.

As I was with my accompanied shaman, I took what was described to me as Ancient Aztec medicine, 5-MeO-DMT derived from the Bufo toad (ICEERS, 2019), and immediately I felt a rush of colors suddenly hit me. A kaleidoscope of images beautifully covered the sky, spinning in front of my eyes until the movements opened up and took me through the entrance of my own existence to discover my true self. I was finally ready.

As the winds blew from the East, I thought I would have so many questions in regards to where I was going. But I really found myself not having many questions at all, but just one solitary defining question: What is my true identity/purpose in this lifetime? As I asked myself that, my past flooded into the atmosphere. All my hurt, all my pain, hit me all at once and reminded me of not only my personal struggles I have dealt with, but the struggles of our people that I carry as a huge burden to solve. And during the process, I didn't realize how much I still let certain life experiences as well as subconscious pre-destined identity messages, guide my present day decision making and block my true self from growing and becoming reality.

There was a moment when I tried to hold back my inner truths, as I believe we all tend to do when life gets way too revealing, and I was very scared. Frightened by seeing what my true self really would look like, my hands were on my face as I wanted to crawl into a ball and hide. My eyes fluttered wildly while grabbing my hair in despair, disbelief and delusion. But in order to break away from those self-imposed chains of identity, I needed to fully accept the message and let go in order to break away to discover my new path, my true vision…my mission.

And then it happened…I let go…all of it. A great feeling of love washed over me like never before and took all the pain away, and as I laid on the ground, the bright yellow sun called out to me. I felt the winds grow stronger, the vibrations and spirits of the lands past surrounded me with love and joy, consuming my spirit and lifted me up to now give me a complete understanding of what I need to do, where I need to go, and really solidified my purpose.

I arose from the ground, my arms as well as my hands tingled intensely, as I saw my seven Chakras (Stetler, 2016). My sensations all over my body were very alert and as I spread out my arms across away from my chest, they became golden wings and my fingers became feathers. I was ready to take flight once more but now with the spirit of an eagle.

As I called out to the bright golden glow of the sun, basking in all its warmth and glory, it also began to transform. A vibrant radiant yellow sun all of a sudden became that of which I did not expect, a noble powerful golden eagle. Its wings grew as big as the sky overlooking the hills of the South Bay, its tail growing long enough to touch the mountain tops. The eagle then became much smaller and more compact as it began to fly directly towards me.

As it finally arrived, the golden eagle came and rested next to me, and we exchanged the purpose, the vision and reason for my journey. Implanting everything I needed to know without words, breathing in the message through my fluttering eyelids…which felt like an eternity, but in all reality was only took a minute's time. The eagle, shimmering in a golden aura, then took flight and flew away into the horizon, and with my new eyes now wide open, I watched until it disappeared into the deep blue evening sky. The trees spoke and humbled me with their branches, soothing and comforting me in the revelation…the color yellow, specifically gold, was my destiny.

I stepped away from my body and symbolically died today, a deep spiritual ride into my own subconscious and personal dimensions. A cleansing and revelation that seemed so hard to reach, yet so simple to achieve if one would only just look deep within one's self for the answers. And as I returned to my body, my surroundings that were intensified by the ceremony, began to go back into hiding, their purpose for showing themselves was now complete. I left the mountain top with new vitality, new direction, new purpose, and I am finally ready for my next chapter with open arms, no boundaries, and no regrets. East Side Hero was now officially born.

East Side Hero

Our Chicano/Latinx, specifically our youth, are looking for an answer, a message of inspiration that creates the power of hope and leads to change. The mission of "East Side Hero" Films/Music and our video/film projects is to serve as a tool to relate to the lives of low-income at-risk youth in under-served schools and neighborhoods. My goal is to inspire our targeted youth to have more positive decision making and resolutions to challenging life situations.

East Side Hero mission and message to our target youth audience:

- To empower low-income at-risk youth in urban communities especially those who attend underserved schools.
- To disrupt the generational cycle of violence between Chicano/Latinx communities in Northern California.
- To show youths that it is possible to break free from the limitations being imposed on their identity from the time they are born.

My mission with "East Side Hero" as with all my video/film projects is to encourage people from diverse, low-income backgrounds to strive for success, inspire creativity and promote education through film entertainment, mentorship programs, and community service.

The time is now to inspire our Chicano/Latinx youth to find themselves in these very uncertain times. To not only transform the East Side of San Jose, but every hood just like mine. And the very decision to stop the pre-destined identity cycle transforms our youth into discovering the person that they truly are and were always meant to be. To show our youth that no matter their personal circumstances, it's really never too late to choose a different path (Osorio, 2017). And so I too chose a different path to get the assistance that I am seeking.

La Virgen De Talpa

Talpa de Allende was founded in 1599 and is a legendary destination that people across Mexico, as well as across the globe for that matter, join in March of every year to experience the purposeful visit to see La Virgen. The shrine at Talpa is dedicated to a manifestation of La Virgen de Guadalupe (Virgin Mary) and it is very well known that a trip in person to this sacred town can be "miracle causing", where many prayers that are asked from the purest of heart and intentions, have amazingly been answered (Gray, 2020).

I have several family members that swear by La Virgen's mystical powers as they too have pilgrimaged on foot to ask for their personal miracles to be granted. My family originates from a small town in Jalisco, San Juan De Amula, which if traveling by foot, takes roughly three and a half days, or roughly 90 plus miles to get to Talpa. The journey takes one through rugged ranch terrain, steep inclined hills and deep dry valleys where one travels by foot in very intense heat by day and chilling cold by night.

It is unequivocally a true test of one's will, spirit, and determination to survive the elements from start to finish. And whether it be suffering from cancer, dire heart disease, or other life and death threatening situations, those who have made the pilgrimage and asked for their miracles with the purest intentions, were rewarded with being granted the most unbelievable miracles and blessings they sought out asking for. Having witnessed their miracles come to fruition first hand was not only unbelievable, but inspirational as well.

So in March 2019, I too decided that it was also my time to take a giant leap of faith, immerse myself into the pilgrimage, and ask for a great miracle. To help me realize the vision and the mission that has been bestowed upon me in the mountains of Gilroy just two years prior. But no one ever said that the road to self-discovery would be easy. And during the journey I was shedding everything I thought I needed, or who I thought I was, and was only moving forward with what I needed, or who I actually wanted to be. On the third day, as I laid on a dirt floor under a tree for shade, bees buzzing all around above, in the middle of nowhere, body breaking down, thirsty, extremely tired, and with nothing but my thoughts to keep me sane and going through the entire journey...it all of a sudden hit me...and I couldn't have been happier.

As we approached the sacred town of Talpa, I knew I was ready. And during three and a half days of grueling, torturous travel, I sprained both my ankles, my left bottom foot skin severely torn through and bleeding, extreme heat exhaustion as well as excrutiating muscle spasms, I literally limped in agony to the finish line. The shrine inside the sacred church had a superior, vibrant golden aura and glow. And with purest of heart and greatest intentions, I painfully hobbled to the altar, got down on both knees, vigorously prayed, and asked La Virgen de Talpa for my miracle...not only for myself, but for those who will accompany me in my journey as well.

Aztec Gold

The road to self-discovery also has led me down the path to do some more research on the color yellow, but specifically on gold and its significance to our Chicano/Latinx people. So I began diving into our history, and through reading certain literature and many google searches, my research led me to one specific poignant moment in our gente's history...Montezuma and the Aztec Gold treasure of Aztlan (Conn, 2021).

According to legend, Montezuma, the king of the Aztecs, in the year of 1520, was imprisoned by Cortes and Spanish conquistadors as Aztlan was being dismantled and taken over. The conquistadors were demanding a ransom in gold, as they wanted to strip every bit of treasure away from our ancestors. But Montezuma had already dispatched to the tribes to hide all the gold to where not even they would be able to find it as he knew that the Aztec empire was nearing its end. With the Spanish unable to successfully recover the coveted treasure, the Aztec Gold, they proceeded to take over the Aztec capitol of Tenochtitlan and kill Montezuma in the process. The Aztec civilization and empire were enslaved, quickly collapsing shortly thereafter, and the great Aztec empire had completely fallen to the Spanish by 1521 (Wikipedia, 2021).

But according to lore, Montezuma wanted the empires treasure so well hidden that it was never to be found by the Spanish, nor anyone else that was not worthy and would attempt to find the coveted Aztec Gold riches, guarded by the dead spirits of Aztec warriors and tribal descendants to watch over it for eternity. It is rumored to be hidden in several places in Mexico as well as throughout Aztlan (the southwestern part of the United States). But researchers, adventurers, and treasure hunters alike have specifically tied the long lost Aztec treasure to be hidden in the desert surrounding Kanab, Utah. Legend also has it that Montezuma's treasure is cursed so that those that thirst for their riches out of lust and greed, regardless of Aztec descent, would be stricken with disease, famine and ultimately death. As a result, the Aztec Gold has yet to be found by anyone successfully (Conn, 2019).

Lowriding into the Future

As I look back on the days of my youth, although my family wasn't well off financially, there was a lot to be proud of and grateful for. And during that time, I could remember my dad making it a point to cut out a piece of the garage wall in order to build a small window to look out of. I recall telling him what was the point, as the gloomy smog layered view only gave me the sight to a heavily spray painted, gang vandalized bridge and garbage littered all over the streets. He simply told me in Spanish, translated, "Don't see what your eyes are telling you to see, but look past that and imagine everything you can see beyond that, if you only just allow yourself to see it". The profoundness of that action and statement still resonates with me.

In keeping with that philosophy, it really is in line with all my work involving lowriding and seeking a better grasp on finding my own personal identity and what it truly means to be Chicano/Latinx. A lowrider by definition is the truest expression of that person who owns the vehicle. It's customized design, alongside intricately colorfully painted murals, tells a wire wheel spoked story rolling on hydraulics that is powerful in its presentation, that is highly entertaining, eye catching, and deeply meaningful to the soul.

But based on Hollywood's skewed societal perception, one does have to get past what you have been taught or told to see in plain sight, and allow yourself the opportunity to look beyond that in order to really see what is truly right in front of you. Your identity, as in lowriding, is not pre-determined on negativity at all. But rather your identity is a visual reflection, as in lowriding, into your true identity that is waiting for you to discover it, so that you can openly display to the world the true beauty and essence of who you really are.

The Aztec Gold, as well as the enslavement of our people's identity, deep history and rich culture, has been similarly hidden from our people for just over 500 years now. But even after all the blood, sweat and tears throughout all the battles to survive in between, our people are now ready to significantly rise again. The discovery of the Aztec gold treasure, as well as our true Chicano/Latinx identity, will ultimately finally be found from the most unlikely chosen one, spreading the message of its discovery and not only share it with all other descendants of Aztlan, but also how to successfully help others find the Aztec gold themselves as well.

The powerful combination of taking lowriding to the next plateau, through culture and finding personal Chicano/Latinx identity, as well as combining the very essence of Aztec Gold and finally discovering it, is what in my eyes and in my heart will ultimately lead us as Chicano/Latinx people to prominently move forward in the U.S., now and for the next generations to come. This is our America, welcome to East Side Hero. "Us Chicanos got a heart...and it's made of Aztec gold" (Chavez, 2019).

References

Arrellano, G. (n.d.). *Latino representation on primetime television in English and Spanish media: A framing analysis.* SJSU ScholarWorks. https://scholarworks.sjsu.edu/etd _theses/4785/

Broder, J. (1997, May 29). *F.T.C. Charges Joe Camel Ad Illegally takes aim at minors.* The New York Times. https://www.nytimes.com/1997/05/29/us/ftc-char ges-joe-camel-ad-illegally-takes-aim-at-minors.html

Castaneda, L. (2018, December 17). *San Jose's disappearing murals: 'It's like wiping away people's history'.* The Mercury News. https://www.mercurynews.com/2018/12/16/ san-joses-disappearing-murals-its-like-wiping-away-peoples-history/amp/

Chavez, N. (2020, July 19). *A paletero was beaten unconscious and another one was killed. Street vendors are on edge.* CNN https://www.cnn.com/2020/07/18/us/street-vendors-attacks-california-texas/index.html

Conn, J. (2019, December 10). *The Wild 100+ year search for Montezuma's treasure in Kanab, Utah.* https://visitsouthernutah.com/blog/the-wild-100-year-search-for-montezumas-treasure-in-kanab-utah/

Chavez, M. (2019). *The message.* USA: East Side Hero Music.

Google. (n.d.). *Hollywood perpetuates Damaging stereotypes about Latinos.* Google. https ://www.time.com/5662739/latino-hollywood-representation/%3famp=true

Gray, Martin (2020, March 15). *Talpa de Allende* sacred sites: World Pilgrimage Guide. https://sacredsites.com/americas/mexico/talpa_de_allende.html

Hackford, T. (Producer), & Hackford, T. (Director). (1993). *Blood in, blood out: Bound by honor.* USA: Buena Vista Pictures.

ICEERS. (2019, September 19). *Bufo alvarius: Basic Info.* https://www.iceers.org/ bufo-alvarius-basic-info

Jordan, M. (2020, October 20). *Migrant workers restricted to farms under one Grower's Virus Lockdown.* The New York Times. https://www.nytimes.com/2020/10/19/us/ coronavirus-tomato-migrant-farm-workers.amp.html

Olmos, E. (Producer), & Olmos, E. (Director). (1992). *American me.* USA: Universal Pictures.

Osorio, D. (2005). *Lowriding in Aztlan.* USA: Code Black Films.

Osorio, D. (2017). *East side hero.* USA: East Side Hero Films.

Palma, B. (2021, May 12). *Did California build 22 prisons and 1 university since 1980?* Snopes.com. https://www.snopes.com/fact-check/california-prisons-universities/

Pineda, D. (2019, December 14). *The life and death of Lowrider, How the Chicano car magazine shaped California*. The Los Angeles Times. https ://www.latimes.com/entertainment-arts/story/2019-12-13/lowrider-magazine-ceases-print%3f_amp=true

Pizarro, S. (2019, January 16). *San Jose's lowrider history finally gets the spotlight*. The Mercury News. https://www.mercurynews.com/2019/01/16/san-joses-lowrider-history-finally-gets-the-spotlight/amp/

RAICES. (2020, May 22). *Help stop family separation at the border*. No Kids in Cages. https://www.raicestexas.org/2020/05/22/video-family-separation-2-0/

Staff, K. T. L. A. D., & Myers, E. (2021, June 18). *Family, community activists mark 1-year anniversary of Andres Guardado's shooting death*. KTLA. https://ktla.com/news/local-news/family-community-activists-mark-1-year-anniversary-of-andres-guardados-shooting-death/amp/

Stetler, G. (2016, December 19). *Chakras: A Beginner's guide to the 7 Chakras*. Healthline. https://www.healthline.com/health/fitness-exercise/7-chakras

Wikipedia. (2021, August 14). *Moctezuma II*. Wikipedia. https://en.m.wikipedia.org/wiki/Moctezuma_II

Wolf, J. (2020, October 20). *Why is progress so slow for Latinos in Hollywood?* UCLA. https://newsroom.ucla.edu/releases/slow-progress-for-latinos-hollywood

4. Our Existence is Resistance

Xris Macias

Lowriders as reclaiming

There is a scene in the movie *La Mission* (Bratt, 2009), where Benjamin Bratt's character Che, who is an OG (Original Gangster) from the La Mission District in San Francisco, is teaching neighborhood kids about Lowrider mural art, he is sitting next to a 1947 Chevrolet Fleetline Aerosedan Lowrider. The scene opens to a candle of the *Virgen de Guadalupe* on a desk. Hands are visible scribbling something on paper. Che is designing a mural for a Lowrider for his son. Two neighborhood kids are in the room, (a garage) observing the design process. They are engaged in conversation until another character, Lena, walks in. The scene goes as follows:

BARRIO YOUTH 1	Where's Tepee-ack anyway?
CHE	*Tepeyac.* It's the mountain where the Virgin first appeared to Juan Diego.
BARRIO YOUTH 2	How come you making her all dark like that?
CHE	Because her original name, her Indian name, was *Tonantzin.* She only became *La Virgen* after the conquerors forced their language and religion on everybody, you know?
BARRIO YOUTH 1	For real? So is she, like, Aztec or something?
CHE	She's *Mexica.* (May-Shee-Ka) Like you and your homie here.
BARRIO YOUTH 1	Hey! That's what's up!
LENA	(Walking into Garage) Hey.
CHE	(gesturing for the youth to leave) All right, all you shorties out of here. The shop| is closed now.
BARRIO YOUTH'S	(exiting the garage, speaking to one another): I'm gonna get a Lowrider just like Che someday. ...
LENA	(now addressing Che) Preparing them for the revolution, I see.
CHE	Ay, the rebrowning of America. (Bratt, 2009)

Although this scene is only in the move to provide context for Che's character, a father rebuilding his relationship with his son after violently disown-
ing him for being gay, the cars, the style of storytelling, the manner in which
Che carries himself is all centered around Lowrider culture. This scene has
always sat with me as an important moment for Lowrider storytelling because
in its simplicity, it connects Lowriders to education in a way that engages
young neighborhood kids; Che makes a clear connection from the art being
created, to their own identities, while simultaneously teaching history and
satisfying their curiosity. He is aware of the larger implications and responsibilities he has, to pass on this knowledge when he says "the rebrowning
of America", implying that America was once brown, or indigenous. Che is
passing down knowledge as a Lowrider; a characteristic of this lifestyle since
its inception. Since their creation, Lowriders have always been tools of resistance from oppression, tools for reclaiming, and tools for education.

Lowrider car culture has created an alternate cultural space for performance, participation and interpretation, one that allows for the reworking
of the limitations placed upon minoritized cultures in the United States
(Chappell, 2001). This space exists as defiance to mainstream white spaces.
Lowriders are vernacular holders of knowledge for the Chicana/o/x community. Lowrider culture is a continuous form of resistance from subjugation
and cultural erasure. It is a teaching tool for forging community solidarity, building collective meaning, and exemplifying shared leadership; values
that are much needed in a society that continually erases Latina/o/x and
Chicana/o/x experiences through systemic means. In the fight against injustice and oppression, educational liberation, calls for creative, complex, and
covert strategies. Survival tactics need to be sustainable and multigenerational, drawn from the wisdom of ancestors and passed on to younger generations (Solorzano & Yosso, 2001). Lowriders are doing exactly that.

Lowriders continue to serve as both a metaphorical escape from reality,
and a very real act of preserving heritage. Today, marginalized groups can use
their struggles and the discrimination they face to create art and emphasize
their efforts or deviance rather than silencing that which society has deemed
unnatural or undesirable. Unwanted are the languages we speak, the stories
we tell, and our collectivist values. The Lowriding community is passionate
about family values, heritage, and honoring the vehicle's influence and beauty
and extending that beyond the cars and objects themselves.

More than half a century ago, when postwar youths sought a means of
expressing their rebelliousness, automobiles provided a distinctly American
outlet. Vehicle rear ends were raised, muscle was added to engines, and customized hot rods became popular. One could hear car radios blaring rock and

roll, and feel the exhaust vibrations as these vehicles approached. Being fast, loud and energetic became almost synonymous with this new generation. For white American youth, these cars spoke to youth rebellion in general, they used them metaphorically to fly past the dreary old symbols of their elders. For Chicana/o/x's, customization meant rebellion also, but the source of this nonconformity was different. They were for the most part, immigrants struggling with poverty and discrimination in the *barrios*, (Mexican slang for neighborhoods) who took a look at these middle-class American icons and saw them in a very different light. Chicana/o/x's instead took a second-hand car that had been in the family for years and payed homage to their parents and grandparents. Their defiance was not so much to dissent their family, but to rebel against a white society that continuously pushed them to the margins. A society that deemed brown bodies, languages, and histories as valueless.

They slowly created a style that would soon be known as Lowriding or Lowriders. Dr. Get Low in Sunday Driver (2005) shares with us that "Since the beginning of cars, man has been changing 'em. And once he found out he could take a roadster and take the springs out of 'em and lay down low... that's low". Lowrider is usually reserved to mean a car, but the term Lowrider can just as easily be placed upon the person behind the wheel of the car. Practitioners of the sport might call it a "lifestyle" (Genat, 2001). Lowrider culture is an example of communities practicing survival, resistance, motion and semiotic protest. "We may lower our cars, but we will not lower our heads, our cars are a statement to the mainstream, that we are not going to have our cars the way they come from Detroit, we are going to change them, we are going to make them our own, and it's going to reflect our identity" (Montañez, 2012).

Lowriding's radical introduction should not be forgotten as integral of its evolution today. It is an incarnation of theory and practice in which Lowriders becomes a "praxis conceived as self-creating and self-generating free human activity" (Darder, Baltodano, & Torres, 2009). The history and rejection of dominant society makes Lowriding fit into the definition of a counter-culture as defined by Solorzano and Delgado Bernal as follows:

> "cultures that rely on the use of counterstories offered by members of marginalized groups who, by virtue of their marginal status, are able to tell stories different from the ones white scholars usually hear. These counterstories can be in the form of dialogues, chronicles, and personal testimonies." (Delgado Bernal, 2001).

Lowriding is a culture whose values and norms of behavior differ substantially from those of mainstream society in opposition to mainstream customs due to their untold perspectives in dominant teachings. The vehicles, the lifestyle, and the people themselves are not found in traditional media. These stories are purposefully left out, thus Lowriding becomes a means of survival through alternative storytelling, through *arte,* and through education via creation.

Lowriders Art in Protest and Reclamation

Some of the most intricate, eye-tantalizing custom paint jobs can be seen on Lowriders. Images of flowers, saints, Aztec warriors, women, historical figures, animals, fictional characters and everything else in between has been featured. They are cars that act as a canvas, sharing art that speaks of struggle, inspiration, family, and history. Cars are meticulously painted in metal flake, candy paint, and layer upon layer of pinstriped glitter, for a look that is not, and will not, be replicated elsewhere. Lowriders let their imaginations run loose and expand their creativity onto their cars, bicycles, and other vehicles. The murals on the vehicles often tell a story or make a statement. Artists use many mediums of expression, but for Lowriders, their canvas is a car (Velarde, 2019). In the world of car paint jobs, Lowriders perhaps stand out as the most meaningful ones. Many tell the life stories of their owners, pay homage to their ancestors or stand in defiance to a system that has continually surveilled and policed their community. No lowrider is the same. A paint job is more than just a paint job, but an added layer of visible manifestation against hegemonic structures. (Gramsci, 1971)

Lowriders are *Arte,* and poetry. *Cultura* manifesting as sacred stories of survival. These *ranflas* we roll low and slow are metaphors for resistance. Audacious aesthetics subverting the status quo. We are *familia.* But more than just art, a creative manifestation of our struggles and physical expression of moving forward in life. One of the stark differences of Lowrider art that separates it from so-called fine art is that this art is mobile (Genat, 2001). Mobility serves as a powerful transcendence of all limitations placed upon Mexican Americans and Chicana/o/x's. Mobility is in itself a defiance of borders.

Lowrider culture and art is hybrid epistemology that draws on Spanish, Mexican, Latin American and Native ways of perceiving, thinking, and knowing (Cowan, 2004). Mainstream art is typically thought of in a visual form such as painting or sculpture, producing works to be appreciated primarily for their beauty or emotional power. This type of art is made for consumption primarily. Many times, it is static. For Lowriders, the mere fact that this lifestyle is mobile and can occupy multiple spaces already challenges the status of mainstream accepted art forms, and thus allows for an evolution of Chicana/o/x folklore and a reinterpretation of border identities (Anzaldua, 1999).

In the 1950s and 1960s Chicana/o/x's were experiencing a renaissance of consciousness and cultural awareness. They created new terms to identify themselves and new ways of communicating this new-found pride. The murals found in Chicana/o/x and Latina/o/x neighborhoods across the U.S. southwest reflect this new identity and political reform.

Murals on the sides of buildings and billboards transformed the space and area they occupy. They served as a way of letting everyone know that they are reclaiming that space sending a direct message to outsiders that Chicana/ox's and Latina/o/x's have a strong presence here and will no longer exist in the shadows.

These pictorial representations of both struggle and pride, made their way onto the cars that were being customized. Murals began to be painted on the hoods, trunks, and side panels. Practically any surface could become a canvas. At times, even the wheels of the vehicles are decorated! Lowriders wanted to share their stories and philosophies with images that connect them to their communities. This created a form of visual literacy that was open to everyone in those neighborhoods, but now made it even more accessible due to their mobility. For many Latina/o/x's and Chicana/o/x's, this system of visual literacy is part of their process of constructing and evolving their cultural identity. With Lowriders being an extension of the community, the ability to interpret, negotiate, and make meaning from information presented via this rolling art, exemplifies the growth and spread of identity (Levitt & Lloyd 2012). Chicana/o/x culture is not about conforming to the mainstream, it is about taking your cultural views, religious beliefs, thoughts and attitudes with you. Actor, art collector and famously proud Chicano, Cheech Marin says: "To me, you have to declare yourself a Chicano in order to be a Chicano. That makes a Chicano a Mexican-American with a defiant political attitude that centers on his or her right to self-definition. I'm a Chicano because I say I am" (Marin, 2012). This self-proclamation and (re)claiming of identity, is powerful because it gives allegory to the idea of customizing even yourself. Lowriders are one of the many physical manifestations of that reclamation. As a founding member of Lowrider Magazine, Sonny Madrid believed that that this style is inspired from indigenous concepts; "The Indians, The Mayans, The *Aztecas,* they were the first Lowriders. . . they used to customize their bodies, and today, they are customizing their cars" (Madrid, 1979). And by customizing a car, whether conscious or not, of it's place as a defiant symbol of white supremacy, colonialism, and American hegemony, a show or a cruise becomes a literal and metaphorical process of changing the space it occupies (Chappell, 2001).

The way this lifestyle transcends time and space is a teaching tool. For Lowriders, the automobile is at the center of a constellation of cultural practices, a mobile canvas for cultural representation and critique. These are representations of cultural values, but also productions of people acting in complex political and economic circumstances (Bright, B.J., Lisa 1995).

Mainstreaming

Today, Lowriders have a negative stereotype associated with them, thanks in large part to the mainstream media. Lowriders have been classified as dangerous in their rebellion and thus, this art form has been purposefully portrayed as undesirable, effectively demonizing our culture. From the early days of Lowriding, they have appeared on television as cars driven by gang members, criminals and young thugs looking for trouble. Criminalization is one tool that perpetuates notions of otherness, which in turn maintains people of color as secondary citizens and justifies penal punishment of them for example (Ulloa, 2019).

Popular movies featuring these cars heavily push that negative image. In the movie *Boyz N the Hood* (Singleton, 1991), the protagonist, "Dough Boy", drove a 1964 Impala Lowrider, that character is a drug dealer. In the movie *Blood In, Blood Out*, a group of young Chicanos are building a lowrider out of a Pontiac GTO, they use it during an ambush where they murder a rival gang leader (Hackford, 1993). In the movie, *Training Day*, Alonzo drives a Chevrolet Monte Carlo Lowrider. Alonzo is a crooked cop who secretly misuses government funds and agents for personal gain (Fuqua, 2001). These among many more, are all movies that feature Lowriders where the protagonists or characters around them are involved in some element of criminality. I could go on naming movies with negative images of Lowriders, they abound.

It is not only in movies that Lowriders are portrayed this way. In music, the Gangsta Rap genre consistently showcases Lowriders in their videos where they push the gang lifestyle, consistently featured alongside illicit activities and a tough guy (macho) image. While each of these forms of media has their place and historical context, they continue to push images of Lowriders into the mainstream world, that do not necessarily reflect the reality of Lowriding (Chappell, 2001). I am not saying that these movies or music are inherently bad, only that the images have made people weary of any car that bounces, is lowered, has a gleaming paint job, and has Chicana/o/x's behind the wheel. This, consequently, has steered people away from seeing the reality and educational potential that this culture has. "Hollywood fiction, functions as documentary fact" (Ulloa, 2019).

Very few media outlets have shown Lowriders in a positive light. In the 1970s show *Chico and the Man*, (Baldwin & Donohue, 1974–1978) the opening credits featured a 1964 Impala Lowrider as a member of the community. The movie *La Mission* mentioned at the beginning of this chapter, does feature several Lowriders heavily and while, the main character is a homophobic ex con, he eventually learns the errors of his ways. Making connections to intersecting thoughts and identities and interpreting a Lowrider Lifestyle (Bratt, 2009).

The Chicano cult classic film, *Selena* (Nava, 1997) has one scene where the drivers of a Lowrider attempt to help the late superstar Selena Quintanilla after her tour bus gets stuck in a ditch. This scene was refreshing change of pace given that the focus, was not on the vehicle itself, but the people behind it being thoughtful, caring citizens. Continuing with the romanticizing of the lifestyle, the song *Lowrider* by War (War, Goldstein, 1975) pays homage to the Lowriders in the most direct of ways. Many oldies style tunes up play the image of owning and cruising these cars. *Swing Low, Sweet Chariot* in its many iterations is an anthem for Lowriders. While not everyone may wish to participate in this culture and many may not see its potential, it is important to accentuate the positive examples and further analyze them in a historical context to better understand how they can serve as constructive tools for education. But we cannot rely on the mainstream examples, positive or negative to tell the whole story. Lowriders can provide a space for families to come together and build something; literally and figuratively. This can teach integrity, commitment, and patience. It can teach the foundations of physics and engineering. The work involved requires a certain industriousness, it allows for creative expression. The cost of building these projects, encourages financial discipline. They can be used to build community, especially in cities with a history of segregation and racism. Many Lowriders are preoccupied with being a positive presence in their communities because of the negative misrepresentation that is portrayed in the mainstream media. At the end of the day Lowriders are mostly working-class people who want to spend time with friends and family and create beautiful cars (Chappell, 2001). This activity creates a space for them to live in temporarily, a space for them to be comfortable, and share ideas, and take a break from the challenges and stresses of having to survive and navigate institutions that are consistently reminding them of their difference. Lowriding is a space for passing down knowledge and stories. This focus on collectivism creates opportunities for education within the culture.

Teaching is crucial to Lowrider expression. As the media continues to decisively erase this important legacy when displaying this culture, they deny the reality that Lowriders are a form of identity, expression, and cultural knowledge.

Lowriders as Storytellers

Lowriders can interrupt traditional oppressive systems of education that perpetuate inequities and hidden curriculum—lessons that are taught informally, and usually unintentionally, in a school system (e.g., behaviors, perspectives, and attitudes) that students pick up while they're at school. Lowrider culture serves "a method of telling the stories of those experiences that are not often told by and about those who are marginalized by society" (Villalpando, 2003). It is a counter-culture that challenges majoritarian stories and privileges. By disrupting the dominant discourse, Lowriders create and share their own perspectives and dispute ahistoricism. In addition, using today's much debated critical race theory as outlined by Solorzano and Yosso, can be a lens from which to view Lowriders as a form of critical knowledge and ways to value its lessons (Solorzano, D.G., & Yosso 2001). For example, the history of Lowriders, began before the cars themselves, it began with the people that eventually would develop and evolve this practice. From Indigenous folks, to farmworkers, to the rebellious well-dressed roots of *Pachucos*. They understood that racism and their responses to it, played a part in the creation of this custom. Critical Race Theory asserts that racism is a permanent component in life, it is embedded into the foundation of our modern ideologies; Chicana/o/x's dealing with racism and erasure of their identities, understanding its permanence, had to find a way to combat it. And still do.

TribalCrit, an offshoot of the broader critical race theory, "honors stories and oral knowledge as real and legitimate forms of data and ways of being...oral stories remind us of our origins and serve as lessons for the younger members of our communities; they have a place in our communities and in our lives" (Brayboy, 2005). These oral histories become embedded in Lowriders as they become symbols of our past, present and future. Street culture counter narratives have a place in our analysis of theory as internalized symbols of pride and resistance as well as physical symbols; our cars.

Lowriders as a New Identity

One casualty of colonization of the Americas is the eradication of diverse forms of human experience and world knowledge. In other words, *one* system of knowledge was manifested as a side effect of conquest. In hindsight, colonization is a misnomer, the reality is that this entire history is that of invasion, destruction, and ransacking of indigenous knowledge (Quijano, 2000). The destruction of whole cultures—in every sense—left the majority of the population lost and struggling to find their identities, a struggle which, for Mexican Americans, continues to this day.

Lowriding is just one of many ways that we took a stand against systems of oppression and made a statement saying we are here, check us out. *Orale.* Just as Nicolas Thomas said "Objects are not what they were made to be but what they have become" (Thomas, 1991). Lowriders are an exceptional example of that. In this case, Detroit mass-produced cars are not enough to satisfy the need and scope of the Chicana/o/x community. A car, a medium for transportation has become a vessel for transformation, it has become a political and cultural statement for identity. From the resurrection of the second-hand or junk car, to the glorification of the velvet and hydraulics customization, Lowriders explore the dynamic of cultures and culture re-definition. This re-appropriation must be interpreted as a mechanism of control, over the car's iconic status. In this case, the car as a symbol of the American assimilation once customized, transforms itself into a new pictogram of the Chicana/o/x identity. The car becomes more a means to resist alienation than a sign of alienation (Høyem, 2007). And gives way to the rebrowning of America. When a lowrider cruise or meet-up is taking place, they are not using the streets the way they are meant to be used. When we low ride, we do it at our own pace, defying the limitations of rules placed on upon the recommended operation of a vehicle. We are using the streets in our own way. We are connecting to our lands with our vehicles. We are taking back the streets even for a night, even for a moment, and reclaiming our culture for our ancestors. Whether it is conscious, or subconscious, Lowriding is anti-colonial land acknowledgement. It is a defiant roar of claiming our land back.

It is important to note, "Borders are set up to define the places that are safe and unsafe, to distinguish us from them. A border is a dividing line, a narrow strip along a steep edge. A borderland is a vague and undetermined place created by the emotional residue of an unnatural boundary. It is in a constant state of transition. The prohibited and forbidden are its inhabitants" (Anzaldua, 1999). *Ni de aqui, ni de alla*—Not from here, nor from there—is a common ideology among Chicanos/as/x's in the Southwestern United States, it is an acknowledgment of forgotten histories and identities. It is an understanding that our lives, languages, cultures, perpetually exist in a border state where each of those intersecting identities are not fully accepted on either side of the border.

Lowriders are border defying, allow for freedom, and anti-imperialist movement.

Lowriders were created by the Chicano community as a response to cultural subordination and marginalization from both sides. Anzaldua tells us that the U.S-Mexican border es *una herida abierta* (an open wound), where the Third World grates against the first and bleeds. And before a scab forms, it hemorrhages again, the lifeblood of two worlds merging to form a third country—a border culture (Anzaldua, 1999). This existence in the third space allows for a new identity and new ways for healing from that open wound. The third space explores the effects of displacement, alienation, exile, diaspora, transnationalism, hybridity, and cosmopolitanism. (Bhaba, 2008) The third space concept is taken from the work of the influential cultural and post-colonial theorist Homi Bhabha; which refers to the inter-workings between colliding cultures, a liminal space "which gives rise to something different, something new and unrecognizable, a new area of negotiation of meaning and representation." (Bhabha, 2008) In this in-between space, that Anzaldua calls *Nepantla,* new cultural identities are formed, reformed, and constantly in a state of becoming (Anzaldua, 1999). The way this was manifested in Lowrider culture is that of the Mexican-American community taking American innovation and creation (automobiles) and adding some Mexican and Mestizo flare to their creations. Lowriding is not just about the cars, but an expression of multiple identities lost and reclaimed. It is an art form that physically embodies the borderlands that encompass our intersecting lives. This lifestyle is a statement from those who instead have learned to become a part of both worlds, worlds whose cultural expectations they are still expected to abide by even when not fully accepted into either. The car might be American, but the customizations and creativity that goes into it, are influenced by a Mexican, and Mexican American lens. Lowriding in the streets, then becomes a connection and an acknowledgement of lost lands.

Latinx's /Hispanics as a whole, continue to outpace other groups in numbers (Bustamante, Lopez, & Krogstad, 2019) With this growth comes the need to forge a different path for a community that challenges the limitations society has placed in front of them. Specifically, being Chicano means, we navigate two worlds; that of preservation of culture and precolonial knowledge, and that of adaptation and survival to modern and postmodernist structures. Chicanismo is that third space. Chicana/o/x's speak a language that is different from the dominant American society that only came to be from the invasive colonization of Europe (Quijano, 2000). This hegemony is then maintained to continue to remove languages and cultures of their own knowledge with power and control. (Gramsci, 1979) and that we can do so while maintaining our culture, traditions, and values. By putting all of that into a car, it becomes an extension of your own experiences.

Lowriders as a Social Navigational Tool

California, Arizona, New Mexico, Nevada, Utah, Texas, as well as parts of Colorado, were part of Mexico until the treaty of Guadalupe Hidalgo was signed in 1848, turning over much of its land to the United States (del Castillo, 1990). When Mexico ceded the huge territory to the U.S., many Mexican families remained on their ancestral lands, continuing to speak Spanish and retain a distinctly Mexican *cultura*. Later, from about 1910 to the mid 1920s, a new wave of Mexican immigrants, approximately 10 percent of the Mexican population, fled the bloody Mexican Revolution and settled in many major urban centers of the Southwest, in cities such as, El Paso, and East Los Angeles. They came, like so many others, seeking stability, peace, and a better life for their children. Immigrant life in the early 20th century was difficult. After the Revolution, Mexicans were brought over to the United States to work in the mines, railroads and in farms as part of the *bracero* program (del Castillo 1990). Many of these new workers were exploited, and without any type of job security or insurance, an illness, loss of employment or other calamity could destroy their lives. Many of these workers formed "mutual aid societies," or social clubs, where they would meet and socialize on a regular basis. The purpose of these groups, however, was survival. For example, when an ailing worker could no longer perform, these groups would collaborate and help the family in need. When workers could not manage transportation to and from the workplace, they arranged carpool services. In fact, many times farmers could tell when a group of workers were on their way to the fields, because the cars would be full of occupants and would be lowered from the weight. This is one way that cars began to be recognized as lowered vehicles.

After individuals come together and identify a need in their community, they begin to research so that they may have a better understanding of the issue and how to aid in its resolution. They also start to recruit other individuals that have a similar passion and interest. This group of people are now part of a formalized association and once basic needs were met, these mutual aid societies began to branch out and form specialty groups, paving the way for official car clubs in coming decades.

Lowriders, like any other subcultures, began with purpose, as part of the social dynamics of identity. Today, because of fear from white dominant society, there is much misinformation and misrepresentation of this lifestyle,

Lowriders have been identified exclusively and erroneously with *cholos*, but as Brenda Bright suggests, gang membership and car clubs do not necessarily go together and in many cases are antagonistic (Bright, B.J., Lisa 1995). Lowrider car clubs are seen as alternative mechanisms to urban gangs, which are aid societies in their own right, but with different purpose. On one hand, gangs are physically limited to the *barrio* where cohort and identity converge and must be protected. On the other, Lowriders overcome those boundaries in a way that, "involves one with others from all over the city in both cooperative and competitive networks" (Bright, B.J., Lisa 1995). Also, Lowriders have made their way far beyond the *barrios* that gave birth to this phenomenon. Today, Lowriders are in every major city of the United States. They have spread to countries like Brazil, Vietnam, Australia, Japan, Thailand, Saudi Arabia and most of the European Union, (Ulloa, 2019) but have mostly kept their Mexican-American roots. For example, it would not be uncommon to see a group of Vietnamese Lowriders sporting American classic cars with Mexican flags draped across the hood of their vehicles! Or you may see Aztec or Mayan depictions of deities on the side panels of cars in the Brazilian *Favelas* (poverty-stricken neighborhoods). Underlying all of this growth, the Chicano identity remains at the forefront. Though anybody with a nice ride is welcome, there is an idea that Mexican-American culture and experience are authoritative in this style. That's part of the value of it. For Alicia Gaspar de Alba, "Lowriding must be interpreted as a status symbol, as a symbol of community affirmation and identification" (Gaspar de Alba, 2003). The cars then, become global symbols of struggles overcome (Ulloa, 2019).

Lowriders as Connections to Our Indigenous Roots

The creation of Lowriders as a culture is credited to Mexican-Americans living in the U.S. Southwest roughly in the late 1930s and early 1940s (Madrid, 1979). However, the concepts that surround Lowriders as we know them today did not originate with the cars themselves. The idea for Lowriding came to be in the 20th century only because of practices and rituals from many centuries earlier. There are two lineages that eventually end up creating what we now call Lowriders. The cultures Indigenous to the Americas, and the Spanish heredity of Chicanos. On the indigenous side, much of the lineage of Mexican Americans can be derived from two major groups of people; the Mayans and the Aztecs. The Mayans that thrived until around 900 AD in the jungles of what is now Mexico and Central America, (where many Chicanos have ancestry) held many concepts of the creation of the universe and time itself. To explain why Lowriders prefer to go slow, we must consider the indigenous concept of *Hunab Ku*, which is described as the "grand architect of the Universe, the giver of life. This idea of creation is not anthropomorphic, it is a scientific concept of the building of the universe in geometric symbols and numbers that comprise the mathematical order of the universe including the concept of time" (Rodriguez, 2010). "[Hunab Ku] is seemingly more complex than the concept of zero. For the Maya, is not the value of nothing, but rather the beginning of everything" (Rodriguez, 2010). This is where I see time as inextricably linked to who we are as a people and to the practice of Lowriding. Both the Mayans and the Aztecs held the idea that time was cyclical, unlike the European version of time which is linear. They also believed that Hunab Ku is intergenerational, meaning that this idea is passed on through memetics; models of cultural information transfer. Memetics describes how an idea can propagate successfully in a given culture or environment (Kantorovich, 2014). In other words, our pre-Hispanic concepts are passed on and still practiced today, even if unbeknownst to the practitioner. This idea, combined with the Yosso's model of cultural wealth that recognizes that the experiential knowledge of People of Color is legitimate, appropriate, and critical to understanding, analyzing and teaching (Yosso, 2005), brings us back to critical race theory that draws explicitly on the lived experiences of People of Color by including such methods as storytelling, family histories, biographies, scenarios, parables, *cuentos, testimonios*, chronicles and narratives. So, even concepts and memories, though not explicit, are still culturally transferred and passed on generationally. This includes our perception of time. Because time was nonlinear, as our ancestors understood it, they knew that they must act in accordance with time. In short, The Hunab Ku is a concept that has existed for millennia from the Mayan culture. It symbolizes creation; and thus, evolution. Hunab Ku is a representation of cyclical time, a direct opposition to western linear understandings of chronology. Time is transcendental, in our culture of indigeneity, we pass on stories and identity through "generational memory" (Anzaldua, 1999; Giroux, 1988) So to me, it makes sense that we keep time in our collective memory, and when it comes to cars, it had to be the descendants of these grand civilizations to hold that idea and take our time, or... go slow. There is no rush to get somewhere (a linear concept) instead there is this idea to cruise and arrive when the grand architect of the Universe wants you to (a cyclical concept). A Lowrider then becomes a semiotic means to connect with our ancestors and embody the concept of Hunab Ku. (Chappell, 2001; Rodriguez, 2010) The thing about Lowriding is that we don't really go anywhere, we just take our time getting there.

Lowriders as Connections to Our Mestizo History

The other ritual that led to Lowriders is on the European side: the Spanish. *Mexicanos* today are the product of the mixing of two cultures, also known as *mestizaje* meaning that they recognize both their indigenous cultures and their Spanish cultural heritage. Mexicans and Mexican-Americans today, have cultural traits that incorporate elements from indigenous and Spanish traditions. One such tradition on the Spanish side that has been passed down intergenerationally is that of *El Paseo*. This is an idea that involves the movement of bodies to sustain oneself and re-energize. The Spanish have always been quite social. El Paseo literally means a stroll. The exact origins of this tradition are not actually known, but it is believed to have started in the 5th century when the Spanish winter was coming to an end and people would finally come out to enjoy the warmer weather, farmers and landowners would exchange livestock, and all of the excess wood from winter storage was burned. People would stroll to see the many bonfires and enjoy the nights for as long as they could. They also used this as a courtship opportunity, where this particular practice actually encouraged couples to take their time and make sure they are right for one another. Paseos not only allow for people to move their sedentary bodies, but it allows us to reconnect with family and friends.

In colonized Mexico, this paseo became manifested as "Charro" culture, Mexican cowboys, who would dress their horses in fancy cloth's and stroll through their *pueblos* to showcase their outfits began to reinterpret the idea of the paseo and make it more than just about having to enjoy yourself, but to showcase something special. "The Romans had their chariots, Mexican Charros had their fancy horses, the modern day Charro, is the Lowrider" (Velarde, 2019).

In the same vein that our indigenous traditions were passed on to us, so were our Spanish customs. The cruise is merely an automotive extension of this ancient tradition, and because colonization of the Americas, led to the eradication of indigenous and even Mestizo experiences, Chicana/o/x's still have the urge to go out and explore our city. To cruise. To exist out of the shadows. To be seen.

Lowriders as Models of Community, Cultural and Self-Preservation

Lowrider culture was born out of rebelliousness and out of a desire to be seen. From the Pachucos in the 1930s and 1940s to today's boulevard cruisers, this lifestyle today holds an outlaw mystique which clings to the cars and their owners, and though this might be considered a social problem for outsiders of Lowrider culture. It can be argued that this particular type of aesthetics is a means to gain visibility for a group of the population who has long suffered from invisibility. But why not instead stick to a less shocking visual narrative? Maybe because—for a group of people who belong to a low status segment of the American population—the outlaw mystique is a valuable source for a liberating feeling of empowerment (Hoyem, 2007). Throughout many Mexican-American neighborhoods, in the Southwestern United States, Lowriders as we know them today emerged from the "zoot suit" fashion, a trend popular among youth. This was a suit with high-waisted, wide-legged, tight-cuffed, pegged trousers, and a long coat with wide lapels and wide padded shoulders. Mexican-American "zooters", cool from slicked back hair to highly polished shoes, called themselves Pachucos. They developed a walk, a talk, and an overall rebellious aesthetic. This persona was a reminder to society that their styles and energy will not be contained. The zoot-suit was a refusal: a subcultural gesture that refused to concede to the manners of subservience (Cosgrove, 1984).

Their clothes were opposite of the contemporary comfortable ideal of clothing fashion, the *pachuco*, by exaggerating the cuts—by creating art of the clothes—made them impractical, and by that turning them into a symbol of resistance towards everything American. This was the beginning of the movement to showcase that Chicanos are present and want to be recognized as distinct. This was the first mass showing of anti-mainstream mentality that eventually aided in the aesthetic of Lowriders cars once customization began.

These Pachucos extended their image into the cars that were available at the time. They cruised beautifully restored, older Chevys, decked out in their oversized zoot suits for a night on the town. "The Boulevards, were not nice places to be, but once Pachucos became Lowriders, the boulevard became something else" (Baca, 2019). Often just the back of a Chevrolet was temporarily lowered, using sandbags hidden in the trunk beneath strategically placed planks of wood, sometimes cinder blocks from parking lots were used to lower their cars (Genat, 2001). Yet another method to lowering a car was to have the suspension springs shortened by cutting the top few coils or heated until they collapsed to a proper cruising height. Then in a flamboyant fashion, they cruised through the streets, honoring El paseo.

There's a kind of knowledge expressed in Lowriding that's not a subject that is taught or valued at school. But it is taught at car club meetings and cruising nights. People who get together around Lowriding tend to share certain things in common: obviously an interest in cars, but also, there is an ethos that this is about more than just a car, but a communal image that needs to be preserved. These sort of informal community building organizations, were created with the understanding that mainstream society and government did not have their best interest in mind. This collectivist culture also spawned the idea that they had to educate themselves.

Lowriding is the artistic representation of resistance. Johnny Gonzales, featured in the series Lowrider Roll Models, explains his connection to his Lowrider community and shares that with his customized vehicle; a green candy painted 1963 Chevrolet Impala SS convertible, he can proclaim; "this is who I am, this is what I stand for" (Velarde, 2019). True education starts with validation of previously held knowledge, such as from one's family and community, an example of Lowrider culture.

Lowriders as Hope

For many, cars are positive confirmations of the human ability to overcome their physical limitation of space (Calvo, 2011). It must have direct impact on the performer or participant of the culture. It must provide a goal, or help to create their own goals. It must be relevant, practical and equally involve learners in defining their own success. It must have hope. Otherwise it will turn into inaction, into hopelessness and despair. Into movements with no foundation and no reason or meaning behind them. Educators need to infuse teaching with action and critical hope (Duncan-Andrade, 2009). At first glance, the art form of Lowriders might seem off-putting to those unfamiliar with the custom, but as we have learned, they helped ease the fears of those living in multiple worlds, and aided in the creation of a new identity. An identity freeing itself from oppression and erasure, and in turn, led many to freedom of expression in a rightful sense. This lifestyle is alive and well today, and continues to give others hope. "[for those] who want to build material hope, must understand that quality is the most significant material resource they have to offer" (Duncan-Andrade, 2009). Material hope as an element of critical hope, comes from the idea that individuals understand their lives and struggles better than anyone else. It also provides hope that they can control their destinies, but not solely at an individual level, but also as a collective in a social group. How someone applies concepts and elements of Lowriders into their own lives is up to each individual, but when Lowriders understand their history and each other, they help provide space to grow, shift, change and rethink what our realities are. It makes teaching and learning relevant and responsive to the languages, literacies, and cultural practices across categories of difference and (in)equality (Freire, 1994). In a space that attempts

Lowrider pedagogy, practitioners become educators and learn to become a part of the lives of others, and be able to exemplify and cultivate solidarity. Those who practice critical hope will be able to better empathize and understand that student and next generations of Lowriders. Developing relationships with others in a community, especially newer, younger generations, is critical to establishing a framework for learning (Freire, 1994; Giroux, 1998). Building something; a car, provides hope for the future. Introducing more intersectional and interdisciplinary curriculum at a young age can help engage their own learning to the point of reclaiming identities beginning at an early stage. We must provide our own truths and create our own futures. Lowrider culture in the classroom and beyond is valuable because it connects various worlds and identities in a new way, attempting to create new pedagogy. It is not just about redefining Lowriders but diving deep into its history, and having a serious purpose. To be a Lowrider today, one must also be a historian and an educator, a person who does in practice what they say in theory. One must be physically and mentally ready twenty-four hours a day, and one must be ready to adopt that lifestyle fully and understand its lineage. (Ulloa, 2019). For too long, the histories, experiences, cultures, and languages of [people of color] have been devalued, misinterpreted, or omitted within formal educational settings (Anzaldua, 1999). Connecting Lowriders to education allows us endure our existence and redefine what counts as knowledge, specifically regarding language, culture, expression, and commitment to communities.

References

Anzaldúa, G. (1999). *Borderlands: La frontera*. Aunt Lute Books.

Anzaldúa, Gloria E. (1999), *Borderlands/La Frontera: The New Mestiza, San Francisco*. 2nd Edition. Aunt Lute Books.

Baldwin, P., & Donohue, J. (1974–1978). *Chico and the man*. Warner Bros. NBC.

Bhaba, H. (2008). *Hybridity and the third space: Paper presented to te oru Rangahau Maori research and development* conference 7–9 July 1998. Massey University: London, Routledge. Retrieved December 02, 2019 from http://lianz.waikato.ac.nz/PAPERS/paul/hybridity.pdf

Bratt, P. (Director). (2009). *La mission* [film] Global Cinema Distribution.

Brayboy, B. M. J. (2005). Toward a tribal critical race theory in education. *The Urban Review*, 425–446. Doi: 10.1007/s11256-005-0018-y

Bright, B. J., & Lisa B. (1995). *Looking high and low: Art and cultural identity*. Tucson: The University of Arizona Press.

Bustamante, L., Lopez, M. H., & Krogstad, J. M. (2019). U.S. Hispanic population surpassed 60 million in 2019, but growth has slowed. *Pew Research Center*.

Chappell, B. (2001). Lowrider cruising spaces. *Américo Paredes Center for Cultural Studies*, University of Texas at Austin. Online dissertation retrieved, November 07, 2019

Cosgrove, S. (1984). The Zoot-suit and style warfare. *History Workshop Journal*, *18*, 77–91.

Cowan, P. (2004). Devils or angels: Literacy and discourse in Lowrider culture. In Jabari Mahiri (ed.), *What they don't learn in school: Literacy in the loves if urban youth* (pp. 47–74). New York, NY: Peter Lang Publishing..

Darder, A., Baltodano, M., & Torres, R. D. (2009). Critical pedagogy: An introduction. In A. Darder, M. Baltodano & R. D. Torres (Eds.), *The critical pedagogy reader* (2nd ed., pp. 1–26). Routledge Falmer.

Del Castillo, R. G. (1990). The treaty of Guadalupe Hidalgo. A legacy of conflict. *University of Oklahoma Press*. Norman Publishing

Delgado Bernal, D. (2001). Critical race theory: Latino critical theory, and critical raced-gendered epistemologies: Recognizing students of color as holders and creators of Knowledge. *Sage Journals*, 8(1), 105–126.

Duncan-Andrade, J. M. R. (2009). Note to educators: Hope required when growing roses in concrete. *Harvard Educational Review, 79*(2), 181–194

Freire, P. (1994). *Pedagogy of the oppressed*. Continuum.

Fuqua, A. (Director). (2001). *Training day.* Village Roadshow Pictures, Outlaw Productions.

Gaspar de Alba, A. (2003). Cruising through lowrider culture. In *VelvetBarrios* (pp. 179–196). Palgrave/Macmillan.

Genat, R. (2001). *Lowriders*. Minnesota: MBI Publishing Company.

Giroux, H., (1988). The hope of radical education: a conversation with Henry Giroux. *The Journal of Education*. Vol 170, No. 2 Pedagogy and Practice (1988) Sage Publications.

Gramsci, A. (1979). *Selections from prison notebooks* (Quinten Hoare & Jeffrey Smith, ed. & trans.). International Publishers .

Hackford, T. (Director). (1993). *Blood in, Blood out* [film]. Hollywood Pictures

Høyem, M. (2007). I want my car to look like a whore: Lowriding and the poetics of outlaw aesthetics. University of Oslo. Online dissertation. Retreived May 2020.

Kantorovich, A. (2014). An evolutionary view of science: Imitation and memetics. *Social Science Information*, *53*(3), 363–373.

Levitt, C., & Lloyd, K. (2012). *Rolling Canvas.* [internet documentary]. Film Lab Productions.

Madrid, S. (Producer). (1979). *Lowriders* [television Broadcast]. Lowrider Magazine

Marin, C. (2012). What is a Chicano?: HuffPost. Retrieved November 2019, from https://www.huffpost.com/entry/what-is-a-chicano_b_1472227

Montañez, V. (2012). Personal Communication. Recorded. April 2012.

Nava, G. (Director). (1997). *Selena.* Q-Productions.

Quijano, A. (2000) Coloniality of power: Eurocentrism and Latin America From *Nepantla; views form the south.*

Rodriguez, R. C. (2010). Amoxtli the xcodex: In lak ech, Panche be & Hunab ku & The forgotten 1524 debate. Eagle Feather Research institute.

Singleton J. (Director). (1991). *Boyz N the Hood*, [film]. Columbia Pictures.

Solorzano, D. G., & Yosso, T. J. (2001). Critical race and Latcrit theory and method: Counterstorytelling Chicana and Chicano graduate school experiences. *International Journal of Qualitative Studies in Education, 14*(4), 471–495

Thomas, N. (1991). *Entangled objects: exchange, material culture, and colonialism in the Pacific.* Harvard University Press.

Ulloa, J. (2019). Professor: San Francisco State University. Personal communication. November 2019.

Velarde, K. (Director). (2019). Lowrider roll models. Lowrider Magazine.

Villalpando, O. (2003). Self-segregation or self-preservation? A critical race theory and Latina/o critical theory analysis of a study of Chicana/o college students. *International Journal of Qualitative Studies in Education, 16*(5), 19–646.

5. Maui the Lowrider: Healing the House of Trouble[1]

LEA LANI KINIKINI AND MARLENA WOLFGRAMM

Introduction

In 1965, the United States immigration system shifted from a quota system that limited Asian and Pacific migration, to an open system privileging family and chain migration. After this pivotal year, many families from Asian and Pacific regions (i.e. Samoan, Tongan, Hawaiian, Marshallese, Filipino, Hmong, Vietnamese, etc. etc.) migrated to the United States. As families arrived to gateway cities such as Honolulu, San Francisco, Los Angeles, and onto other western cities like Sacramento, San Jose, Riverside, San Diego, Reno, Las Vegas, Phoenix, Salt Lake City tied by interstate commercial highways, cars began to connect families. Moreover this deepening and expansive diaspora migration connected Asian and Pacific families to indigenous Chicano families who had birthed the Southwestern, Californian and Coastal Lowrider traditions in the context of post-war, post-industrial America.

Native Hawaiians were the first group of Pacific Islanders to be counted in the U.S. Census in 1960, the year after Hawaii became the fiftieth state (Hixson et al., 2012). Today, there are over 1.2 million NHPIs who make up 1 % (0.40 %) of the entire U.S. population with over half living in Hawaii and California (Hixson et al., 2012). Thanks to NHPI advocates, the Census counted NHPI separately from Asians in 2000 and found that NHPI are one of the fastest growing populations, which increased by 40 percent from 2000 to 2010 and are projected to grow over 2 million by 2030 (Empowering Pacific Islander Communities & Asian Americans Advancing Justice [EPIC & AAAJ], 2014; Hafoka et al., 2020). The disaggregated data further exposed disparities in education attainment, health and socio-economic status that resemble underrepresented and marginalized populations (Hixson et al., 2012; Hafoka et al., 2020).

NHPIs are a relational people with a collective culture, where connections and interpersonal relationships have been maintained throughout Oceania that contrasts the individualistic and competitive American culture (Hau'ofa, 1998; Wolfgramm, 2021). PI cultures are communal, where the family and the community work and learn together for the benefit of the family and the community (Ka'ili, 2008). Similar to PIs, Mexican communities in Tucson, Arizona accumulated funds of knowledge or skills and cultural knowledge that were essential for their household and livelihood, which they shared and exchanged (Moll et al., 1992). With lowriding culture originating in Mexican communities and having similarities to NHPI culture, it comes as no surprise that there is a natural affinity between NHPIs and the lowriding community.

Asian and Pacific families mixed and mingled building inter-family unity within their new homes through a common love of car culture and specifically all the aesthetics and philosophical culture of Lowriding entering into the Lowriding tradition as latecomers, but nonetheless bringing cultural codes with them that emerge as unique contributions and influences. More than anyone, Kita Lealao brought a particular Polynesian ethic and culture, prominently like Chicano cultures, forefronting love and unity. Kita Lealao founded "The Uso Family Car Club" or "The Family" with values of Samoan *alofa* (love), *'ainga* (family and kinship relations). Today despite Kita's passing in March of 2020, the unity which the Uso Car Club with more than 38 club chapters across the globe continues to represent to the fullest.

Class and raced cultural identities, such as lowriders in the social movements of the 1960s, 1970s, and 1980s were part of the liberation movements and social uplift particularly in the urban areas where Uso Family Car Club took flight: San Francisco, San Jose, Los Angeles, San Diego. Class and raced cultural identities, such as lowriders, are conflated with street gangs, syndicated crime families, motorcycle "gangs" etc. and coded as subaltern collectives on the margins of the Anglo-American middle class, often historically erased as criminalized subjectivities. Lowrider and motorcycle clubs are oft conflated in the middle-class public imaginary as subaltern collectives—along with gangs—on the margins of the Anglo-American or white middle class, but lowrider clubs are broader and more culturally permeating—the lowriding tradition is also more than a tradition—it is a movement. This means lowriding as a social movement with a political force and an aesthetic is a transformative line of flight.

> Finally and especially, it [the becoming-animal] incarnates that line of flight the signifying regime cannot tolerate, in other words, an absolute territorialization of the signifying sign, no matter how high it may be. The line of flight is like a

tangent to the circles of significance and the centre of the signifier (Deleuze & Guattari1987).

While the aesthetic and in particular the rebelliousness of lowriders to the status quo, and the lowriding emphasis on civil liberty and freedom on the commercial roads and highways and interstates, and liberation from oppression, lowriders can be seen more as a philosophical blueprint to negotiating and navigating complex sociopolitial disease and disorders, and resisting the political economy of Anglo-American classical liberalism and neoliberalism and a resistance movement to assimilation into neoliberal capitalist sociopolitical structures, while enhancing indigenous art, aesthetics, music, cultural values, worldviews and philosophies. The physical and metaphysical experience of lowriding as resistance to oppression that marginalized peoples face from systemic class oppression, racism, and discrimination can be seen as the reason why love and unity are such important value systems, but moreover why familia/family/'ainga/kainga is such a revolutionary and empowering foundation of Lowrider culture.

Old Heads and Brotherhood: Myth for Healing

To capture this ephemeral and metaphysical or spiritual tradition of brotherhood and social harmony (love) in honor of Kita Lealao and the Uso Family Car Club, in this chapter we look at Maui, the youthful demi-god trickster from Polynesian or Oceanian cultures, whose life encodes several thousand years of indigenous wisdom in risk-taking, young men's place during a liminal epochs between youth and Elders. As an elder statesman of Lowriding, Kita's expansive ability to connect diverse peoples and cultures under an umbrella of love and unity are important aspects to celebrate. Like indigenous culture *Fa'a Samoa* (the Samoan Way), Maui's legends centers respect for Elders, and Elders teaching younger members in a strong, strict, and highly bonded culture of brotherhood (*uso/tokoua* meaning brother in Samoan and Tongan).

Brotherhood as well as Sonship in indigenous Polynesian culture center Elder-younger respect, loyalty, and cohesion. At times of conflict between the young and the Elders, there must be a way to return harmony inclusive and embracing those who are left out, or who fall out, as a way to practice love –an ability to forgive and reconcile peacefully after times of conflict, division, disagreement, disobeying or unrest and social upheaval. Some of the underlying tensions that face Pacific young men has been the emergence and convergence of gangs and the troublesome lifeways that are encapsulated by gang banging, for example. Maui in some legends is known to head the "House of Trouble". Given the high rates of Asian and Pacific Islander incarceration, youth participation in crime and illicit political-economies, and social the emphasis on the positive vision of Kita Lealao addresses how healing the "House of Trouble" (the divergence of young Samoans and Tongans and other youth immigrants into the underworld) from the bone outward through an attention to story is part of living the ethos of Family unity. For although Maui traverses the known worlds, and often entered the dark underworld of Pulotu, he always returned, or in many of the cautionary tales died trying to return, or died by continuing to pursue pushing beyond what the boundary limit could maintain.

This chapter is a narrative meditation through the skin of story, the tissue of myth, and into the blood, veins, guts and ultimately bone of Maui and the House of Trouble. Maui, in contrast to some of the other tricksters from around the world, was definitely human, and he was definitely a youngster—a teenager most likely. That tells us that his life was spoken of for the particular identification and benefit of the young, as a program of thought to model correct behaviour—and warn of becoming too arrogant and convinced of one's invincibility or "specialness". There's no doubt about it: Maui was a youth offender, who thought he was if not above the law, then definitely *beyond* the law. Maui the outlaw-rider.

The Maui is a key in understanding young Polynesian men's cultural footprint and helps explore the Uso Family Car Club values of family and unity. Maui comments specifically on what happens, as a cautionary tale, when the boundaries are pushed, and break. Maui focuses on the dynamic of younger-older sibling and age hierarchy in both Tonga and Samoa and how that plays into the passing down of indigenous wisdom through the practices of Polynesian chieftainship and masculine cultural order-keeping within 'ainga/kainga/'aina, family and kinship networks.

Who is Maui?

The question "Who is Maui" is inappropriate. The better question is "*Which one is Maui?*" because Maui has multiple tellings, multiple beginnings, and multiple endings. Maui leaves traces in many places and across many times—but one thing isn't multiple: Maui is "of" Oceania. *Maui is us.* Maui is an ancient code for healing with love when families get separated or fall out of unity. The progenitor of many Pacific peoples, Maui was first and foremost a young outcast and while highly gifted, was an outsider to the family which accounts for his heroics—trying to earn respect and acceptance.

The story of Maui the Younger, is one that is critical to Polynesian young men, critical to guide various aspects of their soul growth within cultural frameworks, for Maui represents Polynesian society on a macro level, and Maui represents a power dynamic between youth and elders, and between men, thus commenting on the social order of Polynesians as small societies with a strong warrior and priestly traditions, governed by chieftains that helped societies settled on small islands in vast massive trepidatious expanses of volatile oceans survive, and also persist for more than three thousand years, unrivalled and unconquered, through an ethic of strong cultural orders, loyalty, respect which creates a stable distance and love which creates harmony and cohesion. The life evolution of Maui however is how to shape youthful risk and war-making into the wisdom of the elders, where social order is restored, social cohesion and balance maintained.

Maui, whose stories tell of transversals re-member that dissolution or transgressive crossing has the potential to become a space of possibility for potential growth and renewal, a return to the possibility multiple ways to become. Maui legend is a story for healing and growth, as it is a story that is woven from genealogy, imbued with the wisdom of the ancients. The legend of Maui that we have is a great gift and inheritance. There is a great deal of source material on Maui consisting largely of myths and chants now coded into manuscripts and publications. The myths are popular in and are told without tapu (restriction)—Maui myths, it seems were "noa" (unrestricted) and that even "untrained storytellers" could narrate them (Luomala, 1949). The majority of published tissue comes from Aotearoa.

The various exploits and, importantly, transformations enacted by Maui are, as I mentioned above, two characteristics of Maui consciousness. The first aspect is that Maui was an abandoned child—a "throwaway kid" to use a term from popular discourse from the industrial cities of the west. Beyond being thrown away like garbage, there is also the notion of Maui's quest to become reconstituted within his birth family: he yearns for inclusion and longs to fit in. Luomala notes that questions about origin "...reflect Polynesian concern with genealogies and the difficulty of knowing the identity of one's parents due to the customs of adoption and of abandoning unwanted children, particularly those born to parents of different social classes" (Luomala, 1949).

The second aspect of Maui's psychology is that Maui is a younger son, a junior to a hierarchy of elders. In Polynesian societies, the mana of the family was normally conferred in greater degree upon the eldest sons, at the expense of junior sons. However, mana is a power both externally appropriated and, more importantly, internally accessed which is what Maui clearly shows: the potential of the individual who is subjectified within a dense hierarchy.

Luomala writes, "A junior member of a family or a person of low rank may assume important duties if men of superior birth prove lacking in courage, judgement, generosity and accomplishment, the qualities indicative of mana. The concept of mana worked as a leaven in the feudal society of Polynesia and its theoretically rigid class distinctions based on birth. One could lose mana, as well as acquire it" (Luomala, 1949). Like all mythical templates based on likely either an individual or a collective origin tribe, Maui can be taught and re-membered in different ways[2]. Which face of Maui do you want to see? Because he will show you many. . .a multiplicity of forms, for the story of interiority and exteriority is the story of Maui, who is our border-crosser, our tapu-breaker of Oceania. In the Maui legends, there are always multiple Maui: Maui the grandfather, Maui the father and Maui the son; or, a series of Maui who are brothers. Maui's ". . .name crops up in a greater variety of situations than that of any other God or spirit in the Polynesian pantheon" (Luomala, 1949). According to Maori accounts, Maui had three fingers (Luomala, 1949). A Reverend Wohlers, a missionary in Aotearoa in the 19th century, held that Maui ". . .in the present language [te reo Maori] means left, or left-handed" (Luomala, 1949). Other sources say Maui means "life" (Luomala, 1949). One of the stories of Maui describes him as having eight heads (Luomala, 1949). Maui is usually "The Maui", or multiple people; five brothers each named Maui; or as grandfather, father, and son, each named Maui. The Maui is Oceania's way of teaching the spiritual principles transformation and evolution.

Maui is an active resister and agitator to expand the world (fighting, stealing fire to give to humanity, tricking the sun, and braving the ocean swells to fish up islands), pushing boundaries (or lines of flight as Deleuze puts it) through times of social discord and disconnection, through rejection, through distillation of painful experiences, to render the great heights of the mountain –Maui's burden is to be othered in a society that has very tight social cohesion. To enact the transversals, and to bring those on the outside back into alignment and integration into the Family, Maui is a role model of a rebel, but eventually, tells a cautionary tale of contain your growth or else. Growth as a youth, evolves into an elder, and Maui is a necessary evolution of the divine masculine as Maui the younger matures into Maui Motu'a and tells how to go from a young man into an "ulumotu'a" or "Old Head".

Maui began life as a blood clot –an abortion or miscarriage. His mother, having given birth to this blood clot, this un-formed mass, had no recourse except to wrap him in her topknot—her hair bun atop her skull—which she cut—a symbol of both great mourning and indicating hair as a central transmission vehicle of mana—indicating Maui's genetic coding was encased in the most pristine Mana—she cast her blood clot in the sea. Jelly fish succoured him after abandonment and swam with him. Jelly fish are—even for fish—an otherworldly participant, a creature of the deep otherworld wired for a world of darkness. Adrift, Maui floated washed ashore on a distant island ...and like all things Oceanic, no man is an island,—the island belonging to Maui's Grandfather. Maui washed ashore into a tree where he was found.

The exile of Maui—his entire formative years—away from his birth family is an important point. Because of his Maui was reared by the Grandparents—a metaphor for a spiritual home of a world beyond this world—he had access to more "grids" than any other being in all of the legends. He was raised in this non-human realm and yet as he matured, he experienced what can only be surmised as a "homing instinct". One day he returned to the island of his mother and father to take his place as the youngest of several sons. This is not the return of the prodigal son, but the return of the outcast.

Maui's separation from his Family mark him as different. His origins were obscure to him and he was unknown to his parents and siblings; each of his escapades can be read as an attempt by an outcast to receive reintegration into the family collective. As a result, Maui didn't always fit in, and was constantly at odds with authority, playing tricks and exploiting what he knew were the power differentials between the human and the other worlds. He routinely broke tapu after tapu, propelled by a need to shift laws, to test the limits of his capacity as a sort of "second son" who had been gifted a "second sight" from his long exile from home whilst on his grandfather's island. This is Maui's burden, a double consciousness, "born with a veil, and gifted with second sight" (Dubois, 1995).

Interlude

Maui flicks a cigarette on the side of Kamehameha Highway and an abandoned Oldsmobile Rocket Eighty-Eight bursts into flames. As the windows shatter Maui turns to run brightly away from the scene of the crime yelling, "Sistah, what is needed is a new weave!"

"What?" I say, for again I cannot hear above the noise, "A niu weave?"

"No, a NEW weave sistah, A NEW WEAVE!!!"

Maui teaches that a young person must not only surf the highly charged waves, but must also learn to negotiate the low-sides of every life situation. Maui provides young men in particular, the meaning of family, love (self-love), and unity (integration into a positive community). Maui myth like low-riding is about breaking boundaries and codes of space and time, and about transversals of gravity and the epic soul journeys that allow one to transcend space and time that lowriding entail.

Most oceanic accounts say Maui is forever frozen in his youth, for his life is cut short by his foolish attempts to achieve immortality. The storytellers uniformly "...end by telling of his death for having over-reached himself and his own authority" (Luomala, 1949). Maui is punished for living the life listeners only can dream of living. Luomala theorizes that they have persisted as a way to conventionalize and control the vagaries related to hierarchical societies such as the ones found in Polynesia, as well as an imaginative escape from the world, allowing "...conventionalized release from burdens of society and limitations of the physical world" (Luomala, 1949). Mythic characters are often, as Michael Shapiro writes, given "no stable inner character" but remain objects of the speech (Shapiro, 1991). Futa Helu writes hat Maui myth teaches the creative value of risk-taking:

> In fact, all the myths that epitomise the transformation of Maui (Tongan society) declare that culture is invariably the product of resolute effort by perilous enterprise – lands are being torn off from their original moorings, creatures are being subdued and made captive, fire is stolen on a path of death, etc. etc. (Helu, 1999).

Passageways

Even as lowriding deconstructs a factory machine, interrupts and recodes it, so Maui takes a given set of social rules, and breaks them, and by doing so transforms it into new possibility. The ancients educated youngsters with tales of Maui. Maui's exploits and transgressions provide transformations that are in the best interest of a social order that has outgrown its purpose; Maui is bad for good reasons. He disrupts established tapu with the intent to improve the status quo and transform nature. According to Tongan scholar Futa Helu, Maui myth is a metaphor for Polynesian society, a "hypotheses of history". Moreover as a mythic hypothesis, Maui's death is a template that tells of what can happen during periods of social transformation (Helu, 1999). Helu tells of Maui attempting to obtain the secret of immortality from the sleeping Goddess Hine-nui-te-Po by entering her vagina and coming out her mouth again, a transversal of the accepted order of things, or the signifier (Luomala, 1949). Helu reads this demise as such:

> ...a depiction of the body politic and that rebellious spirits who attempt a transmutation of values (represented by the reversal of direction of natural processes in Maui's act) achieve their apotheoses through being sacrificed at the alter of social integrity and permanence (Helu, 1999).

Lowriding as a tricker aesthetic, and a transmutation of values—reversing directions and natural processes. The trickster in their transgressive joyous transborder transformative ecstasy is about exchanges—transforming and transacting inasmuch as one part must be traded. The trickster, who has turned the world on its head, with and through a lowrider consciousness, must also concede to *some* of the limits of the social order, for however the lowrider violates boundaries to humanize and transform the machine, so must they also submit to the ever-changing and external powers that be:

> This is one of the points of the trickster's irony: all that wheeling and dealing, that endless juggling, simply keeps new balls flying through the air in the same order and at the same speed. Even where his only ritual is the telling of his stories, his work is, above all, synchronous. His transforming power has worked in the past to create the present, and it works in the present to make the future reflect the past. He moves past society's circumference to ensure the permanent rediscovery of its center (Pelton, 1980).

Similarly, the lowriding impetus is to make the future reflect the past. Lowrider cars are trickster vehicles, animated, spiritual. The lowriding is a vehicle that is recomposing the past. But to get to that shore is the trickster's journey—and the return is the *trickiest* part for after the journey, for the trickster's role is "to recompose, not simply to expose" (Pelton, 1980) an alternative "social geography":

> [The Trickster] embodies transaction. For this reason he is a mediator specializing in 'exchanges' – a perpetually open passageway. He transforms by no plan except the shape of his own urge to realize the act of dealing, yet because this drive necessarily creates intercourse, he establishes the social geography of the world in the very process of playing out his own inner design (Pelton, 1980).

Lowriding as a form of time-travel or exchanges preserving and reinterpreting the past while also resisting the *transactional* oppression of the factory, the school and centering the *relational* commons of the workshop, the garage, the driveway, the streets. Lowriding deconstructs and recombines the time clock, while centering the hands that repurpose, centering radical aesthetics. Lowriding opens up these passageways to enact a resistance to the grids of order.

Clarissa Pinkola Estes, a Jungian psychoanalyst, poet and cantadora, "a keeper of the old stories" writes:

> In dealing with stories, we are handling archetypal energy...archetype changes us. Archetype infuses a recognizable integrity, a recognizable endurance...we are charged to make certain that people are completely and fully wired for the stories they carry and tell (Estes, 1992).

Lowriding represents the passageway from the past to the future, so does Maui storytelling provided a myth to live (Campbell, 1972) tempering youthful risks into the wisdom of the Elders. The mana—as Kita Lealao had to influence our beliefs about who we are—who we were (the past) and who we are becoming (the past-future). Trickster myths, in particular, develop in the young a capacity for truth-seeking and moral identity (Pelton, 1980). In the Elders, the trickster myth tempers abuses of power by reminding us that spirit travels in all regardless of age or status, and there is particular power and magic in youth that cannot be underestimated.

Conclusion

Maui we have reached the other side! Thank you Maui. Maui the son, Maui the trickster, Maui the transgressor, Maui the bordercrosser, Maui the lowrider, Maui the navigator of new line possibilities, this Maui went off-grid, a burden of crossing, swimming through dangerous dark waters to pull up from the deep blue something to play with: a story on fire, a live bullet it pulsed in my hands, the power transfiguring. . .a story to heal the house of trouble.

The Greek meaning of the word myth is to be "charged with a special seriousness or importance" (Shapiro, 1991). Maui myth as a serious and important one of healing, a myth of redemption, a couple perspectives are useful. Maui myth is a powerful program of thought that contains Polynesian cultural patterns of great antiquity. Roland Barthes sees myth as a "tissue of codes" which controls a text, run by "the order of the signifier" (Shapiro, 1991). Similarly, Joseph Campbell sees myths as ". . .controlled and intended statements of certain spiritual principles. . ." (Campbell, 1949). In Campbell's thought, myths speak in the same archetypal language as dreams, but they are conscious rather than subconscious:

Their [dreams and myths] figures originate from the same sources—the unconscious wells of fantasy—and their grammar is the same, but they are not the spontaneous products of sleep. On the contrary, their [myth] patterns are consciously controlled metaphors. And their function is to serve as a powerful picture language for the communication of traditional wisdom. This is true already of the so-called primitive folk mythologies, metaphors by which they live, and through which they operate, have been brooded upon, searched, and discussed for centuries—even millenniums; they have served whole societies, furthermore, as the mainstays of thought and life. The culture patterns have been shaped to them. The youth have been educated, and the aged rendered wise, through the study, experience, and understanding of their effective initiatory form (Campbell, 1949).

The trickster evolution of Maui generates an awareness of the transformative capacity of healing youth and strengthening into Elders. Pelton writes that tricksters are ironic characters, and irony is the rub of life (Pelton, 1980). To get to the rub of life one must see beyond dialectic pairs. Lowriders like The Maui ride an eternal dialectic between the unbridled boundary-pushing passion of the young and the tempering wisdom of the Ancients.

By raising the Maui legend, this chapter hopes to make space for understanding the *mana* (spiritual power) of Kita Lealao's vision for the Uso Family Car Club. The unity principal for maintaining family connections, reinforcing that when one member of a family is lost, for example to street violence, drug addiction, incarceration and death, that we must search and reintegrate them and adapt the family to unite them into the collective– 'ainga, through alofa/'ofa—love.

Notes

1 This chapter was inspired by the late Kita Lealao, founder of The Uso Family Car Club.
2 A community-based rite of passage program in Hawai'i that does just this in the Maui Hero Project. For details see www.mauihero.com.

References

Barthes, R. (1972). *Critical essays* (Richard Howard Evanston, Trans.). Northwestern University.

Campbell (1949). *The Hero With a Thousand Faces.* Joseph Campbell Foundation: Princeton University Press.

Campbell (1972). *Myths to Live By.* Viking Press.

Deleuze, G., & Guattari, F. (1987). *A thousand plateaus: Capitalism and schizophrenia.* University of Minnesota Press.

Dubois, W. E. B. (1995). *The souls of black folk.* Penguin.

Estes, C. P. (1992). *Women who run with the wolves: Myths and stories of the wild woman archetype.* Ballantine Books.

Hafoka, Inoke. (2020). *From Navigating the Seas to Navigating the Skies: Unloading Tongan Knowledge through the Undercurrents of Airline Employment in the Ano Māsima.* PhD Dissertation: UCLA.

Hau'ofa, E. (1998). "The Ocean in Us", *The Contemporary Pacific.* Vol. 10, No. 2, pp. 392-420. University of Hawai'i Press.

Helu, F. (1999). *Critical essays: Cultural perspectives from the south seas.* The Journal of Pacific History ANU Printing Service.

Hixson, L., Hepler, B., & Kim, M. (2012). *The Native Hawaiian and other Pacific Islander.* population: 2010. U.S. Census.

Ka'ili, T. O. (2008). *Tauhi va: Creating beauty through the art of sociospatial relations.* Unpublished Dissertation.

Luomala, K. (1949). *Maui-of-a-thousand-tricks: His Oceanic and European biographers.* The Bishop Museum.

Moll, L., Amanti, C., Neff, D., & Gonzalez, N. (1992). Funds of knowledge for teaching: Using a qualitative approach to connect homes and classrooms. *Theory Into Practice, 31, 2.*

Pelton, R. D. (1980). The trickster in West Africa: A study of mythic irony and sacred delightt. University of California Press.

Shapiro, M. J. (1991). *Reading the postmodern polity: Political theory as textual practice.* University of Minnesota Press.

Westervelt, W. D. (1910). *Legends of Maui: A demi-god of Polynesia and of his mother.* George Robertson & Company.

Wolfgramm, M. V. (2021). *The Influence of Community Cultural Wealth and Tauhi Vā on the Navigation of Pacific Islanders in Science, Technology, Engineering and Mathematics (STEM).* Doctoral dissertation: The Claremont Graduate University.

6. Car Clubs to Cohorts

DIONICIO MIGUEL GARCIA

Introduction

Lowriding has historically served as a platform of self-expression and belonging for a segment of the Latinx community. Since the implementation of repatriation programs in the 1930s, and before, Latinx communities were stripped of their ancestral and ethnic heritage. Since the 1960s there have been ever increasing numbers of ethnically & socioeconomically diverse students in college. Thus, educators need to reach out to them in innovative ways that address their interests and home communities. Self-expression and building community positively impacts an individual's sense of belonging, thus increasing self-esteem. Lowriding allows students to challenge prescribed social narratives and rewrite them in a way that validates their experience. Institutions of higher learning often lack opportunities for individuals to learn about their background and self, neglecting parts of their identity that make it easier for them to connect to academia as well as find a purpose in society. The structural, economic, and racial forms of oppression faced by many historically marginalized communities often result in non-inclusive campus climates that contribute to current inequalities within the educational system. The purpose of this chapter is to explore the *Low and Slow* lifestyle as a non-traditional pedagogy within counseling and teaching settings in higher education. Connecting students to their culture by making parallels between counseling curriculum and Lowriding in community colleges may increase engagement in historically marginalized youth, thus increasing their sense of belonging and validating their own experiences as a form of empowerment.

Lowriding Background

The history of lowriding originates from the United States since the 1930s when Mexicans were targeted across the country. The Repatriation Act during the Great Depression caused deportation of millions of US citizens to Mexico due to a weak economy resulting in a shortage of jobs and food. The increase of propaganda, much like we see today, portrayed Mexicans as the cause of this failing economy creating tensions amongst White and Latino people. The true form of Lowriding began to shape its identity during the WWII era in the 1940s as a form of resistance from the Anglo societal way of life. Discrimination toward Mexican-Americans resulted in the Zoot Suit Riots when U.S. servicemen beat up Chicanos in places like Oakland, Los Angeles & Chicago for wearing flamboyant attire, which was seen as "unpatriotic" according to the Anglo society. Although they fought on the frontlines during WWII, Mexican-American citizens were disregarded and seen as problematic.

After decades of systemic racism and oppression, the Chicano community began to form its identity by taking the "American Dream" and resisting oppression in the form of music, fashion, cars, and customs to show they belong just as much as the next American citizen. The Lowrider culture was founded on this systemic racism and illustrates a form of social protest, promoting social awareness and activism within lowrider events. In its early years, Lowrider Magazine used its platform, position of power and privilege to convey political conversations. They published articles to editors, promoted political events known as "happenings" to organize people in communities to overcome the oppression that our people experienced for decades.

Personal Background

Background in Lowriding

Lowriding has been a big part of my identity ever since I was a young child. In fact, my parents brought me home from the hospital days after I was born in a lowrider, a 1970 Chevrolet Caprice. Being born and raised in South San Francisco, California, a few miles outside of San Francisco I have plenty of memories involving lowriders at community events. One of my earliest memories of lowriding took place at Orange Park in South San Francisco at a barbeque sponsored by Frisco's Finest, a car club based out of San Francisco. It was there when I watched how the candy paint and pattern flakes on the cars sparkled bright in the sun. As the gold spokes spun as cars rolled on by, I would listen to the music playing out of the trunk of cars and see full smiles of the community members as they danced and gathered for a plate of Carne Asada and Lechon (Filipino pork). Kids ran around playing games such as tug-o-war or relay races and getting their face painted brought plenty of joy to these events. People of various diverse backgrounds and neighborhoods come together for common interest in lowriding, family, and solidarity. This is what has come from my interest in building community and seeing how people come together for a common purpose to thrive as one.

As a child absorbing the lowrider game, I quickly noticed the importance of lowiding and how it positively impacted our communities which were often disrupted due to systemic divides, such as neighborhood gangs. Not only was Lowriding a form of self-expression but also an effort to support our people by encouraging solidarity amongst our divided communities. This was my first introduction into lowriding and has impacted my belief on the importance of building community.

As children, my brothers and I would save our birthday cash to purchase bicycle parts at a local store on Grand Avenue in South San Francisco. Through time, patience, and effort we completed our masterpiece that brought us closer to our culture to attend community events with bicycles of our own. We proudly rode our bikes around the neighborhood and to local car shows to express our individual, authentic selves. I'd think about how I would incorporate my identity into an automotive creation. This passion later led to purchasing my own car to build and proudly display my personal style.

Lowrider Culture

In my younger years, my father took us back-to-school shopping at Siegel's, a clothing store near 19th and Mission streets in San Francisco. We had the choice of buying Ben Davis or Dickies, and a pair of Converse or K-Swiss shoes if it was within our budget due to affordability and durability because we did not have the luxury to buy new clothes frequently. At the time, my father worked two jobs in order to provide for three growing boys so our choice was Ben Davis which was an American-made clothing company that lasted for years. We wore Converse shoes for their affordability; we could not afford big name brand shoes such as Air Jordans. However, during this time, wearing Converse in our communities had a negative image to the angelo society because it resembled gang paraphernalia which added that extra layer of racial profiling from law enforcement. Youth from the community I grew up in dressed in similar fashion creating this image of "gang activity" when in reality we were just dressing with what was financially appropriate and accessible at the time. We used this style of clothing and wore it as a form of resistance similar to the way the Pachucos (a term to prefer to Mexican American men and women during the 1930s & 40's) wore their Zoot Suits.

As a matter of fact, these army surplus and clothier stores were very common in Black and Brown communities. The history behind these army surplus stores stemmed from WWII as the demand of blue collar workers increased in big cities such as San Francisco, Oakland, and Los Angeles. Due to the increased demand of laborers to work on machinery and ships for the war, people of color decided to move to these surrounding areas in search of work and to contribute to the war efforts overseas. It is not uncommon to still see some of the people within these communities adopt this style of clothing as part of their own cultural identity today.

Although lowriding is a huge part of my identity, I hid this lifestyle from my peers in school to avoid being judged. Despite my efforts, I was harassed by school staff, administrators, as well as the local police because of the negative misconceptions about lowriding. I faced discrimination and endured discomfort in educational spaces l when I dressed true to my identity and culture.

As a Chicano male, I was the first in my family to graduate from college. My drive to work with people of color who have traditionally been underrepresented in education comes from a deep personal connection to issues of educational equity. I noticed there is a lack of fair opportunities and challenges that are often ignored by community colleges and universities. Growing up in South San Francisco, I personally lacked accessibility to information and resources that would have led me to higher education. I experienced and overcame some of the same structural, economic, and racial forms of oppression that contribute to the current inequalities within the educational system faced by many students of color today.

The faculty and staff at my high school racially profiled my friends and I based on the neighborhood we grew up in and in many ways prevented us from focusing on our education by sending us to the principal's office. In the eyes of our school administration, we were expected to fail and head in a bad direction due to their judgements based on our appearances. We were accustomed to getting our backpacks and lockers searched and being humiliated in front of our classmates by having our names called on the loudspeaker. These experiences give me a unique understanding of the struggles that people of color encounter in high school providing them with a negative perception on what college would be like. This served as my main motivation to incite change within the educational system to better support these students as they transition into college.

Reflecting back during my senior year in high school, I was encouraged to enroll in an afterschool program called *Hermanos* (Brothers) which served to inspire and assist predominantly Latino males who were first-generation students to pursue higher education by transitioning into two and four-year college institutions. Since going through the *Hermanos* program, I learned first-hand the importance of identity development and building social-cultural capital through mentorship. This inspired me to implement a program geared for Latino men and men of color who may feel disconnected from the education system due to societal and systemic barriers. The Hermanos program opened up various opportunities for me and provided a new outlook on what college was.

Here's Literature to Back It up

My personal background navigating higher education motivated me to focus my research on men of color who are first-generation college students from low income backgrounds. This research guided me to implement a men of color program titled *Brothers Empowering Brothers* at the College of San Mateo primarily to promote academic success and mentorship. This research also guided me to develop my pedagogical practice utilizing the low and slow lifestyle. This is some of the research that I found so I can better support working with men of color and other underrepresented students.

Throughout the last several year(s), the Latino population has been one of the fastest growing ethnic groups across the United States and has quickly become the majority in states like California, Arizona, Texas, and New Mexico. Furthermore, Latinos also have the youngest major ethnic group in the United States. Although the Latino population constitutes for a significant portion of the population, college enrollments among Latino students tend to head in the opposite direction. Latino males are more likely to drop out of high school, have lower college retention rates, and receive fewer Associate degrees compared to Black and White students. Furthermore, Latino women outnumber men across college campuses throughout the US.

While there is a great amount of research on women of color being historically disadvantaged in the educational system, researchers have yet to highlight the various obstacles faced by men of color at the intersection of race and gender. As described by Saenz and Ponjuan (2008), Latino males are "vanish[ing] in the education pipeline" when compared to other ethnic and gender groups. Simply said, Latino males are more likely to drop out of high school, join the workforce, or become institutionalized in the prison system, similar to their African-American peers who face similar challenges. Further, these students of color tend to be academically punished instead of guided toward success. It is clear that Latino males experience "leaks" in the educational pipeline but there is minimal research that showcases programs and/or interventions that are successful in increasing enrollment, retention and persistence rates among this population.

Historically, Latinos are known to face a lack of support in high school, resulting in forming negative views on going to college. Following graduation from high school, Latino students are more likely to attend a community college than traditional 4-year universities. Community colleges tend to be more accessible, cost a fraction of the price compared to a 4-year university and provide you with the opportunity to enroll in classes part-time or full-time. According to Ceja and Hoover (2010), community colleges are currently struggling with overall retention, persistence, degree completion, and successful transfer to a 4-year institution amongst Latino students, more specifically Latino males.

A particular challenge faced by many Latino males is a lack of sense of belonging and mentorship on college campuses, which may lead to feelings of isolation, exclusion and low academic self-esteem. Saenz and Ponjuan found that 28.4 % of Latino males (ages 16–24 years old) dropped out of high school at higher rates when compared with their female counterparts at 18.5 %, 13.5 % of African-American males and 7.1 % White males (2008). It is also important to consider that the overwhelming majority of Latino students are the first in their families to attend college (also referred to as "first-generation college students"). Given that most Latino students are the first in their families to attend college, many do not have access to the knowledge and skills to navigate college which in turn negatively impacts their academic awareness and skills.

Lack of social capital or knowledge from family members has been shown to be critical for successfully navigating through the educational system. First-generation college students face unique challenges that include finding a balance between academic & financial obligations, and lack of cultural relevance implemented into course curriculum. The lack of cohort programs that enable Latino students to use their personal cultural values to learn new skill sets and knowledge to persist in higher education. Given that most Latino men in college are enrolled in community colleges and are the first in their families in higher education, it is critical that community colleges look closely into the barriers Latinos face in college and provide support to overcome these unique hardships. The current academic systems in place are acting as a form of oppression to students of color by not allowing them to fit into their "academic-style."

The purpose of this chapter is to implement the *Low and Slow* lifestyle as an uniquely transformative pedagogy within counseling and teaching settings in higher education. Connecting students to cultural backgrounds through the history of lowriding will bridge the gap between the disconnect in curriculum taught in higher education. Through this increased sense of belonging, the validation of their lived experiences is a form of empowerment and systemic resistance.

Here's How Lowriding Fills the Gaps

Throughout my academic career, I have gained experience by receiving my Bachelor's in Hospitality & Tourism Management and a Master's in Counseling. Through my counseling background, I have been trained to address college students' academic, career, personal and social developmental goals. Fortunately, with these opportunities, I have obtained the highest professional training possible by learning an in-depth concept of multiculturalism and social justice within the educational system. Further, I had the opportunity to work in spaces such as EOPS (Extended Opportunity Programs and Services) who work with underrepresented students at the community college level which was designed to improve access, retention and completion of educational goals for low-income students. As a student, college was a huge transition for me as I lacked experiences needed to successfully acculturate to higher education. Like myself, many Indigenous, Black, and persons of color coming from underrepresented communities, do not have elders who attended college. Typically, education was of least importance as it did not contribute to immediate means of survival. Through my personal experiences and those around me, I understand the unique obstacles and barriers that students encounter.

Through my professional practice, I have the personal obligation to develop innovative ways to teach students about career exploration through a pedagogical practice that resonates with many students from underserved communities. This pedagogy allows the students to challenge the narratives, share their perspectives and go back to their communities to empower one another.

Lowriding Pedagogy

Components of Lowriding Practices: Authenticity, Community, & Healing

My approach as a Counselor and Educator is to pass down knowledge and wisdom through the lens of lowriding. This pedagogical approach is not to force lowriding on to the students, but is used a way to spread awareness using 3 key elements,

- Authenticity
- Community
- Healing

These three pillars help create an environment that is welcoming, safe, and allows the students to explore, reflect & heal past trauma they may have experienced in previous educational settings and in life. Similar to people bouncing their cars up and down at car hops trying to reach new levels of the highest distance possible from the ground up, my goal when working with students is to gradually have them reach the level of healing. True healing takes time, takes many bounces of up and down motions, ultimately resulting in true healing and fulfilment.

Authenticity

My goal, whether I am teaching or counseling, is to put the students first and allow them to be their authentic self. I achieve this by supporting them to gain a better understanding of where they come from and what they are into and what is around them to help navigate their educational and life journeys until they reach their true authentic self. Reflect back on a time where you had to enter a new job or space for the first time and you did not know anyone. What came up for you? Did you feel you would not fit in? Did you think about what if people don't like you? These are similar questions a first time college student would ask themselves if they had to enter a new school for the first time. For many of us that come from underrepresented communities, we are departing one world where we already have an established identity and purpose and are entering another world where we are confused on how to navigate being a college student. It is important for us to provide the necessary tools for our students to succeed in college and evolve into a successful college student.

Many students who are the first in their family to attend college may feel uncomfortable adapting to this new environment for a variety of reasons. Those reasons may range from their cultural differences and the way they dress or appear in the eyes of their peers, lack of preparation for college due to minimal access to resources in low income communities, and eliminating career or major options due to the lack of awareness of skills and access to opportunities. These differences contribute to low levels of academic self-esteem and difficulty adjusting to the college setting. In fact, despite coming from low income communities and very few resources, many of the students that I work with come with an abundance of "non traditional"

experiences. Whether they are navigating life such as taking on work opportunities with their families in order to put food on the table or taking care
of siblings or elders or running errands for a family business all the while
managing school are great ways we can highlight the students' successes on
how they manage to find a balance. Typically students doubt their abilities as
their skillsets are not seen as being of academic importance. Students require
support to translate their skills into ways to become more competitive from a
career standpoint. Building confidence in their own ability to be academically
competitive and successful is foundational.

This will occur with allowing them to be their authentic self and bring
parts of their world into this new space we call a classroom. Higher Self-esteem
is the outcome. We strive for social interactions and belongings however we
need to understand who we are first. How can we stay true to ourselves and
our values as we enter spaces, such as a classroom or counselors office. This is
not an easy task. We push our youth to pursue college and chase their dreams
however we don't provide them the tools necessary to succeed.

Strategies to Reach Authenticity

I will put this into perspective when I am teaching a class, for example,
I begin the first couple of class sessions watching a Lowrider Youtube series
titled "*Lowrider Roll Models*". This online documentary series examines the
lives and challenges of people in the lowrider community. By showcasing
their lowriders or classic cars, they highlight personal milestones that ultimately shaped and impacted the person they have become. I highlight this
series as an example to (1) Show relevance to the struggles people of color face
(2) Breaks down stereotypes society placed on lowriding and people of color
(3) Serve as a way to explore careers through storytelling (4) encourage students to share their own narratives and (5) Express their individual passions.

After the conclusion of the video, we discuss the hardships the person
in the video overcame and reflect on how the story may or may not resonate with us. Creating dialogue amongst the group will allow us to find
our voices, share our unique narrative as Latinos, and how we continue to
overcome them. By sharing our stories, we begin to let down our guards,
trust, and truly begin the process of authenticity. We follow up the group
discussion by putting our stories on paper by creating our own lowriders
using a template of a lowrider of their choice. For their design, students can
showcase life events, cultural backgrounds, and interests, and personalities.
I provide a series of examples of cars with murals, words, and patterns that
represent the owner and their personal backgrounds to highly encourage

them to personalize this car in a meaningful way that expresses their true individuality. I also ask for them to name their car so they collectively create a name that is representative to the uniqueness of the group such as their interests, hobbies, or other factors representing their identities. This project has allowed the students to express their true *self* similar to the way lowriders are designed with candy paint, murals based on stories and loved ones.

Providing them a space and platform to showcase their true identity is highly impactful to one's self-esteem because they will feel more relaxed to speak in front of other individuals without judgement, feel empowered to share their experiences and find validation amongst the classroom. Increasing one's self-esteem will create higher resiliency when encountering barriers, form secure and honest relationships and ability to make decisions without questioning their abilities all of which is highly important in higher education.

Creative a Village

We can all agree that finding a group or sense of belonging and togetherness is highly important to fulfil our social needs. We have experienced this during the worldwide COVID-19 pandemic. Effects of the pandemic caused families to become more distant, separating social groups and removing the actual physical experience of college campuses for students. Approximately 60 % of my students this current academic school year were the first in their families to attend college and already lacked the knowledge on how to navigate the educational system including financial aid literacy, enrolling in support services and finding academic tutoring. Take someone who is the first to navigate any space, ask them to attend and learn from home but still expect and require the same academic success, can create overwhelming and frustrating feelings and in many cases, resulting in a lack of self-confidence or blame. On multiple occasions, students have expressed the lack of empathy and support from professors teaching in distant learning leaving negative impressions on the educational system. It is important that we continue to practice interdependence and togetherness amongst our students and question ourselves: *Who am I in this group? Who are you in this group and who are we together? What can we do and bring to make this group function?* By exploring these questions, the classroom can feel much more safe allowing room for vulnerability and authenticity. The students will gain a better understanding of who they are in the class and how they can rely on others when they need support and vice versa which is critical amongst first generation college students who may need more support personally, academically and socially.

Strategies to Promote Interdependence & Community

We can learn various qualities from car culture within Lowriding, such as interdependence. When looking deeper at the structure of most car clubs, car clubs are a group of people who share common values and interests, not only in vehicles but in life experiences, family values, cultural upbringings and countless amounts of customs we identify as. For example, I belong to Frisco's Finest Car Club. We are based out of San Francisco and the greater Bay Area. We share common values of respect for cars, culture, and family. Car clubs can also be specific to its group such as being all female members and all family relative members. Car clubs can further support a sense of belongingness.

The rules and regulations of the functioning of a club vary on structure; however for the purpose of this example we will take a semi-standard club to explore member roles. Car clubs normally consist of various roles ranging from President, Vice President and board members. This approach allows people to function as one system to maintain as a club. Through organization, traditional car clubs are able to successfully stay together as one unit.

As a community college professor and counselor within the Puente Program, I support a one-year-cohort of predominantly Latino students to transition to a 4-year university. In Puente classrooms, I've adopted and implemented an approach similar to car club alliances. Students are split into groups called their *Familias* ('Family' in English). Students are placed within groups of unknown people which can be extremely challenging when they have not established rapport. Students may fear being judged for their native accents, generational traumas, and concerns of being bullied or laughed at for their interests causing them to disconnect from their peers. In order to practice interdependence and community, it is important for us to reflect and explore who we are as individuals before we can connect as a group. In order to build interdependence, students will need to validate their experiences through open-dialogue. As a community, we come up with agreements to harbor safety and trust, establishing confidentiality and recognizing how a safe conversation feels like. We also discuss how unsuccessful conversations may have been like for them and explore boundaries amongst all members of the community. This is foundational in order to move forward with stepping outside of our comfort zones during these open dialogues. Many of these open dialogues are supported by activities implemented in the classroom, which highlight personal struggles of underrepresented people. This generates conversation of relatability resulting in trust. An example of a class activity is showing students the "*Why I Ride: Low n Slow*" documentary by

Conscious Youth Media Crew. This documentary explores Lowriding in the 1980's in the San Francisco Mission district and the issues Lowriders faced within their neighborhood such as gentrification, police brutality, and the power of activism. We also review a KQED documentary titled *"Everything comes from the streets"* highlighting San Diego's Chicano Park Neighborhood and the decades of systemic barriers they faced. Both films have highlighted the same issues occuring in completely different geographical areas during this era.

As these issues continue to occur nationwide, conversations regarding historical events are important to hold in order to foster radical change in our neighborhoods. I am a strong believer in understanding our community's past in order to better support our future to draw parallels between events our community has faced and continues to face. Discussing these topics, which tend to not be taught in the K-12 educational systems, validate the students' experiences, provide a platform for them to express their views on these issues, and create dialogue on how we can mitigate or overcome these barriers.

Furthermore, to continue harboring interdependence and organization amongst students, I draw inspiration from the car club culture. I ask for groups to choose amongst themselves who will be President (facilitates and keeps group on tasks during discussion), Vice President (keeps track of the time during in class discussions), Note-taker (takes notes on discussion), and Speaker (responsible to report back to the rest of the class regarding their group discussion). These jobs and duties will shift weekly to the next person. Allowing the students to have alternating roles within their *familias* will allow the student to develop a sense of purpose and responsibility amongst their peers resulting in a boost of attendance, accountability, autonomy, and structure within the classroom. During this peer to peer support, students can develop academic skills and learn how to navigate social encounters with other college students. Ultimately it creates a better sense of belonging, a component that is critical to one's experiences in college. Based on my experiences teaching and counseling, there is a strong relationship between a student's level of involvement and their college success because they surround themselves with like-minded people and experiences. Students perform better academically with other students as their support system because they can share common challenges and goals. Additionally, through the direction & support of a counselor/educator, students are able to find a sense of safety, comfort to navigate issues they may have withheld with shame. Supportive peer relationships are connected to the continued pursuit of academic goals and school-appropriate behaviors. When students surround themselves with other students who have the same educational aspirations, they learn to rely on each other by sharing resources and discussing ways to overcome challenges.

Communities of color tend to be more collectivistic however they are also trying to adapt to a white westernized way of life that values the individualistic values/ideals. This creates a troubling disconnect when students enter college because they are not used to the competitive nature within the educational systems. To put this into perspective, we can explore the differences between Maslow's hierarchy of needs and the Blackfoot Nation's First Nations Perspective. Maslow's hierarchy of needs is a developmental theory known in the field of psychology that explores the five levels of human needs ranging from physiological (food and clothing), safety (job security), love and belonging needs (friendship), esteem, and self-actualization. Maslow likes to think of his theory as the shape of a pyramid and humans have to reach the high level in order to reach the top: self-actualization. This theory is most commonly used within westernized American society as it is individualistic. On the contrary, the Blackfoot Nation describes their model of human needs in the shape of a Tipi and self-actualization is placed on the bottom with community actualization placed as higher priority. As an individual surpasses these stages, one reaches "cultural perpetuity" or the ability to leave your legacy behind creating a positive ripple effect for future generations.

Because cultures of color are typically collectivistic, we prioritize community growth. Although we are in a host country focused on individualistic ideals, we struggle with our identity and are able to overcome further separation of our people. To close the equity gap, I have started a mentoring program where educated people share with students starting their academic journey by sharing experiences, amplifying their voices, and sharing knowledge toward success. We begin the healing process by closing the gap of academia perception by validating and reframing our everyday experiences into an academic lens. Our students come with a great amount of experiences that are not viewed in a way that is "academic." For example, scholarship writing is a component implemented into my curriculum which involves writing about personal academic and extracurricular experiences as a student. Every year, the majority of my students have false beliefs that they do not have valid experiences to write about and have very few skills to display on these scholarships. In fact, these students possess various skills, experiences and qualities that are unrecognized in education. Examples of these include taking care of a family friend's child while they work, translating content for parents or relatives in another language, volunteering at church, and fundraising for afterschool sport groups. These are some of the numerous experiences that our students face in everyday life that are not recognized in the academic world resulting in the students feeling imcompetent in their abilities.

Healing, Passion & Paying It Forward

One thing that I appreciate about lowriding is the sense of community or comradery. Comradery and togetherness is a motivating force within Lowriding; without it, very little of cultural and community preservation would exist. Lowrider car clubs take care of their community just as much as they take care of their cars and this is something that I noticed at a young age. As mentioned earlier in this paper, my family and I would go to these free BBQ's at the park hosted by a car club in the area. Frisco's Finest Car Club has hosted an annual BBQ for the community for decades because they believe in giving back to the community and closing the food insecurity gaps. They also noticed that there is a strong need for financial support, so during the winter, we hosted an annual toy drive where we collected toys and were donated to children and families who may lack funds to buy gifts during the holidays. During proms, weddings, quinceaneras, and other monumental events, lowriders will also line up to escort the parties to and from their locations. These are examples of how this car club community comes together and pays it forward to the next person as essentially a form of healing.

Throughout the years of my educational and professional development, I have found that many of my students that I work with come from collectivistic communities similar to the ones I grew up in. These students have strong ties with local community groups such as churches, taking care of elderly members, and guiding youth with their development. Giving back to the community is a huge component that I implement into my classroom and counseling sessions. I also dive deeper into exploring ways students can give back to their communities by understanding the need and equity gaps their people face.

Conclusion

Lowriding used as a pedagogical practice supports students by connecting them to their individual historical roots by allowing them to explore racial and systemic disparities that have caused decades of oppression. Our ancestors unfortunately do not come from scholarly backgrounds that attended prestigious colleges and universities to share their stories around racism and oppression so it is our obligation to reflect upon these events that have taken place in our history and collectively think of innovate ways to grow together as one community much like the car clubs have displayed in low-riding. Although our elders and ancestors did not have a proper place in academia, they had an education from life experiences and the streets which was probably one of the most valuable things anyone can learn from. We as a society value education but we don't see ourselves in education due a lack of academic preparedness, financial hardships, incarceration, not developing a sense of belonging and numerous systemic barriers preventing students from attending college. Now is the time to educate our younger generation as they are the future to create positive change within our communities.

Navigating higher education through the lens of Lowriding through the stages of *Authenticity, Community, Healing* supports students as they begin to question whether they belong in college, what major to pursue, and doubts if college pays off in the long run. You can only imagine what it must feel like to be trying to step into a new setting such as a college campus and wonder if you belong or are smart enough to succeed. Having spaces that allow authenticity is critical for students to gain the self-efficacy to be their true selves without judgement. By doing so, students will be able to focus on college rather than feeling like they do not belong.

Although I serve as their professor and counselor, I also am a member of their community. It is imperative for a person in my professional roles to illustrate the importance of storytelling by sharing my personal narratives on struggles I've encountered growing up. This eliminates the power dynamic between professor and the student by normalizing and validating their experiences, demonstrating vulnerability, and modeling authenticity.

Furthermore, we need to utilize one another and build interdependence as a community so we can overcome the systemic challenges that are set in place to oppress our people of color. We have faced decades of oppression and racism so it is important that we continue to love one another much like the car clubs have done with their communities and create the change we wish to see for the betterment of our future generations.

7. Lowriding as an Ancestral Healing Phenomena

David Escobar

Introduction and Background

A year ago, in the summer of 2020 and prior to the Covid-19 Pandemic, I had one of my essays published in Condition Health News Magazine, which is an online publication that focuses on cutting-edge health news and information. I never intended for the article to be published, only viewed by friends, work colleagues, but in particular my homies in the lowrider community. The article was entitled *Lowriding, Ancestral Healing and Political Resistance*, (Escobar, 2020), to my surprise, it received much attention beyond the lowrider community such as local therapists, unknown folks in academia, and a whole host of folks, which then led me to upload the article on Facebook. The article then took a life of its own among the Facebook Friends network, colleagues at work, health professionals, and even politicians.

Soon after, I then got a call from Hollywood actor Danny De La Paz (aka Big Puppet), who has starred in classic Chican@/X movies such as "Boulevard Nights" and "American Me". For those in the lowrider community, Boulevard Nights and Danny represented and still represents the first time that a Hollywood film placed lowriding and Cholos front and center on the big screen. For some communities, this was a big cognitive shift because the Chicanan@s, and or Latin@s, were now more visible and a slice of the everyday struggle in the barrio was on the big screen for the world to see. To have this Hollywood actor endorse the article was huge. Danny De La Paz was delighted by the article, gave me the thumbs up, some tips to brush it up, and recorded a short endorsement video for me for Facebook. We have since, developed a friendship and respect for each other's work.

The main crux of my article was that: colors painted on exteriors and interior fabrics of lowriders help heal historical trauma and are part of political resistance within the context of a racialized culture. The vehicles themselves serve to cut into and interrupt conventional cognitive norms within a white supremacist society. The posted article, however, was just a minor analysis, of what I believed needed more in-depth exploration to support the original claim. This chapter is by no means a conclusion to my color healing assertions, but, the beginning of a journey and with no particular destination, not only about my healing but the possible healing of others specifically the Chican@, chol@, Indigenous, and lowriding communities. For this chapter, I will use the terms Chican@ Latin@ and Indigenous with a capital I, however, I will make specific remarks prior to or after a specific term if needed.

Disclaimer: I'm not a psychologist or therapist. I lean on ideas and theories from within anthropology, sociology, psychology, and politics, including concepts such as intergenerational trauma and color theory to thread together some ideas already out there and support my claim. Lowriding has many contradictions, tragedies, love, struggles, resistance, resiliency, and a metaphor overall of the hopes and aspirations of a diversity of peoples. In this chapter, I will analyze and discuss intergenerational trauma, healing, and some points on political resistance.

Color is Medicine

So, how did this all happen? While inside an indigenous sweat lodge (Inipi in Lakota language), which is an indigenous ceremonial practice, where participants crawl into a sauna shaped into an igloo-like structure made of canvas and willow branches, water is then poured over hot rocks and hot steam rises and covers the blackened chamber to cleanse the body of impurities. Songs are then sung that allow the body to relax and connect spiritually with your inner source of power and prayer and or good thoughts for your relatives.

While inside the lodge amidst the many beautiful songs being sung, it dawned on me that space, color, and song all come together to produce medicine and healing, very similar to the feeling I always got when I am lowriding. Could it be that lowriding is a type of medicine?

The blackness I experienced inside the sweat lodge reflected darkness like no other and both forced and allowed me to reflect on my defects and shortcomings. It also provided the only space where I could experience and imagine what my ancestors might have seen and felt 500 years ago, before colonization by Europeans in the Americas. By no means do I make a full comparison between the inipi ceremonial practice and lowriding as a complete comparison, only that lowriding is a type of medicine for those grandchildren of indigenous peoples whose ancestral connection has to some degree been severed by colonization. It is almost like, the one beautiful little flower that shoots up out of the concrete in the middle of a busy urban, foot trafficked sidewalk that no one seems to notice or appreciate. Sometimes, life gets so busy that I would imagine that the majority of passersby may never think about how much resilience and effort that precious flower took to reach daylight. It is in this same light that lowriding is medicine and healing.

The original article, mentioned the honor and privilege of having many conversations with healers across the Americas, but specifically, a long-time mentor who, for this writing, we will call Don Juan, who comes from a long lineage of healers within the Maya community of Guatemala. He is a humble individual who deeply knows his community and culture and currently living here in California for almost 20 years. He is renowned as a healer and cultural educator of Mayan philosophy. He is a valued treasure by many intertribal Indigenous communities both here in California and Guatemala. He speaks the truth and I have assisted him as an interpreter in many of his healings with community members and cultural presentations to institutions. A significant part of writing my article and the current essay was the worthiness of experiencing the oral tradition in real-time with Don Juan. The knowledge shared with me has been handed down to Don Juan by his traditional lineage and is unbroken. In this instance when ancient knowledge is being dispensed, I pay attention, much like a soldier who listens to his marching orders.

One day while we were sipping coffee at his kitchen table, I asked Don Juan about color and the different types of color healing that existed within Mayan cosmology. I nudged him a little, about the power of color and how elders in Guatemala utilize this methodology now, he specified quickly that color continues to be used in many healing ceremonies. It is something he said, the West is now catching up to us and beginning to understand that we have much to offer the world.

Don Juan stated that primarily clothing and different colored pieces of cloth are used for certain ceremonies, depending on the illness, to induce a particular physical, psychological, and or spiritual outcome. He then looked up at me and smirked and then said, in the past, the Mayan commoner in society used very simple and gently adorned clothing, "it wasn't until the time of colonization that the indigenous communities began to use and place more elaborate colors, patterns and specific designs" on clothing (D. Juan, 2020, personal communication). As a recount of the article, "Colors, heal the community for both those seeing the color as well as the person wearing the highly-colored clothes. Colors have the power of healing both the psychological, spiritual, and physical, we still are in much need to heal from the trauma of colonization" (Escobar, 2020, p. 1).

Color is everywhere, even when there appears to be no color, there is, it packs a punch, such as the blackness of the sweat lodge, forcing a reflection and a type of introspection like no other moment. The many colors that exist in the world today are gifts, beyond the apparent healing nature of colors, they also evoke and symbolize meaning to people and culture, depending on the society. For example, in a well-known Biblical story, Genesis 9:13–17 (Catholic Book Publishing Corp., 2011), Noah was able to save his family and all of the animal kingdoms from a mass flood that was foretold to him by God. According to the story, it rained continuously for 40 days and 40 nights which destroyed all life on the planet. At the end of the 40 days of storms, however, God sends Noah a sign in the sky of His promise never to bring rains again to destroy the world, today it's known as a rainbow of brilliant colors. This rainbow represents a covenant with humanity forever. Here, we can see that the rainbow not only represented a covenant from God to Noah but was also a symbol of hope and an opportunity and redemption for life on Earth.

Ancestral Trauma

Generally applying the concept of color, healing and space and making a connection with ancestral trauma, to the majority of Latin@ communities in the Americas, but specifically the decedents of indigenous peoples, Chican@s lowriding in California, we may be able to make the correlation between historical trauma and historical trauma response. The connection between lowriders and color, and perhaps de-indianized peoples', conscious or unconsciousness is an attempt to find a modern way to heal and connect with the ancestors. Let us start with the legacy of colonization upon people of color, specifically, taking a look within the Americas, which withstood destruction, bloodshed, and dislocation. Since the very first European boot embedded its impression upon the sands of the Caribbean and beyond, we have now accumulated a plethora of eye witness and written accounts by the survivors of such actions, but now, contemporary analysis of how coloniality was formed, and its insidious and continual recreation of itself within social structures; plus, its ongoing refinement.

Beginning with the supposition that the existing decedents of Indigenous, African, and European "mixed" peoples are carrying an ongoing ancestral trauma, or as traditional Indigenous healers in the Americas call it susto. According to the APA Dictionary,

Susto is a culture-bound syndrome occurring to and among Latinos in the United States and populations in Mexico, Central America, and South

America. After experiencing a frightening event, individuals fear that their soul has left their bodies. Symptoms include weight loss, fatigue, muscle pains, headache, diarrhea, unhappiness, troubled sleep, lack of motivation, and low self-esteem. (American Psychological Association Dictionary, 2020, p. 1054).

Cerdeña (2021) wrote,

> Drawing on original work with the descendants of Holocaust survivors, multiple studies have examined the effects of intergenerational trauma in Indigenous and refugee communities, underscoring how mass traumas such as slavery, genocide, systematic sexual violence, and forced relocation may penetrate subsequent generations. Such work also overlaps with understandings of historical trauma, broadly conceptualized as cumulative wounding across generations. (p. 4)

This framework is particularly resonant for Indigenous communities, who may still suffer the effects of genocide and forced removal from ancestral lands, even across multiple generations. Likewise, African-American descendants of enslaved peoples may continue to feel the traumatic repercussions of the transatlantic slave trade: The concept of post-traumatic slave syndrome is based on understandings of a painful, multigenerational legacy of chattel slavery (Leary, 2017). Colonization itself is a massively traumatic event. According to Treuer (2019), the Spanish were among the most brutal colonial powers, imposing enslavement, physical torture, and sexual violence on the Indigenous peoples of the Americas. Colonial expansion, including the forced migration and labor of African, Asian, and other peoples to Latin America, enforced a system of racialized power that politically and psychologically subjugated racialized peoples (Fanon, 1952). Rather than a distal or unconscious wound, the cyclical reproduction of colonial and racialized violence continues to impact communities across the globe, including Latin Americans and Latinxs (Czyzewski, 2001; Go, 2018). Beyond the painful collective memory of such histories, the lived experiences of Latinxs today reveal contemporary articulations of colonization through the maintenance of White supremacist structures of power. These include violations of Indigenous land and water rights, violence against women and gender sexual minorities, racialized state violence, and incarceration, and unequal access to opportunity, housing, education, and healthcare (Durán & Campos, 2020; Paradies, 2016). Post-colonial Latinx lineages also include European histories of advantage and oppression that add complexity to the portrait of intergenerational trauma in this population. Even among the Spanish, crypto-Jews, or conversos of Sephardic origin who themselves endured suppression, persecution, and forced religious conversion during the Inquisition contribute to the Journal Pre-proof 6 parentage and traumatic histories of Latinx communities

(Perelis, 2009; Velez et al., 2012). These distant traumas reverberate through the collective memory of the Latinx community, contributing to the framework of intergenerational trauma in this population.

The term susto is appropriate from an Indigenous perspective, however, I will use the work of Maria Yellow Horse Braveheart, a scholar and member of the Lakota nation, to better make my point. For several decades now, a new and prevailing theory that's been appealing with many in the psychological, therapeutic communities, along with a great many articles within the academic literature, which is now known as historical trauma (HT), defined as, "cumulative emotional and psychological wounding across generations, including lifespan, which emanates from massive group trauma" (Brave Heart, Elkins, & Altschul, 1998, p. 283).

If we take the next logical step, we then turn to historical trauma response defined as, "a constellation of features associated with a reaction to massive group trauma. Historical unresolved grief, a component of this response is the profound unsettled bereavement resulting from cumulative devastating losses" (Brave Heart, Elkins, & Altschul, 1998, p. 283).

Upon researching for this script, little information is known regarding the dress of the Pre-Columbian Mayan, however, some articles that spoke to the use of color among the Mayan nobility based on the pottery designs and other murals depicted on the temples. For example, according to an article in Archeology Magazine, "Maya kings and queens are typically shown wearing flamboyant headdresses bedecked with masks, quetzal feathers, and jewels as they conjure their ancestors or perform other important rites. However, the most significant element in a ruler's headdress was among its simplest" (Pyne, 2020, p. 1).

I also found this quote from some research regarding the Aztec or more accurately the Mexica-Nahuatl Peoples,

> The more gem decorations on clothes, the higher the noble identity of the wearer. Even with so many luxurious decorations, *current scholarship believes that their clothing styles still were simple,* because these flat garments were loose-fitting and did not completely cover people's body. Some of them were only a piece of fabric or a strip, which were just knotted together. (Steinhilper, 2014, p. 7)

According to Steinhilper (2014), "the only requirement of male clothing was that different people in different levels must wear tilmatli with different length. For example, general male commoners could only wear the simple tilmatli to their knees" (p. 7).

This by no means is a universalizing of Maya and Mexica clothing styles to make my point, but simply, only a possible correlation among indigenous ancient commoners.

Intergenerational trauma also carries an ancestral element that goes in the opposite direction, where collectively our ancestral DNA tries to find ways of repairing ourselves via alternative cultures and identities. The body, mind, and spirit, create and unfolds methodologies of well-being individually and collectively. We have a collective unconscious that, I also believe can lean towards and goes in positive directions.

So, what is the collective unconscious? It's a term introduced by psychiatrist Carl Jung to represent a form of the unconscious (that part of the mind containing memories and impulses of which the individual is not aware) common to mankind as a whole and originating in the inherited structure of the brain. It is distinct from the personal unconscious, which arises from the experience of the individual. According to Jung, the collective unconscious contains archetypes, or universal primordial images and ideas (American Psychological Association Dictionary, 2020). The racial memory on the other hand, also as part of Jung's repertoire, are "thought patterns, feelings, and traces of experiences held to be transmitted from generation to generation and to have an influence on individual minds and behavior. Carl Jung and Sigmund Freud both embraced the concept of a phylogenetic heritage" (American Psychological Association Dictionary, 2020, p. 211).

If centuries of colonization are ongoing, dynamic, and persistent, then, we as a lowrider community who have to some degree, de-indianized, respond to this unresolved grief and or trauma among ourselves and our families in some of the most creative and unforeseen ways the world could not imagine. This collective trauma, the collective unconscious, and collective racial memory, all erupt like an ancient volcano, to respond and heal through our Carruchas or cars and our Chican@ culture. Zepeda (2020) in her writings, speaks to out of Berkeley University Press, turns to Gloria Anzaldua's work, where she quotes, "this proposed recognition of spirit praxis can lead to a 'path of conocimiento' and to sanction or healing of intergenerational trauma for Xicana/x detribalized peoples, without recreating forms of violence or the fear of appropriation" (p. 228), which in this case our non-violent healing are brilliantly colored lowriders, oldies, baggies, brims, and cat-eye makeup.

Healing Through Color

Recent scholarship is now beginning to agree with Don Juan and align itself with what the ancients have been alerting the West, Steven Vasquez (2006) states,

> color may be the most potent therapeutic agent known to humankind. Recent breakthroughs in the use of visual brain stimulation by color within the new method of Emotional Transformation Therapy (ETT) have accomplished

rapid recovery from trauma, depression, physical pain, and spiritual blockages. The new "process color and human consciousness² This blend of quantum physics and interpersonal guidance is supported by research in both physics and psychology. Emotional Transformation Therapy (ETT) uses specific interpersonal guidance in conjunction with the new process of color theory. (p. 192)

One of the key reasons color possesses therapeutic power is that each specific color strongly resonates with specific emotional states. This resonance activates specific emotions so that when appropriate interpersonal guidance takes place the emotional state can progress towards expression and ultimately completion. This is psychologically important because massive recent research in developmental psychology and cognitive sciences now makes it clear that affect regulation is the primary source of integration in many brain functions necessary for the development of the formation of the self and almost all stress-related conditions both psychological and medical. Therefore, through wielding precise activation of emotional states, the impact of significantly altering numerous psychological states, physiological symptoms states can take place.

Vasquez (2006) postulates, "what can color stimulation accomplish therapeutically? When color is used in various combinations, our clinical trials have yielded benefits that apply to a broad range of applications. Breakthroughs primarily in terms of speed of treatment but also as long-term changes have been consistently observed are awaiting" (p. 210).

Conclusion

How is it possible that populations of so-called or named de-indianized peoples begin to organically organize and take old, discarded vehicles and create such masterpieces of art? We could just say, color has always been part of Mexican, Chinan@, LatinX culture and we are simply creating a transactional anthropological operation of culture exchange and diffusion within urban contemporary societies. Perhaps it could be a mere coincidence over the course of 500 years of ongoing enormity of trials, we as cholos and lowriders so happen to collectively come together and just think all this up, just to look cool. I do not think so! There is much to be said about an ancestral spiritual force that is flowing throughout the culture that has been manifested for centuries which includes clothing, language, music, and art within Chican@X culture as both subtle and outright resistance.

Lowriders are not just part of a healing methodology, but also part of a long trajectory of exercises in self-acknowledgment of our indigenous ancestry and humanity, a barrier against alienation in a primarily racist country, and a type of political resistance. Our lowriders fight the invisibility imposed upon us and become a beacon of light that has to be noticed by the world. Lowrider healing is much more than color, it's multifaceted, dynamic and always adjusting itself to fit the present and full of contradictions. Lowrider healing is a sarape laid upon the table of coloniality a banner of upheaval to racism and the colonial project it's an interruption to the senses of regulated spaces. The mere fact, not just of the existence of lowriders, but the sheer existence of the brown bodies who drive them, is a cognitive shock to mainstream society, our bodies and lowriders are as symbolic as the flags that were stuck onto indigenous soil by Europeans five centuries years ago. Together our bodies and cars become both flags and navigational banners for the next generations of lowriders to come. Colors, cars, clothing, oldies music, language, murals, tattoos, tortillas, and a whole host of other elements, all mix into medicine. This medicine permeates and soothes our ancestral DNA that thirsts for justice and remembrance. This is medicine homies! Hasta La Victoria Siempre!

References

American Psychological Association Dictionary. (2020). https://dictionary.apa.org/col lective-unconscious.

Brave Heart, Y. H., Chase, J., Elkins, J., & Altschul, P. (1998). *Historical trauma among indigenous peoples of the Americas: Concepts, research, and clinical considerations. Journal of Psychoactive Drugs, 43*(4), 282–290.

Catholic Book Publishing Corp. (2011). *New American bible.*

Cerdeña, J., Rivera, L., & Spak, J. (2021). Intergenerational trauma in mental health America Latinxs: A scoping review. *Social Science & Medicine, 270,* 113662. https://www.academia.edu/44975470/Intergenerational_Trauma_in_Latinxs_A_Scoping_Review?auto=citations&from=cover_page

Czyzewski, K. (2001). Colonialism as a broader social determinant of health. *International Indigenous Policy Journal; London, 2*(1), n/a. http//dx.doi.org/10.1854/iij.2011.21.5

Duran, R. J., & Campos, J. A. (2020). Gangs, gansters and the impact of settler colonialism on the Latina/a experience. *Sociology Compass, 14*(3), e12765. https://doi.org/10.1111/soc4.12765.

Escobar, D. (2020). *Lowriding: Ancestral healing and political resistance. Condition Health News.* https://conditionhealthnews.com/lowriding-ancestral-healing-and-political-resistance/

Fanon, F. (1952). *Black skin, white masks.* Grove Press.

Go, J. (2018). Postcolonial possibilities for the sociology of race. *Sociology of Race and Ethnicity, 4*(4), 439–451. https://doi.org/10.117/2332649218793982

Paradies, Y. (2016). Conolisation, racism and indigenous health. *Journal of Population Research, 33*(1), 83–96. https://doi.org/10.1039/ntr/ntw295

Perelis, J. (2009). "These indians are Jews!": Lost tribes, Crypto-Jews, and Jewish self-fashioning in Antonio de Motezino's Relacion of 1644. *In Atlantic Diasporas: Jews, Conversos, and Crypto-Jews in the Age of Mercantilism, 1500–1800.* John Hopkins University Press.

Pyne, L. (2020, June 9). Maya clothing. *Archeology,* 1–2. https://www.archaeology.org/issues/387-2007/features/maya-clothing

Steinhilper, D. (2014). Clothing and identity about symbolic meanings of the pre-hispanic costume a research paper. *Mapa de Cuahtinchan No. 2 (898).*

Vazquez, S. (2006). COLOR: Its therapeutic power for rapid healing. *Subtle Energies & Energy Medicine Journal Archives, 17,* 210.

Velez, C., Palmara, P.F., Guevara-Aguire, J., Hao, L., Karafet,T., Guevara-Aguire, M., Pearlman, A., Oddoux, C., Hammer, M., Burns, E, Pe'er, I., Atzmon, G., & Ostrer, H. (2012). The impact of converso jewson the genomes of modern Latin Americans. *Human Genetics, 131*(2), 251–263. https://doi.org/10.1007/s00439-011-1072-z

8. It's Not a Hobby, It's My Culture

Juan Roman-Medina

Introduction

We, who are part of the Lowrider lifestyle, have often been asked where the birthplace of lowriding is and how it started. In my opinion I feel that lowriding started in our very own backyards here in the barrios of Aztlán, and has manifested throughout the world. There are many different families, friends and communities that have come together to form this Chicano/American hybrid culture. These communities have helped frame and lay the architectural blueprint that has kept the lowrider culture and the dynasty alive. As Lowriders it is our obligation to pass this legacy on to our future generations. Lowriding is a passion, lifestyle, a feeling that nothing else can give you. It has been passed on through generations between: fathers, mothers, children etc. Lowriding is a family affair in which everyone participates proudly. It is important that we lead our actions with our own stories so that we can define ourselves instead of allowing others to define us. Beyond the overview of lowriding as a culture it is apparent that Lowriders need to create a narrative in which we grab hold of our stories and tell them through our own voice. This is key because it leads us down a path of self-reflection and forces us to become clear with our interest and allows us to explore our motivations. This paper will investigate the question of how lowriding is not just a hobby? How does music, language, art, customization, and community play in the role of lowriding?

Thesis

As the western world becomes interconnected and easily accessible with the advancement of technology such as social media, Internet, satellite television and reality shows, a false image of the Lowrider culture has taken shape. As a lifelong Lowrider, raised in this lifestyle and now as a college student, I will examine lowriding through a sociological lense in an effort to understand how and why lowriding has grown from a handful of practitioners during the 1940s to a cultural phenomena in the present day United States; growing from a hobby of expedience into a culture and lifestyle that transcends geographical boundaries and nationalism.

First, it's important to define the term "culture" before going much further. Culture is how we see and make sense of our unique individual worlds. Without our respective cultures, we would be blind to interpreting daily events. It's also important to understand that in a multicultural setting, one individual or group's cultural orientation may clash with the established norm, creating confusion, even tension (Irving, 1984, p. 138).

Along with defining the difference between hobby and culture, I will seek to define the components that define Lowrider culture. I will use the sociological lens to identify four aspects of the Lowrider culture: music, language, art, and style of clothes. In addition, I will explore cruising, cultural stereotypes, and preconceptions. This analysis will be completed through a thorough analysis of scholarly discourse along with information gathered through personal interviews of those who participate in the Lowrider culture.

Literature Review

In order to determine the influence and meaning of lowriding and what makes it a culture, it is important to study the areas of music, art, language and style of clothes. These genres of academic literature and lenses through which to analyze lowriding are important and provide much insight to the culture. In addition, by illustrating these cultural dynamics, we begin to understand the pillars lifting lowriding from a mere hobby or pastime to the heights of cultural relevance. Lowriding is not a new phenomenon and the studies fall short to explain and define Lowriding culture. In specific the research fails to explore: How and why the world has not recognized lowriding as a culture as opposed to an expensive hobby, the idea of Lowriding as a weekend car show, nor does it address the preconception of Lowriding as gang-bangers with outrageous cars.

There are few academic sources presently found on the topic of lowriding. These sources were found in academic journals, scholarly books, and insightful documentaries. Below I will review the literature on lowriding, paying attention to how scholars define this activity. Some of these various sources of lowrider literature, including documentaries, peer-reviewed articles, and scholarly books, will be studied for relevance under an academic gaze.

During the early 1970s, two bands, *Tierra* and *Los Lobos*, emerged as Lowrider favorites. Using lyrics evoking a romanticized past of Aztlan, pachucos, and raza while integrating contemporary images of cholos, lowriders and barrio life, *Tierra* and *Los Lobos* were quickly embraced by the Chicano/Latino communities, but especially by lowriders. By 1975 the band *War* released the hit single *Low Rider*, a tribute and celebration of the Chicano car customizers, owners, drivers, and the lifestyle itself. There had been cruising music before but this era ushered in popular mainstream music that was being written and broadcast. This cultural shift reached Lowriders through airplay. Music specifically associated with their culture was being integrated into the mainstream. Prior to the release of *War* there was no specific music addressing the Lowriding culture and instead Lowriders listened to Soul, R&B, and Oldies. With the release of *War*, Lowriders were suddenly empowered with an anthem that gave voice to a culture (Lipsitz, 2012, pp. 193–207).

The notion that music has the ability to harness communities is not a new idea. According to Oliver Wang, the song *Viva Tirado* by the band *El Chicano* became another very influential song. *Viva Tirado* was able to inter-twine Chicano and Lowriding cultures through music and precipitated a shift in music that continues to this day. According to Wang, "the full richness of "Viva Tirado" is best appreciated in a fuller exploration of it's tri-iteration offering and evocative example of the unpredictable power of music to link different communities together in a web of genealogies and solidarities". While music is a great unifier it is important to explore the notion of culture and how Lowriding is defined.

In *Mexican American Lowriders*, Brenda Bright wrote, "The point of her research on Low Riders is not to define a subculture, but to identify cultural expressions relative to a process of cultural inscription and the assertion of cultural/historical continuity located within residual culture" (Bright, 1997, p. 18). She asserts that lowriding is neither a culture or subculture, but a product of cultural creation. She points out that lowriders as a popular phenomenon was constructed through the popularity of *LowRider Magazine*. She also illustrates that the term *"Low Rider"* is popular in itself. Brights' claims beg the following question: Does it matter how lowriding became culturally relevant? Do Bright's claims negate the fact that over several decades lowriding has developed its own culture, music, art, and language? Do Bright's assertions negate the fact that Lowriding has transcended geographic and cultural boundaries? Lowriding has been relevant since the post World War II economic boom. Lowriding has gained *more* popularity over time, not less, eventually becoming a lifestyle for the Lowriders. Lowriding is a part of the cultural fabric that has not dissipated over time but continues to grow and evolve.

Compare Bright's stance to that of Michael Chavez, in *The Performance of Chicano Masculinity in Lowrider Car Culture*. Chavez assumes no fixed or generalizable definitions of what or who a lowrider is (Chavez, 2013). Chavez then tries to define the cultural expression without any direction of what it is or what it consists of but argues that it is a "fluid and dynamic construction which relies on various factors including both environmental verification and individual labeling" (Chavez, 2013). In other words, it may be defined in one direction or multiple directions without correctly defining it. Chavez continues to argue and support the idea that there is no one clear definition.

In exploring the definition of a lowrider, Chavez searches in different avenues. He states "lowriding as a series of political practices which cannot be narrowly defined by the constraints of an aesthetic" (Chavez, 2013). Chavez defined a lowriding vehicle using the research of two researchers. One explanation was having either a stock or custom low-slung vehicle, usually an older 1940s to 1970s General Motors model. Another explanation refers to any automobile, van, or pick-up truck, motorcycle, or bicycle lowered to within a few inches of the road. While Chavez asserts there is no one true definition he uses the work of two researchers as an attempt to provide a definition. Lowriding culture whether defined or not is found through the individual association with the culture and the manifestation of how individuals come together as a community.

Martin Hoyem, in *I Want My Low Rider to Look Like a Whore*, defines lowriders as strange things with pristine paint jobs, clean ornate interiors of chrome and gold: everything contrasted in the crude mechanical dances (Hoyem, 2007, p. 31). In his analysis, Hoyem describes the same as what Brenda Bright is suggesting in quoting the *The New Oxford American Dictionary* definition of a lowrider: "a customized vehicle with hydraulic jacks that allow the chassis to be lowered nearly to the road" (Hoyem, 2007). Hoyem describes a lowriding vehicle, but he does not define what lowriding truly is. The specific definition of a lowrider vehicle does not allow for the context in which that car is restored, shown, driven, and valued. Definition of a word does not allow for exploration of the culture surrounding the vehicle.

Hoyem states that most people he interviewed stated that "a lowrider is characterized by the car being raised or lowered using hydraulics, has wired wheels, an expensive paint job, and a flawless interior" (Hoyem, 2007). In the opinions of Bright and Chavez, it is the car that makes the lowrider. Hoyem's opinion is in agreement in that lowriding is centered on the automobile. Hoyem argues that the traditional traits of lowriding are American cars, stating, "Still there are some clearly visible trends, or preferences, among those who spend their time with these cars" (Hoyem, 2007). While Bright, Chavez, and Hoyem all found that the Lowriding identity was inherently tied to a vehicle they did not speak to the various components that encompass the culture. They also fail to address that any kind of motor vehicle including Japanese and European cars, are used and frequently entered into Lowrider car shows. "Lowriding is about pride and culture, for instance; or to describe lowriding as "positive" and to tell me about how "it's a family thing," often going to great lengths to characterize the style as entailing a depth of commitment that made it something more substantial than a "fad" or a consumption trend, representing instead a distinctive subjectivity or "lifestyle""" (Chappell, 2012).

"Lowriding as a version of Mexican American identity became possible when Mexican Americans joined the U.S. car culture. This was a convergence of two developments: on one hand, the rise of Mexican Americans as a consumer market, and on the other, the expansion of the automobile class (Chappell, 2012). During World War II there were two factors which saw the expansion of access to vehicle ownership: (1) postwar surpluses in production (2) and measures such as the G.I. Bill which was building the U.S. middle class. The expanding availability of used cars spurred the development of customization of automobiles. This in turn spurred the trend of the hot rod and cruising scenes that are now iconically associated with the 1950's" (Chappell, 2012).

Denise Sandoval, in *Cruising Through Low Rider Culture*, agrees that the lowrider started germinating after WWII in working class neighborhoods. Sandoval states that by giving our "identity" or our "culture" values of existence that certain rituals are practiced on a regular basis. Some of these rituals include the car club itself as well as the beliefs and practices of the members of the car club, which allows for the creation of a different "identity" that separates the 'white' American from all others (Sandoval, 2003). Interviews done by Ben Chappell argue that some of the car club members thought of themselves as American, although first identifying as Mexican-American. "I drive an American classic, not a foreign plastic" (Sandoval, 2003). What is more American than a reused classic car that is American made? I think this is another way of looking at it, which is also purchasing and using American techniques on their Lowrider vehicles.

Methodology

For this research project I reviewed scholarly articles, books, and documentaries about lowriding. I also conducted in-depth interviews, engaged in participant observations, and took many photographs while conducting ethnographic research. I interviewed three individuals. For the purposes of confidentiality I will use a pseudonym for the interviewees. Two interviews, El Carnal, age 50, and The Judge, age 50, were twenty-seven minutes in length each and took place in a park located in Stockton, California. The other interview was thirty-four minutes in length, by Lowrider Weatherboy, age 50, which was recorded in my home—Santa Rosa, California. El Carnal and The Judge stated that they grew up in lowriding, while Lowrider Weatherboy stated that for him, it started around the age of thirteen.

Throughout this journey of exploration, I conducted qualitative interviews of subjects that live within lowrider culture. These subjects have first hand experience enabling us to get a better understanding of what it means to be a lowrider. The qualitative interview method was chosen in order to allow for the gathering of information that is best expressed in a non-structured method in which the interviewee can freely express their thoughts and experiences. The freedom of dialog provided a more accurate picture of the lowriding culture. Authentic content was obtained which included interviewee's values and attitudes. Questionnaires would not have provided for the ease of dialog that was created by using the qualitative interview method. Each individual's own experiences in living as a lowrider, its traditions, cars, art, customizations, and their involvement in the lowrider community was collected through these series of interviews. The process of the qualitative interview permitted me the chance to ask my respondents to touch upon personal narratives, experiences, expressions, and feelings, which also allowed them to narrate the story of the lowrider through their eyes.

A second round of interviews were recorded of two of the subjects. I used a second in-depth interview instead using a semi-structured interview framework, a social science method. These second interviews were conducted in order to build a more comfortable relationship which would in turn allow me to more freely ask in depth questions. The second interview allowed me to construct additional questions that more closely explored the topics of: family structure, social structure, and personal discipline. In-depth qualitative interviews were needed in order to gather more specific data. The open ended discovery-oriented method was used in order to provide questions but allow for the interviewee to respond at length. Information gathered through the second pass of interviews provided for rich background information that helped shape further questions on the topic

Along with interviews my own experiences as an active member of the lowrider culture will be incorporated in my analysis. I will use my participation observations to explain and give examples through the lens as a participant within the culture. I will explore my own experiences of the practices and rit-uals by providing examples of my participation in cruising, building lowrider cars, congregating in a car club, as well as participating in car shows. This will be complemented with the academic literature knowledge on culture and lowriding culture, I will be able to apply academic social science theories to everyday life in and out of the lowrider community.

Third photographs taken at car shows will be included within the analysis portion of this paper in order to support my findings. Images play a signifi-cant role in the development of values and beliefs, including the perception of gender, sexuality, ethnicity, and class. Social Science considers this method as Visual Culture, which happens to be art, painting sculptures, and film pic-tures. For example, pictures are very visually impactful and they tend to tell different stories, interpretations, and meanings.

Findings

Through the articles written regarding lowriding culture in combination with data procured through interviews I was able to pinpoint three factors that were not part of the articles already published. There is far more to this culture than one could imagine at first glance. First, stress is one big factor that no one ever talks about. Second, the unwritten rules are a very important part of this culture. For example, Lowrider Weatherboy said, "cleanliness it's a must, you must make sure everything is detailed and clean. Whether you have a car that's nicely painted or if you have a work in progress car, this rule applies to both show cars and streetcars". Third, there is the notion of confi-dentiality among those who participate in the car culture.

Stress

Stress is an inherent part of the lowrider cultural fabric. From personal expe-rience and via interview data I have been able to reach the conclusion that there is a rule where those who compete do not speak about the stressors caused by participation in the Lowriding culture. The anxiety and nerves prior to a car show are not to be spoken about or shown. The stress is pushed back in order to put forth a façade of strength and infallibility. This unwritten rule is corroborated as part of the definition of masculinity encapsulated by this culture.

The research shows that the predominant opinion in regards to Lowriding is that it is a male dominated sport. The macho attitude is that we do not get stressed and fold under pressure, nor do we ever talk about it. Personally, as a participant of this culture, I never express the way I feel or how stressed a car show can get me because I want everything perfect. This includes items such as, cleanliness and shininess of the vehicle. Items such as the extended amount of time put into the vehicle, making sure the paint has several layers of wax and the chrome is not dull, ensuring that the windows are sparkly and crystal clear are all major stressors. When conducting my second interview, I interviewed El Carnal and The Judge from Stockton, California. I asked them how they felt the night before a show and both individuals stated that the week or even a month before there was anxiety. He referred to this emotion as having "butterflies," like a child on Christmas day. When compared to Sandoval's article, I believe she stresses the fact that women are highly sexualized and objectified in *LowRider Magazine* but she does not mention anything of the vulnerable state that men experience through stress. I believe that both genders tend to fall victim to vulnerability when dealing with the demand of high expectations: important because it does not question masculinity but invokes that we are human.

Unwritten Rules

My second finding was the concept of unwritten rules. Unwritten rules are those which govern and are known by all within the culture and yet they are rules that are not written. These rules must be explicitly followed in order to be part of the Lowrider culture. For example, confidentiality happens to be also known as "whatever happens in the car club, whether it's politics within itself, you're not to discuss it outside the car club or family" (The Judge). Although this notion is not written in any rulebooks, it is encouraged and practiced. This confidentiality can be such as when a car is being built, no one is to talk about the process nor the kinds of customization that are being done to it, or the kind of classification the vehicle will be entering. So when the car is going to be introduced into the lowrider sports arena it will be a shock to the people competing. "Nobody speaks until the big reveal, you want no one to see or get ideas on your project, you want the car to be unique" (The Judge).

Cleanliness

The third finding was the need for cars to be clean and neat. This is a reference back to the working class ideals instilled at a young age. Even if one's clothes were holey they were clean and pressed. Along with a neat appearance good personal hygiene was also instilled at a young age as important.

Those same sensibilities are seen in the lowriding culture. Owners of lowrider cars take immense pleasure in keeping their cars in pristine condition, clean. Lowrider Weather Boy talked on this issue during his interview.

As a child, I was brought up in a working poor household, where I was conditioned to be aware of my personal cleanliness and making sure I looked presentable. Although our family was poor and we wore clothes with holes in them, we were aware to look our best. Our clothes were to be neat and pressed, our appearance was to look nice and neat as well as our personal hygiene—clean and smelling nice was something my family practiced. This runs parallel with the lowrider culture, being that the lowrider culture comes out of the barrios. The owner of this car also encompasses the idea of cleanliness because the car reflects their craftsmanship as well as bits of their personalities. Endless hours are spent attending to every detail of the car including: cleaning white walls on tires, cleaning bumper to bumper, polishing each nook and cranny in the interior, waxing, and buffing their cars to a shine.

Analysis

Through personal observation at various car shows spanning between September 2013—November 2013, I was able to clearly see the link between music and the Lowriding culture. On first observation almost all cars were playing War's low riding anthem through their car stereos as they entered the car show arena. This is significant and correlates directly to War being the first song that implicitly used and referred to Lowriding. In 1975 it was a revelation to have a song hit the airwaves that sang about Lowriding yet my observations show that the connection to War as a lowriding anthem is as strong today as it was in 1975. Geroge Lipsitz found that War suddenly gave lowriders an anthem and voice which still rings through the speakers today (Lipsitz, 2012, pp. 193–207).

Beyond the notion of War's song *Lowrider* as an anthem I found that a certain genre of music, Oldies, was most closely identified with Lowriding culture. As I walked around and conducted interviews I clearly noticed that Oldies were either being played as a background to the action taking place or else people were humming the melodies of Oldies songs. This became a recurring theme in every show I attended throughout the season. This clearly showcases the link between music and identity in Lowriding culture. For example when asked of the importance of music in lowriding, La Cosa, a life-long Lowrider said, "Every Lowrider you see today, what are they bumping? Oldies. So that's the main music that I like, and you know, I grew up with it". With La Cosa's first memory of finding the lowriding culture at 8 years of age he also clearly remembers Oldies as a piece of the Lowriding fabric. One without the other does not exist.

The correlation between music and lowriding is clear but for an example of Oldies style of music, the original soundtrack from the film American Graffiti is a fine example of Cruising Music. The music from this film is found on most Lowriders' playlists. The music from this era is showcased through slow ballads and love songs from the late 1950s to early 1960s. When asked why Oldies is so popular with Lowriders? The Judge replied, "Cuz that's Cruising Music". When asked if it is possible to cruise without music? The Judge answered emphatically "No!" Those within the Lowriding culture accept that Oldies are as much a part of their identities as Lowriders as the car themselves.

Oldies as part of the Lowrider culture is further shown through this quote from The Judge, "Like I told you, anytime you go to a car show, you watch a guy taking his car off the trailer, what's the first thing he's gonna do? Turn on the music, and you've got to have the right song to turn it on" he continued. The Judge explained that years ago, he would make sure he had the right CDs, or 8-Track tapes, set up in the correct order to "make sure it's set up for the right song when you're cruising into the show." Why is music so important? "It sets the mood," said The Judge. "First impressions is all. You gotta have it. And like I said... Lowriders take music to heart. Most people don't take it to heart. We take music to heart". Feel, showmanship, and mood all play important roles in creating the atmosphere of the car show competition and as exemplified by the Judge, Lowriders take music choice as an important part of the car show and cruising process.

Still, beyond the notion of integrating music as an important part of the Lowrider culture why is the genre of music preferred Oldies? One assumption is that many cars are older and from the era where Oldies originated, but I found that there was a more important reason for choosing to identify with Oldies. Oldies consist of slow and mellow music which fits the mood of a slow, leisurely cruise around town. To quote The Judge, "Cruising Music is usually slow, relaxed... You're taking your time, setting the mood on a date. When you're with the lowrider, that's your woman right there. What more do you need? That's why it's called Cruising". Music sets the pace and mood of the cruise and of the car show. With those two motivators it is easy to see how Lowriders most closely identify Lowriding with Oldies.

Music sets the mood and pace of the Lowriding culture yet Language also plays a significant role. Language and culture go hand in hand. If you ignore one you can never fully understand the other. During my interviews with La Cosa, Lowrider Weatherboy, and through personal observations throughout the car shows I noticed several examples of code switching. The interviewees would effortlessly pepper their English with Spanish words, phrases, or idioms such as La Raza. Also, I noticed perfect pronunciation when naming Spanish surnames, or the name of a city such as Sacramento. Some nonverbal codes consisted of pinstriping or gold-leafing abstracts on the vehicle paint jobs. These are signatures of various artists in plain view, yet hidden from sight. A person may observe such codes many times but without ever realizing or registering what they have seen, so carefully done are these personal signatures or markings. These verbal and non verbal cues are important parts of the Lowrider culture which further solidify their connection to each other. Those who do not know the language can never be included as an insider to the culture. For example Calo is a language that has roots from the Pachuco era, the slang of the barrio. Denise Sandoval states that the low-rider culture has its own language through the media, we as a consumer have to identify with something in the advertising when reading or simply looking at the page of *Low Rider Magazine* (Sandoval, 2003, p. 180). It is through the various facets of language that those within the Lowriding community forge a stronger sense of community and tie to each other.

Beyond music and language I also found art as a recurring theme throughout my research. Murals were painted on the trunks of vehicles, in between door jams, or underneath the trunk. Each person had chosen the art work and location as an expression of themselves. This notion of customization is a prominent thread among Lowriders. While some customizations are performed in order to solve a problem, others are chosen as part of an extensive work to improve the vehicle's artistic show value. The process of customization is an art form that allows the lowrider to reinvent themselves through creative means. In customization and modification, a lowrider with unique features is the ultimate goal, beside the need to keep the vehicle immaculate at all times. Examples include a new mural or custom engraving by a well-known, respected, and celebrated vehicle painter. The goal of creating something nobody's ever thought of before, such as a lowriding bicycle or custom painted, fully detailed and flawless peddle car for toddlers are all part of the guiding principles of Lowrider art and customization. Throughout my observations I was unable to find one car where the owner had not taken painstaking time to make their car a work of art that shined beyond the paint job.

This is something that Hoyem spoke to when describing lowriders in his book *I Want My Low Rider to Look Like a Whore* in which he states that

lowriders are characterized by the car being raised or lowered via hydraulics, having wired wheels, expensive paint jobs and a flawless interior. This
merely describes the aesthetics of an expensive vehicle but where is the soul?
Hoyem's definition fails to address the driver, components of Lowrider
culture, hours of labor invested in car restoration, and instead solely focus
on image. Hoyem's version of the lowrider is nothing more than a gaudy
pimpmobile. Whereas Hoyem offered a narrow view on the definition of a
Lowrider I found that his observations were flawed and were not an accurate
depiction of what I observed and found through interviews.

Using that narrow definition of lowriding, Hoyem's, Chavez and Bright's
scholarly research seems nothing more than flipping through a copy of *Low
Rider Magazine* or a reference to *The New Oxford American Dictionary*.
Without a driver, culture and language, the lowrider is just an object. To
understand why seemingly sane individuals, families, car clubs, etc. invest
thousands of dollars and hours laboring to restore a vintage automobile the
layperson would have to understand that this is a communal effort. There is
no culture without community. One person may own the vehicle, but the
entire car club (familia) has a hand in that vehicle's success at a car show and
simple joy and satisfaction one derives while cruising. The literature found on
Lowriding negates what my field observations showcased; Lowriding is multi
dimensional and continues to fluctuate like all cultures.

Along with music, language, and art, style of clothes are an equally
important component of the culture. Literature indicates that there is a
discrepancy of understanding when the Lowriding culture was first seen.
Some people argue that lowriding started before WWII, while others argue
it started *after* WWII. Sandoval stated that Lowriding began after WWII.
This is most logical because at that time young servicemen were coming back
from the war and saw cars as an important status symbol for the working class
families (Sandoval, 2003, p. 183). This was a time in the American history
where more cars were being sought in order for middle class families and
those aspiring to be part of the middle class to show inclusion into the middle
class social status. It is also from this era that we see the style of clothes worn
by Lowriders originate. The Zoot Suits, Fedora, Pachuco, Calcos (shoes),
Pendletons, dresses, make-up, and hairstyle all stem from the era in which
lowriding originated. La Cosa and Lowrider Weatherboy both indicated that
style of clothes are a key factor in partaking in the Lowrider culture. Through
my observations I found that not all car owners and participants wear clothes
in the Lowrider style yet they all accepted the clothing as an integral part of
the culture.

Conclusion

Lowriding as a culture has many misconceptions and stereotypes. The academic research published regarding Lowriding does little to negate those negative stereotypes, instead they reinforce them. Through my research I was able to find that there is a rich history and culture which is often lost when researchers attempt to define Lowriding as a culture or cultural phenomena. As an insider I am provided a different lens and enter into a world in which others cannot enter. It is with this knowledge that I was able to push the research beyond the surface in which other researchers have failed. As part of the research process I learned that while researchers have not been able to fully develop into the Lowrider culture, I also found that precious few Lowriders have taken hold of their own narrative.

In the presence of mainstream advertising, the explicitly political edge of the 70's has been lost (Sandoval, 2003, p. 194). I am strongly aware of this, and as lowriders, I feel it is our obligation to pass this legacy on to our future generations. Since the birth of *Lowrider Rider Magazine*, in 1977, many Chicano readers responded enthusiastically to the creation of a cultural space through the magazine that documented working class barrio life (Sandoval, 2003). I feel it is important that we lead our actions with our own stories so that we define ourselves instead of letting others define us. Grabbing a hold of our personal narrative is also important because it leads us down a path of self-reflection, it forces us to become clear with our interest and the meaning of why we do what we do and our motivations. Once the magazine was sold in 1997 to the largest publishing group in the United States, we no longer told the story. This is important for us because we are defining our own history, our ability to tell the story and be respected. I have discovered the values that lowriders hold so dearly, which are hard work, dedication, and loyalty.

Together we can create a legacy of our Chicano and Chicana culture in our home and schools that we may share with the world. This becomes important to us so that we never go back to feeling irrelevant, being banned, and feeling sanctioned from different cities. We want our dignity to be reflected in the legends we create. Only we can take our past, present, and our future and provide an accurate depiction. I push the academic community to push beyond the stereotype and push to truly understand the Lowrider community and what makes it tick. It is only if both the Lowriders and researchers combined choose to push beyond the veneer of the car can we get to the heart of the culture where the Lowrider story can be fully told.

References

Allatson, P. (2007). *Key terms in Latino/a, cultural and literary studies*. Blackwell Publishing.

Bright, B. J. (1997). *Nightmares in the new metropolis: The cinematic poetics of low riders. Studies in Latin American Popular Culture*, 16, 16, 18.

Chappell, B. (2012). *Lowrider space: Aesthetics and politics of Mexican American Custom Cars*. University of Texas Press.

Chavez, M. J. (2013). *Dissertation: The performance of Chicano masculinity in lowrider car culture: The erotic triangle, visual sovereignty, and rasquachismo*. University of California, Riverside.

Hebdige, D. (1979). *Subculture the meaning of style*. Routledge.

Hoyem, M. (2007). *I want my car to look like a whore: Lowriding and poetics of outlaw aesthetics*. University of Oslo.

Irving, K. (1984). Cross cultural awareness and the English-as-a-second-language classroom. *Theory Into Practice*, 138.

Lipsitz, G. (2012). Cruising around the historical bloc: Postmodernism and popular music in East Los Angeles. *Modernity and Modernism, Postmodernity and Postmodernism*. 5, 157–177.

Massey, D. (1994). *Space, place & gender*. University of Minnesota Press.

Mendoza, R. (2012). *Cruising art and culture in Aztlan: Lowriding in the Mexican American southwest*. Universitatsverlag.

Minkov, M., & Hofstede, G. (2013). Cross-Cultural analysis: The science and Art of Comparing the World's Modern Societies and Their Cultures. SAGE Publications, Inc.

Sandoval, D. M. (2003). Cruising through low rider culture: Chicana/o identity in the marketing of low rider magazine. In A. G. Alba (Ed.), *Velvet barrios*. (pp. 179–196). Palgrave Macmillan.

Tatum, C. M. (2011). *Lowriders in Chicano culture: From low to slow to show santa Barbara*. ABC-CLIO.

9. *El Campesino Project: Conciencia y las Raices de Tu Causa*

MARTÍN MORALES RAMÍREZ

Introduction

This piece begins with another day en la memoria, between King City and Greenfield, in the Salinas Valley where espiritus I can hear, roam every day. Where there are more than 70 unsolved murders dating back to 1999 (KION546 News Team, 2018). Too many names to say, they keep calling me and other survivors by name. From the grave, dead in flesh, with much to say. The spirits of an unusual number of children and young adults call us to an unresolved purpose. Still, those spirits run from their demons. *Fuck it!* Many say it's their fault, until the spirits call their own name. Beyond the news, the young deaths are rarely discussed publicly. Yet, I hear them in my consciousness recalling a homies' love for one-another, telling me they see me running, trying to keep their name out of my mind. *Not even the long hours of field work will make you or I forget. Yes, it is me. Do you remember that day? I miss you! I hope to see you one day. I see you passing the Campo Santo, or did you forget that I am here? After all, it was only yesterday. Please do not forget my name. If you dare, say my name, and give me peace.* This piece is an attempt to reach the reader with a mirror and ask if they relate to the pain. Our ancestors used to say, *Tu eres mi otro Yo (In Lak'ech),* so I will keep calling names of the spirits, in an attempt to understand the unresolved purpose. Revenge is part of this reality. Yet sometimes it is not an option when death is caused by youthful misfortune, drug use, and abuse. Karma, some say. Is there anyone to blame? Gangs? Violence is too often the perpetrator. Por qué? Is it because the community lives in fear, or simply has accepted this condition? For many this reality is a part of life; others disagree. This suspect remains at-large. Unsolved deaths in Greenfield reveal a collective pain that plunges this community. How can we better understand? Es más, what can we do to stop this madness?

Background and History

Campesinos (farm workers) largely from México live in the Salinas Valley. They are immigrants with sons and daughters born in Salinas or South Monterey County. Some children immigrated for the states as infants to "el norte" from Central American countries. Others migrated seasonally with roots across the southwest and northwestern U.S., more specifically, Texas, Arizona, New Mexico, Colorado, Oregon, and Washington. There also remain Chicanos (Mexican Americans) and Filipino Mexicanos who have worked this valley for generations. These are the parents that sacrificed their livelihood and moved north to provide a better future for their children. Some have been integrated in the economy as farm foremans, service sector workers, bus drivers, factory workers, and more recently, prison guards. Some were the sons and daughters of Braceros who crossed the border as contracted farm laborers in the 1940's or later, parents with desires, visions, and goals of their children fulfilling the American dream. As my mother would say, "Para hacer un peso/to make a dollar" (G. M. Ramírez, 1995). Working long hours is not uncommon for most campesino parents with children that were raised in the Salinas Valley since forever until the present. Beginning their workday as early as 4 a.m. and ending in the late hours of the evening, they labored Monday through Sunday (del Lunes hasta Domingo), seven days a week from spring to fall. As a result, many children do not spend quality time with their parents or extended family.

School friends became part of the familia, providing a bond that sometimes became more powerful or more important to youth than their immediate family. Some male youth described this connection as "carnalismo" (brotherhood), while others named it a "set" or barrio after the local gang culture that has been evolving in the Salinas Valley, reinforced by urban media and the popular culture of movies, music, and style. Families with positive values focused on hard work, love, respect and providing for their families are now exposed to violence and fractured by domestic issues and poverty. The growing assimilation of children and their parents' old-world traditions causes generational cultural conflict. The identity of children and youth of campesinos takes on many directions regardless of "good" or "bad" families.

These bonds created on the streets and schools amongst these youth became a force to be respected. Today, bonds are reinforced and influenced by a prison culture of mass incarceration born in 1946 with the California Department of Corrections Camp Center in Soledad, which eventually expanded in 1958 into the California Training Facility. From its inception, Soledad Prison held a link to years of regional institutionalized racism and inadequate funding for educational institutions. Influenced by social factors and cultural differences, the children of the essential agricultural labor force of the Salinas Valley had long been ignored by educational establishment. For Mexican-origin students, a sense of belonging to educational institutions and relevant cultural histories were often nonexistent, which created the need for positive cultural reinforcement.

By the early 1970's Soledad Prison had become infamous for its racial violence. There were four major prison gangs: the Aryan Brotherhood, Black Guerrilla Family, Mexican Mafia, and most significant to the Salinas Valley, the Nuestra Familia. All were engaged in bloody war. The Nuestra Familia would evolve and provide a call for cultural unity and direction for rural Mexican-origin youth whose families were largely farm workers. This delivered the cultural reinforcement and belonging that many youth were looking for and could not find in their community. It also became the glue that attracted many youth to become part of local barrio gangs that were evolving. As a result, the sons and daughters of campesinos became the prime target for recruitment and membership into gangs under the eventual control of organized crime. The cultural conflicts that many youths had experienced within their communities, specifically educational institutions, made the streets, gangs, and ultimately prison gangs attractive and key to gaining a sense of false dignity. Poverty and lack of economic opportunities in the Salinas Valley also influenced the relationship with such experiences. For many it provided a method to earn money on the streets from the sale of drugs, and to gain a reputation and status in the process.

Rural Gang Violence in the Salinas Valley

They call it the Salad Bowl. The Salinas Valley annually creates millions in revenue for growers. Yet, farm labor continues to live in poverty. Hence, children and youth of farm laborers are left to struggle for opportunity out of familial and often generational poverty. For some youth, the urge for respect, status, protection, and financial gains greatly influenced the decision to join a gang. Those youth who do join, do so at a great sacrifice for themselves and their families, leading to school failure, incarceration, community violence, and divisions amongst peers arising from gang activity to name the obvious. What was once called resistance to cultural assimilation, racism and classism has become both complex and simple. It is simple in that it is no longer a choice as much as a need—a longing for Mexican-origin youth to gain respect, status, protection, and to "come up." It is complex because the cost to belong to a gang is rarely spoken. Here the prison gang became the gatekeeper of the direction neighborhood street gangs moved. Northern California is the domain of the Nuestra Familia—Norte.

The Norteño (North) and Sureño (South) rivalry stems from a Chicano prison dispute in San Quentin in the 1970's over a pair of shoes and continues to plague thousands of Mexican communities. Norteños are considered residents of Northern California who wear red colors and use the number 14. In addition, most Norteños are affiliated with the Nuestra Familia (NF) prison gang. On the other hand, Sureños are considered Southern California residents who wear blue colors and use the number 13. Most Sureños fall under the Mexican Mafia (La Eme). Both are responsible for much violence and drug distribution that continues to increase, resulting in a vast number of violent attacks and homicides against each other and others on the streets and in the prison system. There is much history within each faction of North and South. Warfare between the NF and La Eme and the rivalry between street gangs that they control continues, as does a rise in internal politics in and out of the prison system. This conflict is found in the Salinas Valley.

The issue of gangs in California, North, South, or now Central Valley, centers on World War II in the L.A. area with the original Pachucos and Zoot Suit "riots" during the early 1940's. This historical moment is critical to understanding the present formation and function of gangs. The early formations of Mexican origin youth gangs were simply social groups of youth that felt as outcasts from mainstream society, alienated by their cultural differences, racial discrimination, and language. Their style of dress, talk and behavior was an affront to American society and its WASP (White Anglo Saxon Protestant) cultural formation. However, it became more than a social group of youths. The focus on Mexican-origin youth who presented themselves in any manner other than WASP caused conflict, the most extreme leading to juvenile hall. From this point forward, it has only become more complex. The result is the largest prison system in the industrialized world, the California Department of Corrections and Rehabilitation.

In the Salinas Valley, neighborhood or local gangs became a form of protection, a sense of belonging and clearly an acceptance for many youths. Acts of violence deriving from those attempting to gain status and respect led them deeper into negative behaviors, as lifestyle often overshadows any elements of positive past or present relationships. Eventually, being labeled by authorities as belonging to a gang, "at risk" of having no positive direction, made such youth targets of law enforcement. Thereby school failure, juvenile incarnation, or being placed on formal probation also made specific areas of the community being perceived as gang "hot-spots" by police. Likewise, a potential threat to other neighborhood gangs due to significant numbers of these youth claiming association with Norte and hence, the Nuestra Familia.

The proximity to Salinas, the Monterey County seat, from Greenfield plays a major role and influence on the entire Salinas Valley, not because of employment opportunities, but because of the authority the Nuestra Familia has on Northern California gangs. The gang culture of Salinas parallels the prison gang politics found in California prisons. Soledad or "Chole" as it is known to Mexican- origin inmates has long held Northern California inmate domination, thus became a Nuestra Familia stronghold. Its rival counterpart, the Mexican Mafia, has other prisons under its control. Soledad Prison has much history in the conflict between Northern and Southern California inmates. Since the infamous wars fought on the Soledad prison yards in the 1970's, prison politics and organization has grown stronger and climbed over the prison walls onto the streets. In California, prison politics have become street politics, leaving youth in and around the Salinas Valley with little choice but to become part of the politics.

Today, the increase of gang violence continues to plague communities, including small rural towns like Greenfield, my hometown located in the Central Coast of California. Growing up, I experienced first-hand knowledge about gang influences and the consequences resulting from joining a gang. In 1995, at the age of 13 years old I had witnessed beatings, drug sales, and riots. In my later youth, I would observe shootings. In fact, I witnessed several incidents involving shootings and gang fights. I thought most incidents were unavoidable because they were part of my community, penetrating school activities, sporting events, dances, and parties. I estimate that half of the adolescent population during my youth was involved in such activities. As a result, several of my childhood and neighborhood friends were killed. Still, others continue to embrace and continue to be deeply loyal to the prison gang lifestyle as adults. This clearly persists and affects Greenfield's youth today.

Gang culture has become part of mainstream America in states across the nation, affecting rural, suburban, and urban settings with an increase in violence. As youth say, "get in, where you fit in." One way presents itself in public. The increase of youth involved in gang activity derives from many factors in households, communities, and self. For Mexican-origin youth involved in gangs or not, their present and futures continue to be conditioned by a sense of displacement from mainstream America, where white middle class is portrayed as a normal way of life. In contrast, millions of Mexicans in the U.S. live in poverty, with inadequate housing, minimal access to health care and unequal educational opportunities for both children and adults. Mexican immigrant children and youth, and those born here, encounter negative experiences or racial microaggressions in their K-12 academic journeys with teachers, counselors and other staff (Irizarry & Donaldson, 2012; Solórzano,

1998; Yosso et al., 2009). The English language may not be their primary language and a historic racist curriculum greatly disconnects students from a humanizing educational experience. Academic challenges are often linked with behavioral issues and continually masks the school failure of Mexican-origin students. Education is socialization in American society.

In a rural community, agricultural employment has long been seen as a future for lack of school success. However, the perennial issue of immigration has unfortunately become more stable in the negative and thus, the children of farm workers overwhelmingly seek futures outside of agriculture employment. Being a child of Mexican immigrants has never been welcomed in rural California, nor urban centers for that matter. The national debate and politics surrounding the immigration issue condition their lives. The children of farm workers often lack consistent guidance from their essential hard-working parents during harvest season. This reality has been a mental health stressor, an unspoken generational trauma for many children and youth of farm worker parents. They move in all directions, some assimilate, some not, some stay local, while others move away, some go to college, others leave school, most work, and some join gangs.

La Tierra es de Quien la Trabaja

The issue of gangs in the Salinas Valley however significant has forever been linked to agriculture and the exploitation of farm labor. As has been presented above, the children of farm laborers have equally been exploited through the residual effects of poverty, stigma, and stereotype of being the offspring of a farm worker family. Yet, the economic motor that drives the Salinas Valley and state of California is agriculture. Without this essential workforce at the state level, billions of dollars generated annually by agriculture and agribusiness could simply not happen.

The Bracero Program (1942–1964) brought over five million contracted farm laborers from Mexico to fill farm labor shortages caused by WWII. Mexican bracero laborers created an economy in California that propelled the state into international dominance and was therefore used beyond WWII. Braceros would also establish many of the Mexican origin enclaves found throughout rural California, many would stay in the U.S., marry, and begin families. This is the story of the Salinas Valley. On September 29, 1942, the first 500 farm workers arrived in Stockton, California. It was a bilateral agreement between the Mexican and U.S. governments. From its inception there were horrendous levels of exploitation of Braceros. For example, in the beginning of their gathering at Empalme, Sonora, México, they'd often be forced to wait long periods to cross the border. Many went without food or shelter, only to be sprayed down while nude with DDT (a harsh chemical agent) as part of the medical examination process to enter the U.S. to work and finally, be placed in barracks-like housing conditions to live, often sleeping on metal cots.

The Salinas Valley became one of the major receivers of bracero labor. Its proximity to the San Joaquin Valley, Santa Clara Valley, Pajaro Valley, and Central Coast ranches and fields with their diverse crops and orchards made "the next ranch" easy access for Braceros. Still, it was the need for labor with its diverse crops that kept Braceros in demand in the Salinas Valley. The Salinas Growers Farm Labor Association (GFLA) would negotiate and manage contracts for Braceros on behalf of the growers in the Salinas Valley. There was much demand for cheap bracero farm labor justified by the profits that would now be reached with this unprecedented labor force. Therefore, over the duration of the 22 years of the Bracero Program in the Salinas Valley was extremely monetarily fruitful for growers. The program would end after a tragic farm labor transportation accident in the Salinas Valley town of Chualar.

In the early morning hours of 17 September 1963, the crew of male Mexican guest workers (or braceros) who lived at the Earl Meyers Company labor camp in Salinas, California, boarded a bus to begin their work in two local vegetable fields (Flores, 2013). After a more than eight-hour workday they reboarded the vehicle near the town of Chualar, south of Salinas. The "bus" was actually a flatbed truck with a wooden frame attached to an unfastened canopy and two wooden benches for workers to sit and provide an illusion of a transportation vehicle. Fifty-seven men crammed into the back with all their equipment as the makeshift back door was closed and locked with a chain. They could not communicate with the driver, their foreman, or co-foreman sitting in the passenger seat. When they approached an unmarked railroad crossing, the driver stopped and moved over the tracks until he heard the whistle of an oncoming train much too late. The impact sheared the truck in half and sent the bodies of its passengers flying in all directions. When it was all over, some 33 farm workers would be dead. This was the deadliest farm labor transportation accident in U.S. history, not because of it being a rare occurrence but because of the fatalities at one time (Flores, 2013). Accidents in the transportation of farm laborers are not rare, only there have been less fatalities during incidents. This was the Salinas Valley during an era when profit overshadowed the safety of essential workforce.

Little has changed for farm laborers. Exploitation continues into the 21st century, yet it was in the 20th century that it became highly organized and structured in favor of the growers. The Bracero Program employed such an extensive work force that the logic of profit drove all growers in California to exploit workers in their favor. Despite government sponsored hearings and advocacy groups bringing attention to the exploitation of farm laborers and the conditions in which they worked and lived, profits only increased. Alarmingly, slavery-like conditions prevailed to maintain a modern-day caste system in which racial segregation is prevalent in prison systems today (Alexander, 2010). For example, in Monterey County, hundreds landed in farm labor housing such as Camphora Camp, located next to Soledad Prison, where grandparents and great-grandparents endured great abuse by growers. Many camps like Camphora have been closed but still have left a bad memory on children (now parents themselves) of farm workers who grew up or were born in Monterey County. In many cases growers sold overpriced food and other items to braceros and families at the camp store, which they owned, beyond charging them rent to live there. Often growers did not pay workers for the exact number of hours they worked, leaving single men or those with families to struggle to eat and cover the most basic of necessities. As the sons and daughters of farm laborers came of age, the second generation made plans to leave farm labor. However, often with limited education, some left the area to seek non-agricultural employment and others themselves entered the fields. Thus, generational poverty continued to be reality.

In contrast, there is now a gira (a tour, migrant trail) that has led youth from Salinas Valley High Schools into University of California, California State University, Community College, and California Polytechnic campuses. Many of these youth return to the Salinas Valley as professionals. These trends are promising, and both community organizing and strategic advocacy at the state capital and educational leadership, including educators and students, will be crucial in continuing to positively impact the future of youth throughout the Salinas Valley. I quote the interview in which Godoy (2017) captured Dolores Huerta's espiritu and who coined the palabras, "We can do it. I can do it. *Si Se Puede.*"

The relationship between rural gangs and agriculture remains to be looked upon in serious study. What we do offer the Salinas Valley and other parts of California is El Campesino Project. We now turn our focus on an attempt to provide hope and a counter narrative to the campesino struggle through Lowriding Culture.

El Campesino Project through a Latino Critical (LatCrit) Theoretical Framework

The focus of this project is to encourage youth to question their original beliefs of what they believe "La Causa" means to them through the

Lowriding Culture but through a LatCrit framework. LatCrit recognizes the relationship between race, racism, wealth, and power (Delgado & Stefancic, 2017). LatCrit Theory affirms the experiences and intersectionalities of Raza populations (del Rosal et al., 2018). It serves as a guiding theory that provides a lens on how race and racism affect the lives of Raza within the context of the agricultural experiences and lowriding culture. LatCrit proponents argue that Raza has engaged in transformational resistance in creating *counterspaces*, which allow them to connect with supportive and strong spaces that acknowledge their cultural knowledge and therefore sustain and ground them (Solórzano & Delgado Bernal, 2001; Yosso et al., 2009). As a result of their experiences in negative climates, Raza has built communities and pursued spaces that represent and reflect their home cultural wealth (Yosso et al., 2009). In this context, El Campesino provides a *counterspace* of transformational resistance for our Raza.

In finding the truth, some students/youth may not be happy; others may be shocked and or surprised. The reality is that many youth who grew up in rural parts of Northern California may realize that what their tio, tia, amigo, amiga, mother, father or abuelo/a told them was actually not the most accurate account of where "La Causa" was born. The original "Causa" was born in the fields. A result of abuse by growers, Cesar Chavez and Dolores Huerta organized a strike that eventually gained national attention. Wages that kept families in poverty-stricken conditions and unsafe working conditions led Mexican American farmworkers and allies to fight back for dignity. Montoya (2016) states, "La Causa -- 'the cause,' as the farmworkers' quest for unionization became known -- was an important inspiration to Mexican Americans everywhere because they closely identified with the strikers; they saw themselves, or their parents, or their grandparents" (p. 40). Palabra! At this point in our history/herstory x our ancestors demanded dignity y los de abajo/masses both rural and urban took notice. This became el grito that greatly influenced the Chicano Movement. In contrary, "Nuestra Familia highjacked the original movement and used the campesinos flag "UFW-Aztec Eagle" and momentum to recruit youth into their "cause" that was masked by conflicting ideologies, greed, institutionalized racism, lies and betrayal" (Anonymous, personal communication, 2000). As a result, "The Cause" for many youth became a different struggle that often turned many recent Mexican immigrants, Mexican American or Chicano youth on each other. Eventually, youth that were convinced about the NF CAUSA became owned by the well-organized structured gang that continues to have strong roots in communities throughout Aztlan, state and now federal prisons. El Campesino Project's priority is to strategically encourage youth, adults, our

Raza, to reflect on our core values that are sometimes easily influenced in our childhood. At that time, during our parent's prolonged absence due to their work schedules, as children we do not develop a strong sense of belonging in our schools, homes and communities. Their causa, purpose and/or identity becomes authored by others. El Campesino Project's goal is to challenge youth's sense of cultural identity and encourage youth to ask questions and practice critical thinking. Como dijo mi padre, "Piensa" (Lara, 1994). That is the ultimate goal: to make people a bit uncomfortable so they can "think" and reflect on their own journey and identify with something positive that they can fight for. The goal here is to support youth on building a critical consciousness about their community and their core values or immediate families. As a result, our youth and communities will work towards achieving "conscientization" to become critically aware of their social reality and their place in the world so that they can make their own decisions about how they live their lives and not have them made for them (Freire, 1970).

To make this a reality, this project intends to inspire youth to use their own creativity to capture and imagine their own causa. Students would be taken on a historical cruise about how Lowriding became a vehicle for communities to resist racism and micro and macroaggressions from law enforcement and biased laws. Participating youth would receive "flecha" on how Lowriding has origins in resistance and serves as a form of self-empowerment "con orgullo" that fought against mainstream society that attempted to sideline our people or force us to assimilate "a huevo." Eventually youth would be asked to study "El Campesino Project" and the theme that this lowrider represents, "La Causa." In the process, youth will learn about the original "Causa" that was born out of the Chicano/a Movement in the 60's, a cause focused on nonviolence, education, justice, and sacrifice. Matthiessen (2014) quotes Cesar E. Chavez's words, "It is my deepest belief that only by giving our lives do we find life" (p. xxiii). Hence, El Campesino Project is focused on inspiring youth to sacrifice and advocate for political, economic, and social awareness so institutionalized racism is derailed and more members of our community benefit from equitable opportunities, fair wages, empowering education, healthcare, and affordable housing.

Students will learn the story of how "El Campesino Project" was born. The initial seed that gave life to this project was planted in 1993 when I was 11 years old. As a kid, I noticed that many kids within my circles were being pulled in two different directions. Unos al Norte y otros al Sur. I did not go either way and for many years after this I made an attempt to stay in the middle. It was a very challenging task. One decision on any given day had the possibility to be deadly. Being at the wrong place with unexpected visitors could end my corrido/ballad/story. This meant being very careful of where I would visit and who I decided to associate with, including childhood friends. Years later when I was 15 years old I would take notice of who was pulling the strings and heavily influencing our childhood and community. After experiencing several years of violence, murders, my father's unexpected passing, drug and alcohol abuse, I realized that I had to detach myself from the madness or suffer the consequences. At this point, I enrolled into a Chicano/a Studies course at the age of 19 which inspired me to do something to heal the wounds that I was carrying on a daily basis and give a voice to all my childhood relations. Here is where El Campesino Project was born. Since 2000, I have been in search of different strategies to touch el corazon y la mente de nuestra raza. It has now been more than two decades since I began my "spiritual re-encounter with our cultural roots" (p. 87) as Figueroa (2002) reinforces in his book. As previously mentioned, de chiripada I enrolled into a Chicano/a Studies course in Sacramento, CA and poco a poco se me fue borrando la "P" que tenia en la frente as Dr. Rodolfo Acuña, Professor at California State University, Northridge nos enseño in his lecture as part of the Chicano Studies 445 course (personal communication, January, 2003). My exposure to the Chicano/a Studies, including the Chicano Movement and historical accounts dating back to the Mother Culture of Mexico, the Olmeca and everything in between, inspired me to create El Campesino Project to inspire youth. At this point I reached out to maestros/artistas and campesinos that I met on my journey and asked them to support the development of El Campesino Project. From day one, my goal was to target nuestros morritos and morritas in an attempt to provide them with a sense of cultural identity and reinforce our struggle over 500 years by using el arte. My objective was to construct una ranfla, but not just any ranfla, a lowrider that represents el grito de Miguel Hidalgo, Cuauhtémoc, Dolores Huerta and the millions of mujeres, hombres and X that have died para la causa.

At this point, I decided that El Campesino Project would be used as an educational vehicle to inspire our youth to learn/search for their raices and be critical of causes that they believe in. The goal is to continue presenting this project in Northern Califas, Aztlan/southwest and perhaps other parts of the country. But, the journey will begin in our barrios. For example, the plan is for El Campesino Project to visit K-8 schools, after school programs, car shows, parks and boulevards, and provide kids and youth the ability to take an inspirational journey into the past, present, and future. With the help of a small book that is part of this project, youth would be able to imagine their own cause and potentially identify abuelos, abuelas, tios, o tias, fathers and mothers or maybe brothers/sisters that worked in the fields and sacrificed for their family, so they could have a better future. Additionally, youth would meet the different artists that contributed to this lowrider and helped to create the collage of images representing "La Causa." Other students would have the ability to learn about "El Campesino Project" virtually via Zoom. The goal would be to share this lowrider with youth so they can be inspired to pursue their own causa that is centered in their personal passion and aspirations. Participating youth learning at a school site, for example, would be asked to draw images that represent their own cause or images of their relatives that worked in the fields or sacrificed for their families. For some youth, this exercise will spark childhood memories; for others it will spark new ideas that create joy, memories of love, healing and sometimes pain. The ultimate goal is to create community, hope and empowerment for our youth and honor los de abajo, all our relations and our mothers and fathers that still live. This project is also intended to honor fathers like mine who passed away in the struggle to provide a better future for the next generation and members of the United Farm Workers Union that were part of the frontlines in the struggle to provide the best for their children and families. I quote, "Remember, as a young Chicano, I'd say everything starts at home, sometimes the parents are hard workers and want the best for the children. But after school 3:00 pm to 9:00 pm is important if one is not in sports, baseball, soccer, basketball etc...Where is he at? That's where it starts so after school programs are extremely important especially in a Mexican community" (Anonymous, personal communication, 2003).

The original questions posed to artists, maestros, amigos, and campesinos that contributed to this project were: What is "La Causa"? How would you represent "La Causa" in an 8 x 11 size image? Taking it back from the Olmeca period to the most recent immigrant struggles, supporters were asked to share one piece of arte that represents la causa to them or our pueblo through their point of view. The art pieces that were shared represented many forms. For one community member, the item that was shared to represent "La Causa" was a three-D "Aztec Eagle" pencil or pen holder that was made from wood. Another community member shared a picture of his tio, posing with a "pica" on asparagus fields because his uncle was considered the Heisman Trophy Champion at cutting the most asparagus on any given day. The speed, quickness, and hard work ethic that this campesino exhibited was unmatched. This accomplishment came with "orgullo" pride, admiration, and dignity. With the supporters' permission, the shared images, items, and self-portraits became part of a collage on the 1963 Impala that is the heart of this project. In total, 14 different supporters helped provide a definition of what "La Causa" represents through their lens/imagination. The vehicle eventually was painted a victory red color with an original Impala interior. The color represents the blood that has been shed by our community on each other and the constant racist acts by the colonizer that have, as declared by the title of Acuña (2000) book, "Occupied America." Again, the victory red paint represents the blood that continues to run in the halls of penitentiaries, streets, school classrooms, files, border walls, bedrooms, parks, backyards, garages and behind closed doors. By our gente on each other! Que desgracia! "Amaliciala" dijo mi padre! (Lara, 1993). The EZLN Zapatistas (Ramirez, 2003) say, "Ya Basta!"(p. 151) mi Raza. It is time to change our course and change direction for seven generations atras y siete adelante. For this reason, the art on the car was my attempt to capture a collective effort by community members to define "La Causa" and provide youth with multiple examples of what "La Causa" can represent. For some, "La Causa" represents taking care of their families and breaking the chains of mental slavery that sometimes hold us back from aspiring to accomplish our goals. I quote Marcus Garvey, "We are going to emancipate ourselves from mental slavery because whilst others might free the body, none but ourselves can free the mind" (Tattrie, 2017).

The display that is part of this project honors different aspects of the campesino journey; it provides a glimpse to the tools and life that community members experienced to provide for their families. El Campesino Project display includes a thermos, picas to cut asparagus, bolsas pa el lonche, guantes de algodon, palas, asadones, tijeras para la apoda and the famous cortito o mano del diablo "the short hand hoe" that was outlawed from the fields. These are only a few of the items that are included as part of the display when El Campesino Project is presented. The hope is the future generations will learn about the campesino experience during the 40's, 50's, 60's, 70's, 80's, 90's and 2000's and be able to imagine the sacrifice and life that our ancestors lived and endured. With each campesino tool or relic that was donated to this project, a small plaque has been created to humanize each campesino; included on the plaque is a short biography on the life of each campesino. The trunk includes a nicho that is accompanied by an altar and two small caskets that replicate the casket that Cesar E. Chavez was buried in. Outside of the trunk a small church bench is displayed for prayer which replicates a bench from the Holy Trinity Church in Greenfield, CA. This part of the project makes an attempt to duplicate the temporary altar that was created by the UFW when the organization would hold mass in the fields during picketing. Like in the past, this altar is focused on providing our community with hope/esperanza and the opportunity to connect with our descendants and those still living. Also included on this altar is a picture of Larry Itliong with Cesar E. Chavez. Mr. Itliong was a Filipino labor organizer who led his union to begin the Delano Grape Strike. Eventually, Mr. Itliong would invite Cesar E. Chavez to join his cause.

The fact that we poison our own, kill our own, and exploit our own is apparent. Again, the primary goal of this project is to take youth on a cruise down the street and back up the block into our genetically imprinted DNA. If anything, within our own palabras the answers exist to the demons that we sometimes ignore. "La Cultura Cura" dicen las comadres y compadres (The National Compadres Network, 2014). Or, can amor within our own families be the answer? Padres y madres taking the time to hug and kiss their morritos, morritas and X children every day, putting la botellita to the side. Perhaps it will take the sacred circle to help our community heal from all the pain resulting from untimely murders of youth and historical traumas that sometimes are passed on by past generations. Since the beginning of time, people have gathered in circulos, to honor each other, and to preserve the harmony of the community and the natural rhythm and movement of life (The National Compadres Network, 2014).

Demanding culturally relevant curriculum in our schools has also proven to be effective to engage RAZA and inspire youth to be empowered, not be brainwashed by false causes and or be manipulated, and learn about our roots/raices and beautiful histories dating back to the idea that we derive from la, Raza Cosmica. Boredom and being left out or ostracized in our schools by racist Eurocentric teaching strategies and curriculum, has not effectively inspired a majority of youth to remain engaged by building on their wealth of capital (Yosso, 2005). This project on the contrary provides youth with a Chicano/a/x Studies perspective on a historical period that is rich in lessons of self-determination, sacrifice, justice, and education.

El Campesino Project highlights the potential that Critical Lowriding Pedagogy has to influence and empower future generations of youth through our Lowriding tradition. As Xris Macias mentioned at the Save The Kids 1st International Lowrider Studies Conference (electronic communication, January 29, 2021) the goal is to develop a Lowrider Critical Pedagogy. Indeed, we need a "critical theory of schooling" that can embrace our Lowrider tradition to empower and humanize our experience in schools and society (Lam, 2019). Lowriding has proven to have roots of perseverance, resistance, empowerment, self-expression, and heart to support los de abajo. Here I argue that Lowriding, again, has the caliber to break down barriers between the walls, in our towns and classrooms, and up and down our barrios, including state lines. It is possible. As La Profe Sandoval (2000) says,

"Moving low and slow across the land of a thousand freeways, their ranflas have helped to break down some of the barriers that separate the inhabitants of our city" (p. 7). As in the past, Lowriding continues to prove that its craft and creativity is unmatched; hence, I argue that it can become a tool to influence youth to identify a causa and/or reflect on their "CAUSA," one that is not owned or manipulated by anyone but their corazon, passion, talents, and raices de bronze. A causa that is focused on not forgetting our roots and giving back to our communities through philanthropy, education not schooling, both professional and peer mentoring, and community centered organizing, focused on empowering current and future generations. I reference Tupac when he quoted Eldridge Cleaver: "You're either part of the solution or part of the problem" (Joseph, 2006, p. 41).

CAUSA

Here, again, I propose that it is time to take a deep self-reflection on our "CAUSA" through Lowriding. In his lecture delivered as part of the Chicano Studies 445 course at California State University, Northridge, Professor R. Acuña (2003) stated, "The they is us." This self-reflection can begin by listening to our youth and providing sunlight as we do with our plantas in our jardín. Sharing what Figueroa (2002) captured in his book, "...the dual prophecy of the last Mexica ruler, Cuauhtémoc, will be fulfilled, that our Sun will shine again and that the greatness of Mexico/Tenochtitlán will never perish" (p. 11). Agua y sabiduría para compartir palabra seria el siguiente paso para comensar el proceso de curar las heridas. Creating medicine in the process is the objective; we can support each other emotionally, helping to heal wounds attributed by injustice and childhood experiences. Una cosa bonita. A group of community members, lowriders, including youth/students with a common purpose: growth, support, and change for our community. Juntxs we can brainstorm visions of change in education, group projects, and community empowerment. Full circle as el millennial Julio Parra says (2020). It had to be the circle to heal hell, el Maestro Jose Montoya wrote (2005, stanza 2). As a collective, taking ownership of our responsibilities and not allowing any one individual or group to pollute our streets with synthetic drugs, guns or elements that are unhealthy to our youth and community.

The power of words is unimaginable. Words like "CAUSA" can definitely plant the seed of a rebirth for one, two, or many individuals. In this case causa is defined to be "struggle." How liberating and empowering is this one term? For me it gave me hope and it empowered me to believe above and beyond what I dreamed for myself as a young man of 19 years old. The power of words is, indeed, unimaginable, so embrace ideas, words, terms that may be distant but can empower you to experience a rebirth. Freire (1970) stated, "Freedom is not an ideal located outside of man; nor is it an idea which becomes myth. It is rather the indispensable condition for the quest for human completion" (p. 47). Facing the fear to embrace a new idea to describe who we are or can become is key. This can be the beginning of a new chapter in your life as you already know that "CAUSA" gave me life and ganas/grit. Palabra! Word! Orale!

Positive Change

It takes courage, character, palabra, and vision to be different and change history and herstory. We all have choices that have consequences, but not even the best choice does not prevent the end of our physical journey on mother earth. So, be the change that you want to see in your family and our town; this process begins with reflecting on past choices and creating an action plan to change future outcomes here in Grinfas, and beyond- in your local community. Be the voice that does not forget our brothers, sisters, fathers, mothers and grandparents that have already been sacrificed. The reality is that we need to begin learning from examples like members in our communities who are striving to make positive change, individuals who were not afraid to take a different road and change the course of history. Organizations such as AVILA VICTORY BOXING INC. and U.N.I.D.O.S 831 from Greenfield, CA and MILPA from Salas, Santa Cruz Barrios Unidos, Lowrider Commissions or Coalitions, Brown Issues, Self-Awareness and Recovery, The National Compadres Network, Lowrider Clubs and California Association of Latino Superintendents and Administrators need our support. Our communities need time to heal, not only from yesterday's loss but from the loss of so many of our family members who have passed. Help yourself if you walk around with cargas/baggage. Do not pass your cargas/negative/culture energy to our future generations. How many more tragedies like the 1963 Chualar Bracero accident do we need to unite? "Ya basta" (Ramirez, 2003, p. 151) mi Raza! El pueblo unido jamas sera vencido! Remember, in the song titled *Karma*, Paez (1999) says, "El que al cielo escupe la cara le cai." We must not forget the lessons from our Salinas Valley, be different, smile, con respeto, put on some good rolas, dress your best, always take care of each other and take a cruise down El Camino Blvd and Broadway in your lowrider. El Compa Edgar Zapata (Mexico, 2018) dice, "Zapata vive, la lucha sigue!" (p. 22). Tu causa es mi causa! Con Safos! C/S

References

Acuña, R. (2000). *Occupied America: A history of Chicanos* (4th ed.). Addison Wesley Longman.

Alexander, M. (2010). *The new Jim Crow: Mass incarceration in the age of colorblindness.* The New Press.

del Rosal, K., Roman, D., Basaraba, D. (2018). Debemos escuchar a los maestros: Perspectives of bilingual teacher candidates in teacher education partnerships. *Bilingual Research Journal, 41*(2), 187–205. https://doi.org/10.1080/15235882.2018.1456986

Delgado, R., & Stefancic, J. (2017). *Critical race theory: An introduction.* New York University Press.

Figueroa, A. A. (2002). *Ancient footprints of the Colorado River: La Cuna de Aztlan.* Aztec Printing Company.

Flores, A. L. (2013). A town full of dead Mexicans: The Salinas Valley Bracero tragedy of 1963, the end of the Bracero Program, and the evolution of the California's Chicano Movement. *Western Historical Quarterly, 44*(2), 126–127.

Freire, P. (1970). *Pedagogy of the oppressed.* The Continuum International Publishing Group Inc.

Godoy, M. (2017). *Dolores Huerta: The civil rights icon who showed farmers 'Sí Se Puede'.* NPR: The Salt. Retrieved from: https://www.npr.org/sections/thesalt/2017/09/17/551490281/dolores-huerta-the-civil-rights-icon-who-showed-farmworkers-si-se-puede

Irizarry, J., & Donaldson, M. L. (2012). Teach for América: the Latinization of U.S. schools and the critical shortage of Latina/o teachers. *American Educational Research Journal, 49*(1), 155–194. https://doi.org/10.3102/0002831211434764

Joseph, J. (2006). *Tupac Shakur: Legacy.* Atria Publishing Group.

KION546 News Team. (2018). *South County Major Crimes Unit highlights unsolved murder cases.* KION546 News Channel. Retrieved from: https://kion 546.com/news/2018/05/21/south-county-major-crimes-unit-highlights-unsolved-murder-cases/

Lam, D. K. (2019). The Oxford Research Encyclopedia Education. Doi: 10.1093/acrefore/9780190264093.013.382

Lara, L. (1993). Personal communication.

Matthiessen, P. (2014). *Sal si puedes: Escape if you can.* University of California Press. Mexico. LXIII Legislatura de la H. Camara de Diputados. (2018). *Ofrenda: A la memoria de Emiliano Zapata.* Impreso y hecho en Mexico.

Montoya, Jose. (2005). El Circulo.

Montoya, M. (2016). *Chicano movement: For beginners.* For Beginners LLC. The National Compadres Network. (2014). *La Cultura cura: Transformational health & healing* [Pamphlet]. [San Jose, CA]: Jerry Tello/NCN.

Paez, K. (1999). Karma. *On b-side players: Culture of resistance* [CD]. [United States]: Players/Rollin West Publishing.

Ramirez, M. G. (2003). EZLN 20 y 10: *El fuego y la palabra.* Quebecor World Graficas Monte Albán S.A. de C.V.

Sandoval, D., & Polk, A. P. (2000). *Arte y estilo: The lowriding tradition.* Palace Press International.

Solórzano, D. (1998). Critical race theory, race and gender microaggressions, and the experience of Chicana and Chicano scholars. *International Journal of Qualitative Studies in Education, 11*(1), 121–136. https://doi.org/10.1080/095183998236926

Solórzano, D. & Delgado Bernal, D. (2001). Examining transformational resistance through a Critical Race and Latcrit Theory Framework: Chicana and Chicano students in an urban context. *Urban Education, 36*(3), 308–342. https://doi.org/10.1177/0042085901363002

Tattrie, J. (2017). *The African Nova Scotian roots of Bob Marley's "Redemption Song."* The Canadian Encyclopedia. https://www.thecanadianencyclopedia.ca/en/article/the-african-nova-scotian-roots-of-bob-marleys-redemption-song

Yosso, T. (2005) Whose culture has capital? A critical race theory discussion of community cultural wealth, Race Ethnicity and Education, 8:1, 69-91, DOI:10.1080/1361332052000341006

Yosso, T., Smith, W., Ceja, M., & Solórzano, D. (2009). Critical race theory, racial microaggressions, and campus racial climate for Latina/o undergraduates. *Harvard Educational Review, 79*(4), 659–691. https://doi.org/10.17763/haer.79.4.m6867014157m7071

10. Raza's Membership in Lowrider Car Clubs

ELIZABETH G. RAMOS

Introduction

Despite experiences of legal injustices, exploitation, and discrimination, *Raza* has been able to persevere by working together as communities (Acuña, 1981; Alaniz & Cornish, 2008; Almaguer, 1971, 2009; Duncombe, 2002; Palomares, 1971). Raza has been defined as a hypernym for all Latin American people (Acuña, 1995; Zavala, 2013). For this study, the term Raza was more narrowly defined as individuals of Mexican descent. *Lowriding* is one aspect of Raza's history that exemplifies both resilience and *rasquachismo*. Rasquachismo has been defined as praxis and an attitude of resourcefulness and adaptability by Raza that demonstrates the tenacity and desire to do the best they can with what they have. Lowriding is the practice of designing, building, and maintaining customized lowrider cars, trucks, vans, and bicycles (Best, 2006; Lowrider Network, 2002a; Tatum, 2011). Lowriding is also the product of creativity and flexibility of thought, which involves using what others discard or adapting to meet specific needs. Today, lowriding is known for the unconventional and innovative transformations of modern or classic cars, trucks, vans, or bikes into living pieces of art that continue to evolve (Calvo, 2011; Padilla, 1999; Penland, 2003; Tatum, 2011; Zaragoza, 2015).

Characteristics of lowriders—from the art and symbolism to the language and clothes associated with lowriding—can be found in many books, magazines, newspapers, and even mainstream media, popular videos, commercials, movies and television shows. Studies in various disciplines have been done to learn more about the practices and culture. Gradante (1982) examined the history, politics, and practices of the lowriding culture. Bright (1994) reported that lowriding is an expression of culture and sociopolitical struggles. Sandoval (2003) described how Raza's identity has been influenced and expressed through lowriding practices and values. What remains constant is that lowriding, as a practice and lifestyle, is a source of strength and resilience for Raza. It is an opportunity for them to display their culture, pride, creativity, work ethic, and unity (Ides, 2009; Moran-Zejli, 2007; López Pulido & Reyes, 2017). This study focused on the people who made lowriding their lifestyle and what it means to them. Through their perspective and voice, I explain how being a member of a lowrider car club has influenced Raza's identity and helped them cope with stigma and psychosocial stressors.

By targeting Raza specifically, this study helped explain why lowriders hold on to their history and roots while adapting to modern times and social changes. I explain how Raza demonstrates pride in self, community, and heritage. I describe how Raza works together, emphasizes brotherhood or sisterhood, and can still display a competitive spirit. I hope to add to the field of psychology by presenting both the struggle of Raza and the progress (metal wellness) they achieve through their membership in lowrider car clubs. Allowing Raza to share their experiences helped clarify erroneous generalizations that they are criminals or gang members and highlighted the positive impact of lowriding on the Chicano community and world.

Background

This section includes a synopsis of Raza's history and American politics in the evolution of lowrider culture and a review of events that changed lowriding. This phenomenon continues to be purported as a source of cultural resistance, passion, and self-expression for all who participate in it (Fregoso, 1980; Padilla, 1999; Tatum, 2011; Usner, 2016).

Roots of Lowriding

Lowriding as a hobby, trade, and lifestyle began making its presence in the 1940s (Miner, 2014; Penland, 2003). Its place of origin continues to be debated. Some believe lowriding first emerged in Los Angeles, California (Penland, 2003; Tatum, 2011), while others believe it was in Española, New Mexico (Miner, 2014; Usner, 2016) or the border towns of El Paso, Texas, and Juarez, Mexico (Arredondo, 2016; Boyle, 2016). World War II created a booming economy and gave rise to new opportunities (Meier, 2016). Raza returned from their wartime deployments with a G.I. Bill and new trade skills. For countless others with minimal education, they remained limited to low-paying jobs in agriculture, industry, or the railroad (Acuña, 1981). While

White youth were racing hot-rods, Raza's pursuit of the American dream edged them on to own a vehicle (Best, 2006; Frost, 2002; Padilla, 1999). However, purchasing a car often meant looking at older models that often needed work.

As they struggled to help their families make money, Raza began organizing collaboratives (Acuña, 1981; Alaniz & Cornish, 2008; Tatum, 2011). Large family-sized cars (typically Chevy or GM because they were cheaper) were used to transport groups of people to and from work. On the weekends, as hot-rods were making their presence known for their speed, Raza began customizing their cars to cruise low and slow around their *barrio*. A barrio is a Spanish-language term used to describe relatively small-sized neighborhoods that were often densely populated by Raza (Alaniz & Cornish, 2008; Penland, 2003). These impoverished, yet overpriced, barrios were an example of the ongoing exploitation Raza experienced (Acuña, 1981, 1995). Many families shared a car because they could not afford one and public transportation was often not a viable option due to their limited routes. With their snappy names and cool jackets, Lowrider car clubs began to make their presence known too.

Early Conflicts: 1940s and 1950s

The practice of lowering cars and crafting them to display unique qualities and capabilities burgeoned in response to sociopolitical clashes in East Los Angeles and neighboring communities across California and the country (Lowrider Network, 2002a; Penland, 2003; Tatum, 2011). Poverty and post-war racial tensions coupled with media sensationalism resulted in two major incidents in 1943. The end of the Sleepy Lagoon case and the Zoot Suit riots inflamed negative stereotypes of gang violence among Raza youth or *pachucos* that continue to the present day (McWilliams, 2016; Salomon, 2003; Sanchez, 1943).

Racial tensions between Raza and law enforcement continued into the 1950s. Due to wartime economic opportunities, Raza was better able to customize their lowriders (Lowrider Network, 2002b). They became visible in more significant numbers, meeting at local hang-outs, cruising the boulevards, and attending community events. The media again began using inflammatory language to describe Raza as gang members intruding into otherwise peaceful neighborhoods with their cars. They were reported to be instigating violence, destroying pavements, and disrupting traffic. (Penland, 2003; Salomon, 2003; Tatum, 2011)

In 1959, in an effort to limit cruising by lowriders, California introduced vehicle code § 24008, which limited how low a car could sit (CVC, 1959; Lowrider Network, 2002c). Raza, demonstrating their rasquachismo, moved from placing rocks or sandbags in the trunk or cutting springs to developing hydraulics using discarded plane parts and skills acquired during World War II. This innovation allowed them to cruise low while still making their cars appear street legal when the police were present (Penland, 2003; Tatum, 2011)

Call for Unity During the 1960s

After decades of aggressions against La Raza, political protests united Raza to create positive social change. The limited options for better housing, barriers to education, and narrowed opportunities for higher-paying jobs left Raza laborers and youth feeling defeated. Raza continued to organize to address these disparities. The Chicano Movement was one such effort, and it worked in solidarity with other Latino/Hispanic, Native American, Asian American, Arab-American, and African American civil rights groups and farm workers' movements. Together, these disenfranchised groups struggled to acknowledge the contributions minorities made in agriculture, industry, and the military (Acuña, 1981; Almaguer, 1971, 2009; Martinez, 1991). This chaotic time also saw the first in a series of restrictions on cruising and car shows in Los Angeles and across the southwestern states (Best, 2006; Penland, 2003). Many who came together over issues such as the war in Vietnam and ongoing civil rights violations also united to keep lowriding alive (Alba Cutler, 2009; Martinez, 1991; Penland, 2003).

The 1970s

Lowriding began gaining more attention through an increase in media attention. In 1974, NBC aired a sitcom that featured a lowrider (*Gypsy Rose*) in its introduction (Frost, 2002; Lowrider Network, 2002a; Simpson, 2015). In 1977, Lowrider Magazine sparked a new conversation about lowriders that continues to flourish today (Lowrider Network, 2002a; Lowrider Network, 2011). The 1978 movie, *Up in Smoke* debuted a rasquache-looking lowrider (Tatum, 2011). However, it also negatively characterized the owner, further stigmatizing the lowrider community. The following year, *Boulevard Nights* depicted life in the barrios of Los Angeles, but not without criticism that it was exploiting Raza (LoBianco, 2016; Tatum, 2011). Both movies continue to impact the rules and bylaws of lowrider car clubs today.

New Generation of Lowriders

In the late 1970s and early 1980s, lowriders began making greater strides in crossing racial lines. While lowriding had been associated with La Raza, lowriding culture was also represented in the African American community and spreading throughout other ethnic groups and countries (Penland, 2003; Tatum, 2011). This became most evident as lowriders began being featured in music videos (Frost, 2002; Kercher, 2015; Penland, 2003). In 1990, the Smithsonian National Museum of American History acquired *Dave's Dream*, a lowrider from New Mexico with a significant legacy (Boyle, 2016; Frost, 2002). As a result of cars like *Gypsy Rose* and *Dave's Dream*, museums began displaying lowriders and their galleries and exhibitions (Penland, 2003; Usner, 2016).

In 1992, because of the dangers of car-jacking and gang violence, lowrider car club members reached out to car clubs nationwide to safeguard car shows and community events so that they could continue (Lowrider Network, 2002d, 2002e; Penland, 2003; Zaragoza, 2015). Despite the protests and barriers Raza experienced, such as being banned from mainstream car shows and restrictions on cruising, interest in lowriding continued to grow through the 1990s. Cruising, car shows, and hanging out at the park were revitalized by music labels associated with lowriding. Thump Records offered popular titles in genres like freestyle and hip hop (Olson, 1999; Tatum, 2011), and Art LaBoe created compilations such as *Oldies but Goodies* and *Dedicated to You*, further popularizing the *East Side Story* compilations first released in the late 70s. Finally, the internet helped lowriders gain national and international acclaim (Kercher, 2015; Penland, 2003; Tatum, 2011).

However, what was once known for its fierce competitions and rivals between car clubs and solo-riders, began to change towards the late 1990s. Being in a lowrider car club has, for many, been a family tradition (Aguilar, 2014; Lowrider Network, 2002a). Therefore, keeping with family values, lowrider car clubs began to focus on respect for one another and loyalty to their club and the lifestyle. What has remained consistent has been the expression of self, community, and culture (LaBelle, 2008; Miner, 2014).

Lowrider Identity Development

Whether Raza sees themselves as shy, outgoing, or insecure, when they choose to become a member of a lowrider car club, they begin to identify with aspects of the club culture and the people around them. Generally speaking, Raza looks for something that will provide them a safe place to explore different world views, celebrate their heritage, and cultivate their own identity. Many have dreamed about the car or truck they want to restore, grown-up following certain car clubs, and are eager to "fly a plaque." The support and acceptance they receive from their club and the lowrider community as a whole contribute to their self-concept and sense of belonging (López Pulido & Reyes, 2017; Sandoval, 2014).

Raza and lowriders have historically been branded with negative stereotypes, such as *cholos*, *gangbangers*, and drug users (Almaguer, 1971; Chappell, 2012; McWilliams, 2016). Instead, lowrider car clubs have provided this marginalized group with an opportunity to demonstrate that they are competent, skilled, tenacious, and resilient (Aguilar, 2014; Best, 2006; Bright, 1994; Madriaga, 2014; Tatum, 2011). They see their membership as an honor and an opportunity to give back to others and their community. Their priorities are simple—family, job, faith, and club. Despite using lowriding as a platform to express culture and heritage, the identity they most relate to is one absent of color lines and focused on inclusion, empowerment, and their passion for classic cars.

It is, therefore, their lived experiences and participation that sometimes brings out the leadership, creativity, and determination that defines their true identity. Raza has faced decades of oppression and negative attitudes (Ahadi & Puente-Díaz, 2011; Alaniz & Cornish, 2008; Plascencia, 1983). However, Raza has reported discovering a different side of themselves after joining a car club. For some, they are no longer afraid to speak their native language and sometimes learn more about their heritage by speaking to the elders in the lowrider community. Still, others say the club pushes them to do things they would not otherwise do. For example, they may have started a club or chapter and feel humbled and proud to continue their leadership role decades later. Some have described taking on organizational or leadership roles within their community outside of their car club. As their identity development evolves and they become grounded in who they are and how they see the world around them, Raza also becomes more satisfied and happier in other aspects of their life—work, family, relationships, or spirituality. Lowriding, despite having its roots in Raza culture, is no longer primarily about ethnic pride. For Raza, lowriding is about being part of something bigger than oneself—a community, a movement, a love for classic cars.

The building of a lowrider demonstrates aspects of resistance through the customization of cars, trucks, and motorcycles. As Raza continues to progress and evolve, their achievements and pride can also be seen through their unique designs, use of unconventional materials, elaborate styles in the paintwork, customized parts and bodywork, or even in selecting the name given to the car. The networks they build with other lowriders aid in expanding their view of the world around them, encourage them to consider alternative perspectives, and empower them to test their own limits. Where it was once primarily about competition, it is now more about the lifestyle. That means some may restore a classic car to its original look, while others will alter the body, add engraved chrome, and give it a name—like *Miss Jackson, Taste of Kandy,* or *Gypsy Rose.* They resist the pressures to assimilate, become a stereotype, follow the crowd, and be left in the shadows.

Men

For some men, creating their lowrider identity started with them trying to figure out how to meet girls and get noticed. Much like how Raza used to dress up and congregate at their local park, men describe their early days in a lowrider car club as a way to get noticed at the weekend parties, especially by the females. Others described experiencing difficulty finding themselves during their youth or understanding the world around them. This turmoil likely resulted in conflicts at home, school, work, or within their community. Raza reported that being part of a lowrider car club saved them. Whether they were engaging in unlawful behaviors, had difficulty with relationships, or were isolative, lowriding provided structure, acceptance, and purpose.

Many times, because of all the struggles men faced, they recounted how being part of a car club helped them gain confidence in themselves and taught them how to deal with different personalities. Whether it was blasting their music as loud as possible, rolling in on three wheels, or having people approach them about their car, cruising their lowrider offered a sense of accomplishment and pride. Simple gestures such as having someone shake their hand and demonstrate an interest in their lowrider are both empowering and rewarding. Most car clubs require new members to have a lowrider ready to roll and represent the club. Men take pride in describing the effort it took to find the right car, build it with their own hands, find the right people for paint and upholstery, and the meaning their particular selection had to them. At times, lowriders were a reminder of a lost parent or loved one, part of a childhood memory, or partnership with a spouse or child.

Women

For females, identifying as a lowrider has inherently presented its unique challenges. Among Raza, ladies may contend with extra intrapersonal and interpersonal difficulties when identifying as a lowrider. They often go against cultural roles, such as being seen but not heard and staying at home to raise a family and tend to household duties. These females also have to prove they are knowledgeable about their car, capable of building/designing it, and even maintaining it themselves. Fortunately, women in lowriding are gaining recognition for their cars, crafts (like designing and painting), and skills (like hopping or mechanics).

Some women have had to try multiple car clubs before finding one that was a good fit for them because men did not believe they should have a say in club politics or joined with a spouse and were never officially given the title of "member" due to their gender. Women have even started creating all-female car clubs because of the problems they experienced. For some, it is important that they are seen as "ladies" and take pride in presenting themselves in a feminine manner rather than wearing men's shirts with their club logos. Comparable to what the men shared, being a member of a lowrider car club is less about ethnic pride and more about a passion for classic cars. For others, being a member of an all-female lowrider car club rather than a mixed club is principal. Women take pride in being themselves and not having to fit into a mold developed by men.

Core Values

For Raza, being a member of a lowrider car club means identifying with a group of people that share their values (e.g., familia, pride, giving back, respect, and comradery) and their interest. These five values are reflected in stories shared by Raza, who are members of lowrider car clubs and identify with this lifestyle. This may or may not align with other roles in their life, but it helps keep them grounded. What is important to them is staying humble, being driven to prove themselves, and become better versions of themselves—paving the way for others and making the streets safer. Lowrider car clubs use group dynamics positively and constructively by competing, innovating, and participating in community enhancements (Lowrider Network, 2002d; Penland, 2003). They collaborate on social activities such as fundraisers, parades, cruise nights, and car shows. Members within and across clubs support each other in times of need, such as illness, death, mechanical breakdowns, and celebrating milestones.

Familia/Family

Lowriding used to be viewed in terms of competition and rivals between clubs, towns, and ethnic groups. It was a male-dominated phenomenon.

However, more recently, it has become a lifestyle and has also become increasingly referred to as a family-oriented experience. *Familia* has become the most central part of the lowriding community. Familismo/Familism is the practice and attitude of putting a family's needs before personal or individual needs (Constante et al., 2018; Hernandez & Bámaca-Colbert, 2016) and where the family works together as a unit (Ingolsby, 1991). Being family-oriented means that spouses and children clean the cars, set up displays at car shows, ride along during cruises, and wear club gear. Children are even encouraged to participate by building lowrider bikes, pedal cars, or remote control cars. When clubs have their annual picnics, it truly becomes a family affair, and everyone is welcomed and embraced as family. It is not uncommon for kids to refer to club members as aunts, uncles, or even grandparents. This bond emphasizes a sense of trust, commitment, and belonging experienced by Raza who are members of lowrider car clubs.

Pride

Sandoval (2003) discussed how Raza has always attempted to make something of themselves or for themselves despite their limited resources. The decades of dealing with negative stereotypes, oppression, and marginalization have only encouraged Raza to have pride in their culture and strive to be and do better. While ethnic identification has been a point of contention for many, identification with culture has not. Raza, who are members of lowrider car clubs, demonstrate their dedication to the empowerment and betterment of their community through culture and heritage. The reward for working together has become worldwide acclaim and following.

Pride can have both positive and negative connotations and can be focused on either the process to achieve triumph or the display of vanity or self-aggrandizing (Dickens & Robins, 2020; Tracy & Robins, 2014). Raza overwhelmingly describe lowrider pride in terms of their passion for cars, attributions of their club, and creating positive social change. Listening to Raza describe their lived experience, their pride was evident in their voice, body language, and expressed words. While they gleefully shared their accomplishments, they became animated in discussing what the club or chapter did together. The pride in their club was further supported by how many individuals mentioned the growing number of lowrider car clubs, while remaining steadfast in their commitment to their club.

Bright (1994) and Stone (1990) described how Raza experienced pride in their lowrider car club and themselves. While styles may change depending on geography or socioeconomic status, what remains consistent is that while

Raza makes efforts to customize and maintain their lowriders, as individuals, they try to stay humble and true to their roots (whatever that means to them). Some may build a car in memory of a loved one and others may reflect personal interests. Staying within their financial means may sometimes mean bartering with others for parts or services. Regardless of their reason, building a lowrider allows Raza to "be different," self-expressive, and try new things—learning through each modification and from those helping them. Pride then comes in terms of experience and expertise. Worn like a badge of honor, Raza enjoy talking about what it feels like to have the "youngsters" (younger generation) seek them out and ask questions.

Giving Back

For Raza, joining a car club has evolved from being part of social enclave to expanding their family and feeling connected to something bigger than themselves. They described pride as less of a feeling and more of a value or belief system that helped them learn and grow. These two core values (familismo and pride) lend themselves to the third—giving back to others and their community. Many are humbled by the opportunities they have been afforded by being part of a lowrider car club that they make efforts to pay it forward. The community—talking about their clubs, tagging pictures they posted online, and showcasing individuals—has helped demonstrate what a positive phenomenon and support system this has become, both locally and internationally. They make concerted efforts to give back to their communities by participating in cultural events such as Cinco de Mayo festivals, community events such as Christmas parades, and fundraisers to help sponsor scholarships for school organizations or fund local charities. They also follow strict codes of conduct that preclude them from engaging in any criminal activities, including but not limited to gangs and illicit drug use. They sponsor events like car shows or cruise nights that promote outdoor activities and help stimulate spending at local businesses. Taking part in feeding the homeless or handing out coats and blankets is equally as important as enlisting their children and grandchildren to dress-up and walk in a parade because it helps them teach the next generation about values, empathy, and gratitude.

Respect

The concept of respect has been widely studied (Clucas, 2020; Dillon, 2010; Prestwich & Lalljee, 2009), especially with regard to distinguishing it from the concept of liking someone (Prestwich & Lalljee, 2009). Getting noticed and building a positive name for themselves is how Raza, who are members of lowrider car clubs, curb the tendency for people to see them as gang members, drug users, or self-promoting individuals that are only in it for the fame and glory. It has become such a vital part of their mission that car clubs create constitutions and bylaws that emphasize respect. While pride is a value that reflects a desire to succeed, respect was described as a value that emphasizes treating others with dignity. Without respect, there can be no pride. For example, Raza may create a new customized part, style, or technique. By sharing it with others, it gets noticed, and people respect the contribution as much as the contributor. The positive feedback was experienced as pride—in self, but also for the positive attention given to the club.

Janis (1971, 1972) said that groups might come together around a core set of values that espouse harmony and solidarity. This resonates with Raza who believe that "to get respect you have to give respect". Participants in this study spoke about how the lowriding culture has changed (for the better) in that it stresses inclusion, acceptance, and solidarity. If Raza sees a lowrider pulled over on the side of the road, they will pull over and offer help, regardless of what club they belong to or where they come from. This show of solidarity can have lasting effects—not just for the individual but their respective car club as well. Raza shared stories about being invited to schools to be part of a panel that spoke to students. Others described feeling humbled by the turnout at their car show, especially when it was on a military base—earning the respect of mainstream America. Respect, therefore, was about maintaining a positive self- and group-image, empowering one another, and creating positive social change both within and outside the lowrider community. Embracing respect as a core value also contributes to the betterment of the lowrider community and culture.

Comradery

While there are those who are adamant about the bonds they have created with their club members, they also see their lowrider car club as a social-community organization that enjoys classic American cars. They may use the term brotherhood loosely but maintain their association as one that augments their lives rather than defines their lives. Wilkins (2019) discussed comradery in terms of groups providing shared interests, cultural experiences, opportunities for resources, and imparting knowledge. Solidarity is paramount for Raza. Participation in the lowrider community may be compartmentalized and separate from family. Membership may simply be about spending time with others who share their interests. Some lowriders identify as solo riders – not affiliated with a car club. But for those who are club members, all lowriders are afforded goodwill and acceptance – like family.

Seaton et al. (2019) described comradery as individuals working together, helping each other, and building lasting bonds. Whether viewed as a brother- or sisterhood or just a social network, comradery contributes to mental wellness, acceptance, and a sense of belonging. Durkheim (1951) explained that a sense of belonging and acceptance by a larger whole can help people deal with depression and can even prevent suicide. As members of a lowrider car club, Raza have gone from being part of an enclave to a broader, more global community. Their networks are far-reaching. They share experiences, expertise, and knowledge. With chapters in multiple states, lowrider car clubs are not just representing a local community anymore. They are a growing community that crosses gender lines, racial lines, and geographic lines. Raza credited their experience with making new connections, networking capabilities, and opportunities to learn from others. Chavez (2013) described how networking between clubs and members could sometimes result in a "homie hook-up" or discounts given simply by mentioning someone's name or association. Some may continue to associate lowriding with gang members or thugs cruising in their cars, smoking marijuana, and listening to rap. However, Raza's experience is a healthy, supportive, legal, and safe means for them to maintain old traditions, embrace new perspectives, and celebrate each other.

Discussion

When I set out to do this study, I was curious about what it means for Raza to be a member of a lowrider car club and how it impacts their identity—how they see themselves and the world around them (Erikson, 1968, 1978). Growing up, I remember lowriding being referred to as a "Chicano thing", but I didn't fully understand what that meant. An overview of the events and circumstances that contributed to the evolution of lowriders since the 1940s was provided to demonstrate how the struggles and the achievements of Raza have shaped who lowriders are today. From experimental techniques to deliberate designs (e.g., murals, engravings, and unique decorative styles), the methods may have changed, but the principles remain. Do whatever it takes to make your car stand out, to make you and your club stand out, and to make the lifestyles continue to shine and feel relevant.

It was important for me to interview both males and females of Mexican descent (Raza) because females have long been absent from the dialog associated with being a lowrider or being a member of a car club. They have been and continue to be as much a part of the lowriding culture as men. Thirteen men and women were interviewed. They were from three states—California, New Mexico, and Georgia. While most participants were in their 50s, the youngest was 22 years old, and the oldest was 65. Some did not have stable employment (mainly due to the pandemic) and others held professional jobs. Most identified as Hispanic or Mexican American. Many participants grew up in either a diverse neighborhood, came from intact families, and were married, but not necessarily from all three. More than half of them have been a member of a lowrider car club for more than 15 years.

I shared a laugh with one woman who initially struggled with describing herself and her club experience. When I compared her being a business owner with being the president of her car club, she had plenty to say. This happened a few other times. It was easier for them to describe themselves in terms of the group than as an individual, which is common among Raza. Once they started to open up and share, they described becoming more outgoing, self-driven, compassionate, or even determined due to their club experiences. They described being a member of a lowrider car club as something beautiful, an honor, a lifesaver, and overall, a great experience. They reported having life-changing experiences, such as participating in a toy drive for a children's hospital and seeing the excitement on the faces of children whose illness would likely cut their life short. Others spoke about the negative experiences they had in previous car clubs and how it has impacted how they interact with their current club and how they see the world outside the lowriding community. Raza, who are members of lowrider car clubs, advocate for community involvement, and empower members to be autonomous and innovative. They offer support to one another during happy life transitions, such as weddings, christenings, significant accomplishments, as well as difficult or troubling times, such as funerals or grieving for a loved one, loss of employment, and personal struggles such as addiction, depression, or divorce.

What does this all mean? This study showed that Raza, who chose to be members of lowrider car clubs, do not fit a specific mold. They do not all share the same background or experiences. Some reported they felt like they were "born into it," while others said they joined to meet girls or guys and enjoyed hanging out with people with similar interests. Another interesting finding was that being in their car club offered them a safe forum to express themselves—heritage, individuality, and pride. Many participants spoke about their dislike for club-hoppers while demonstrating compassion and understanding for their unwillingness or inability to commit to a club. In a world where they may be labeled inappropriately or feel limited by social pressures, lowriding affords them acceptance, belonging, and empowerment. In their everyday life, they may be physicians, law enforcement, cooks, teachers, business owners, firefighters, mental health professionals, or any-thing in between. However, when they put on their club shirt, they are just a lowrider. Their race, age, socioeconomic status, even their past is insignifi-cant. They are among family.

Lowrider identity or what it means to be a lowrider was reviewed. Differences between men and women were highlighted. Let me clarify. To be a lowrider, it does not matter what gender, race, or sexual orientation you identify with. What is different is their experience and what that means to them. Women feel the extra pressure to prove they own and maintain their lowrider. For some, they simply enjoy the sisterhood, much like the men enjoy the brotherhood and choose to be part of an all-female car club. Therefore, as the men do, they adapt, and they make it work because what is important is that they just want to be a lowrider in the end. Finally, five core values echoed in their stories and descriptions of their experience—familia, pride, giving back, respect, and comradery. These values are the backbone of how Raza experiences being a member of a lowrider car club. They guide, define, and explain the lowrider experience for Raza.

Conclusion

I thought it was powerful that all participants agreed that being a member of their lowrider car club was not like belonging to a fantasy football league, the Parent-Teacher Association (PTA) or Gardening Club. It was a privilege and something that was a great source of pride for them. They were more excited to describe how they give back to their community and what made their car club special to them than to recall the various trophies, accolades, or publi-cations they had received. While ethnicity was not explicitly linked to their identity, it was implicitly tied through culture and heritage. And while many denied their experiences as a member of a lowrider car club changed them, I posit that it has. Perhaps it has not changed their core values, which resonate within their car club or even the lowriding culture, but it has changed the way they interact with the world around them.

Vega (2001) reported that lowriders had once been prevented from partici-pating in community events. Communities are now supporting events hosted by lowrider car clubs and associated businesses. Due to the pandemic, car shows were canceled. As communities started to open up again, cruise nights were hosted to encourage the public to socialize outdoors and patronize local businesses. These events are not exclusive to lowriders but instead promoted the inclusion of hot-rods and all other custom cars, trucks, and motorcycles. These gestures exemplify their respect, solidarity, and determination to create positive social change by disproving the age-old stereotypes and misconceptions and sharing their passion with others.

This study aimed to explore the lived experience of Raza who are members of lowrider car clubs. A review of their shared meaning and perceptions was provided to better understand how this lifestyle has influenced Raza life. Being part of something bigger than themselves aligns itself with Raza's roots and history. The participants were excited to have an opportunity to deliver a positive message about lowriding and Raza. They also wanted others to know that lowriders are not gangsters and that members of car clubs generally hold strict codes of conduct. Despite the pressures, stigmas, negative stereotypes, and misconceptions associated with lowriding, they are committed to this lifestyle, this identity, and wear it like a badge of honor.

References

Acuña, R. F. (1981). *Occupied America: A history of Chicanos* (2nd ed.). Harper & Row Publishers.

Acuña, R. F. (1995). *Anything but Mexican: Chicanos in contemporary Los Angeles.* Verso.

Aguilar, R. (2014, August). Latinas get attention in male-led lowrider clubs. *USA Today:HispanicLiving.*http://www.usatoday.com/story/money/cars/2014/08/30/latinas-in-lowrider-clubs/14795077/

Ahadi, S. A., & Puente-Díaz, R. (2011). Acculturation, personality, and psychological adjustment. *Psychological Reports, 109*(3), 842–862. https://doi.org/10.2466/02.07.17.20.PR0.109.6.842-862

Alaniz, Y., & Cornish, M. (2008). *Viva la Raza: A history of Chicano identity and resistance.* Red Letter Press.

Alba Cutler, J. (2009). Disappeared men: Chicana/o authenticity and the American war in Viet Nam. *American Literature, 81*(3), 583–611. https://doi.org/10.1215/00029831-2009-027

Almaguer, T. (1971). Toward the study of Chicano colonialism. *Aztlan: Chicano Journal of the Social Sciences and the Arts, 2*(1), 7–21.

Almaguer, T. (2009). *Racial fault lines: The historical origins of white supremacy in California.* University of California Press.

Arredondo, D. (2016). Lowrider history. *ConvictedArtist.com.* http://www.convictedartist.com/lowrider_history.html

Best, A. L. (2006). *Fast cars, cool rides: The accelerating world of youth and their cars.* New York University Press.

Boyle, M. (2016). Take a little trip: A cruise through lowrider history in New Mexico. *The New Mexican's Weekly Magazine of Arts, Entertainment & Culture.* http://www.santafenewmexican.com/pasatiempo/art/museum_shows/take-a-little-trip-a-cruise-through-lowrider-history-in/article_484e1da9-103d-5c93-877a-8b15747aa721.html

Bright, B. J. (1994). *Mexican American low riders: An anthropological approach to popular culture* (Publication No. 9514155) [Doctoral dissertation, Rice University]. ProQuest Dissertations & Theses Global database.

Calvo, W. (2011). *Lowriding: Cruising the color line.* (Publication No. 3466266) [Doctoral dissertation, Arizona State University]. ProQuest Dissertations & Theses Global database.

Chappell, B. (2012). *Lowrider space: Aesthetics and politics of Mexican American custom cars.* University of Texas Press.

Chavez, M. J. (2013). *The performance of Chicano masculinity in lowrider car culture: The erotic triangle, visual sovereignty, and rasquachismo* (Publication No. 3559921) [Doctoral dissertation, University of California – Riverside]. ProQuest Dissertations & Theses Global database.

Clucas, C. (2020).Understanding self-respect and its relationship to self-esteem. *Personality and Social Psychology Bulletin, 46*(6), 839–855. https://doi.org/10.1177/01461 67219879115

Constante, K., Marchand, A. D., Cross, F. L., & Rivas-Drake, D. (2018). Understanding the promotive role of familism in the link between ethnic-racial identity and Latino youth school engagement. *Journal of Latina/o Psychology, 7*(3), 230–244. https://doi.org/10.1037/lat0000117

Dickens, L. R., & Robins, R. W. (2020). Pride: A meta-analytic project. *Emotions, (advanced online publication),* 1–17. http://dx.doi.org/10.1037/emo0000905

Dillon, R. S. (2010). Respect for persons, identity, and information technology. *Ethics and Information Technology, 12,* 17–28. https://doi.org/10.1007/s10676-009-9188-8

Duncombe, S. (2002). *Cultural resistance reader.* Verso.

Durkheim, E. (1951). *Suicide: A study in sociology* (J. A. Spaulding & G. Simpson, Trans.). Free Press.

Erikson, E. H. (1968). *Identity: Youth and crisis.* Norton & Company.

Erikson, E. H. (1978). *Adulthood.* Norton & Company.

Fregoso, L. (Host). (1980, September 8). Lowriding: The fusion of cultural symbols and the diffusion of cultural myths (No. 41) [Audio podcast episode]. In *Onda Latina.* The University of Texas at Austin. http://www.laits.utexas.edu/onda_latina/prog ram?sernum=000536356&term=

Frost, B. (2002). Low & slow: The history of lowriders. *The History Channel Magazine.* http ://www.historyaccess.com/historyoflowride.html

Gradante, W. (1982). Low and slow, mean and clean. *Natural History, 91*(4), 28–39.

Hernandez, M. M., & Bámaca-Colbert, M. Y. (2016). Behavioral process model of familism. *Journal of Family Theory & Review, 8*(4), 463–483. https://doi.org/10.1111/jftr.12166

Ides, M. A. (2009). *Cruising for community: Youth culture and politics in Los Angeles, 1910–1970* (Publication No. 3354175) [Doctoral dissertation, University of Michigan]. ProQuest Dissertations & Theses Global database.

Janis, I. L. (1971). Groupthink. *Psychology Today, 5*(6), 43–46.

Janis, I. L. (1972). *Victims of groupthink: A psychological study of foreign-policy decisions and fiascoes.* Houghton Mifflin

Kercher, S. (2015). Lowriding culture goes global. *New York Times, p.* 12. https://www.nytimes.com/2015/12/06/fashion/lowriding-culture-goes-global.html

LaBelle, B. (2008). Pump up the bass – Rhythm, cars, and auditory scaffolding. *The Senses and Society, 3*(2), 187–203. https://doi.org/10.2752/174589308X306420

LoBianco, L. (2016). Boulevard nights. *Turner Classic Movies.* https ://www.tcm.com/watchtcm/movies/69473/Boulevard-Nights/

López Pulido, A., & Reyes, R. (2017). *San Diego lowriders: A history of cars and cruising.* The History Press.

Lowrider Network. (2002a, July). Chapter one: The roots of lowriding. In Lowrider Network (Ed.), *Lowrider History Book.* http://www.lowrider.com/features/0000lrm-history1/

Lowrider Network. (2002b, July). Chapter two: The emerging styles. In Lowrider Network (Ed.), *Lowrider History Book.* http://www.lowrider.com/features/0000lrm-history2/

Lowrider Network. (2002c, July). Chapter three: Cruising into history under the law's nose. In Lowrider Network (Ed.), *Lowrider History Book.* http://www.lowrider.com/features/0000lrm-history3/

Lowrider Network. (2002d, July). Chapter four: Cruising into the eye of the revolution. In Lowrider Network (Ed.), *Lowrider History Book.* http://www.lowrider.com/features/0000lrm-history4/

Lowrider Network. (2002e, July). Chapter nine: By the time I get to Arizona. In Lowrider Network (Ed.), *Lowrider History Book.* http://www.lowrider.com/features/0000lrm-history09/

Lowrider Network. (2011). *35 Years in the Life of Lowrider Magazine* – editor's letter. http://www.lowrider.com/features/1201-lrmp-35-years-lowrider-magazine/

Madriaga, M. (2014). Lowriders at Chicano Park Day: Born into the Klique. *San Diego Reader.* http://www.sandiegoreader.com/news/2014/apr/23/stringers-lowriders-shot-chicano-park-day/

Martinez, E. (1991). 500 years of Chicano history in pictures. SouthWest Organizing Project (SWOP).

McWilliams, C. (2016). North from Mexico: The Spanish-speaking people of the Unites States (3rd ed.). Praeger.

Meier, M. S. (2016). Chicano leadership and organization. In C. McWilliams & A. M. Garcia (Eds.), North from Mexico: The Spanish-speaking people of the Unites States (3rd ed., pp. 249–262). Praeger.

Miner, D. A. (2014). *Creating Aztlán: Chicano art, indigenous sovereignty, and lowriding across turtle islan*d. The University of Arizona Press.

Moran-Zejli, G. M. (2007). *Cruising into the future: Women and lowrider culture* [Unpublished master's thesis]. University of California, Santa Cruz.

Olson, C. A. (1999). Thump lends lowriders rhythm. *Billboard, 111*(26), 73.

Padilla, C. (1999). *Low 'n slow: Lowriding in New Mexico.* Museum of New Mexico Press.

Palomares, U. H. (1971). Viva la Raza! *Personnel and Guidance Journal, 50*(2), 118–129.

Penland, R. P. (2003). *Lowrider: History, pride, culture.* Motorbooks International.

Plascencia, L. F. B. (1983). Low riding in the Southwest: Cultural symbols in the Mexican community. In M. T. Garcia, F. Lomeli, M. Barrera, E. Escobar, & J. Garcia (Eds.), *History, culture, and society: Chicano Studies in the 1980s.* Bilingual Press/Editorial Bilingüe.

Prestwich, A., & Lalljee, M. (2009). The determinants and consequences of intra-group respect: An examination within a sporting context. *Journal of Applied Social Psychology, 39*(5), 1229–1253. https://doi.org/10.1111/j.1559-1816.2009.00480.x

Salomon, L. R. (2003). *Roots of Justice: Stories of organizing in communities of color.* Jossey-Bass.

Sanchez, G. (1943, Autumn). Pachucos in the making. *Common Ground,* 13–20. http://www.unz.org/Pub/CommonGround-1943q3-00013

Sandoval, D. (2003). *Bajito y suavecito/Low and slow: Cruising through Lowrider culture* (Publication No. 3086760) [Doctoral dissertation, Claremont Graduate University]. ProQuest Dissertations & Theses Global database.

Sandoval, D. M. (2014). The politics of low and slow/bajito y suavecito: Black and Chicano lowriders in Los Angeles, from the 1960s through the 1970s. In J. Kun & L. Pulido (Eds.), *Black and brown in Los Angeles: Beyond conflict and coalition* (pp. 176–201). University of California Press.

Seaton, C. L., Bottorff, J. L., Oliffe, J. L., Medhurst, K., & DeLeenheer, D. (2019). Mental health promotion in male-dominated workplaces: Perspectives of male employees and workplace representatives. *Psychology of Men & Masculinities, 20*(4), 541–552. http://dx.doi.org/10.1037/men0000182

Simpson, I. (2015, July 24). How the Gypsy Rose became the most famous lowrider in the world. *LA Weekly.* http://www.laweekly.com/arts/how-the-gypsy-rose-became-the-most-famous-lowrider-in-the-world-5774408

Stone, M. C. (1990). Bajito y suavecito (low and slow): Low riding and the 'class' of class. *Studies in Latin American Popular Culture, 9,* 85–126.

Tatum, C. M. (2011). *Lowriders in Chicano culture: From low to slow to show.* Greenwood.

Tracy, J. L., & Robins, R. W. (2014). Emerging insights into the nature and function of pride. *Current Directions in Psychological Science, 16*(3), 147–150. https://doi.org/10.1111/j.1467-8721.2007.00493.x

Usner, D. J. (2016). *¡Órale! Lowrider: Custom made in New Mexico.* Museum of New Mexico Press.

Vega, C. M. (2001). Salute to the Route becomes event unto itself. *DailyBulletin.com.* http ://lang.dailybulletin.com/socal/route66/news/salute083101.asp

Zaragoza, B. (2015, August). Lowriders in San Diego: Jose Romero tells the history. *South Bay Compass.* http://sandiegofreepress.org/2015/08/lowriders-in-san-diego-jose-romero-tells-the-history/

Zavala, M. (2013). What do we mean by decolonizing research strategies? Lessons from decolonizing indigenous research in New Zealand and Latin America. *Decolonization: Indigeneity, Education & Society, 2*(1), 55–71.

11. Lowriding Murals: Freeways, Automobiles and Mobility

GUILLERMO AVILES-RODRIGUEZ

Introduction

From the first recorded broadcasting of a lowrider on the 1970s sitcom *Chico and the Man* to any number of other present-day hip-hop music videos, lowriders are deployed by various groups as signs of wealth, sexual appeal and urban excess. For example, Marilyn Manson's 2001 music video titled *Tainted Love* begins with the band pulling up to a party in a custom black lowrider with a front license plate reading "Goth Thug." A 2017 film featuring Academy Award nominated actor Demian Bichir about a teen forced to choose between a good or an evil path, takes *Lowriders* as its title. The 2018 Lowrider Super Show Japan is indistinguishable from a low rider show in Los Angeles, Phoenix or San Diego. However, these are incomplete notions of a cultural phenomenon born in the Chicana/o community of Southern California, that has now managed to resonate across the globe in literal and figurative ways.

A standard definition of a lowrider is any aesthetically modified vehicle lowered to within a few inches off the ground that is often equipped with a hydraulic suspension system. It is also now a term used to describe the adornment of not only cars but other objects such as: home furnishings, clothes, art, and even toilet seats. "Lowrider" is also used to describe the owner of or the participant in the lowrider scene. The distinction between what are known as muscle cars, or hot rods is important, these two types of modified vehicles privilege large frames and fast speeds. Lowriders proffer slow and tight motion in place of fast and loose movement. To more fully understand lowriding one must understand the singular way that lowriders have become vehicles for a mobile metonymy where thug life, the struggle between good and evil and counterculture are all mobilized. Here movement and mobility are to be understood as a resistance to the immobility's (economic, social, geographic) imposed on subaltern communities. Movement aids the lowrider enthusiast to maneuver into, out of, and through exclusionary spaces and define an alternate identity for Chicana/os that presents them not as immigrants, but as indigenous people who after the Invasion of Mexico became detribalized natives.

America moves fast and worships speed and, by extension, its most available form: the automobile. It is this addiction to speediness that has made the automobile or the opportunity to own one "the most attractive promise of American democratic capitalism." An idea that positioned car ownership in the Chicana/o community as a key down payments on both practical and material equality of living (Flink, 1975) and so past generations of Mexican migrants embraced this part of the American Dream. Unfortunately, they learned this Dream only exists in sleep. First the capitalist and now the neoliberal promise of economic rewards were not delivered through the increased capacity to buy into the American consumerist culture. As Enda Duffy puts it "The personal thrill of the new-century motor speeds and politics of late imperial capitalism turn out to be unexpectedly and uncannily related." (Duffy, 2009) The descendants of early Mexican Americans have grown up understanding this notion instinctively and have opted to meet the hot rods and muscle car's rapidity and power with the lowrider's lowness and slowness. Opting not to remove themselves from Anglo's perpetual need for speed, but to elegantly resist it. In this way contrasting hot rods and muscle cars from lowriders necessitates an understanding of their relative velocity more than their material differences.

The artwork on lowrider cars can feature images ranging from expressions of religious zeal to historical episodes in Chicana/o culture and are also often charged with a legacy of political and social resistance. Consequently, here lowrider art is framed as a *portable mural* (Tatum, 2001, p. 174) and subsequently examined for the unique ways that these murals in motion contribute to a reshaping of the urban geography in communities with large Chicana/o populations. As Brenda Jo Bright has put it "Chicano car murals draw on a variety of relevant sources, such as Catholic imagery, Aztec mythology and American popular culture, to create visual narratives about identity, experience and fantasy" (Abrams, 2000, p. 41). Regardless of the thematic content of the art on lowriders the defining characteristic in the art emblazoned upon them is the attention given to the representation of images that are classic, idealized and in many cases picturesque. The vehicles alone are a work of art but when decorated lowriders become a thing of beauty, but that does not eclipse the beauty that is to ride inside of one.

It is well documented by science that as motion accelerates our sense of reality morphs proportionally to it, but this same morphing occurs in deceleration and in a prolonged state of slow motion. Slow motion is a valuable form of expression in lowriding because it's effect, as in film, allows for action to be paced in such a way that it can be absorbed and most importantly enjoyed. The images on a low rider are not created to be blurred by swiftness but rather to be accentuated by meditative observance or observation that sways and rocks the viewer's gaze into a hypnotic state of being. One sees differently when art moves and when one is moving as one sees. Lowriders cruise to be seen, but they also enjoy seeing the spectators see. It is in this mutual seeing, that both are moved, literally and figuratively.

Consequently, to think of slow motion enables us to consider the ways that moving slowly changes how Chicana/os experience identity- of self and others. The right and the choice to move then is a right to use space to make it one's own, to inhabit space is one of the most valuable of all freedoms, with movement one can control and navigate, without movement one is fixed, affixed and contained. The power that lowriders provided the past generations of Chicana/os could not be left unchecked: as early as 1959 the first California law prohibited cars from riding on streets if any of their components were lower than the bottom edge of the wheel rim was implemented (Calvo, 2011, p. 4). This law however would have the unintentional consequence of inspiring an early lowrider named Ron Aguirre to develop a new hydraulic technique to lower and raise a car through the use of a flip of a switch, enabling Chicana/o lowrider drivers to move themselves in an out of the law's reach.

Despite this and other tactics to discourage this form of cultural expression lowriders show up in many ways and in many places on the terrain of Chicana/o identity: movies, books, television shows, stories, poems, plays, and music have all to one extent or another been a stop on lowriding's historical cruising across the American cultural landscape. As Ben Chappell has put it "Through all of these manifestations, low riding has remained a site of Mexican American cultural authority for several generations of participants" (Chappell, 2012, p. 3). In an emic perspective then, Chicana/os use mobility to shift from caricature to self-portrait, this self-representation plays out in how, where and when Chicana/os move—or don't move. Thus, motion is the characteristic feature of Chicana/o identity.

Movement however is not exclusively physical. The way Chicana/os have used various labels to define their identity is especially illustrative. The historical fluidity of this group's nomenclature has seen Chicana/os go from *Mexica*, to *Indios*, to Spanish, to Mexican to Mexican-American, to Hispanic, to Xicano, to Chicano, to Chicana/o, to Latino, to Latina/o, to Latinx, to Latine. Chicana/os then are a people whose foundational myth is one of movement be it in the concrete form of migration or in the more metaphorical form of nomenclature. Here then is a reason why the place granted to the automobile in the Chicana/o community is so privileged. It is the automobile that caries the expression of motion and movement to a material state, the auto enables, facilitates and is motion. It is true that many other ethnic groups have formed intimate relationships with the car, but few can claim to have elevated the car to the same height as Chicana/os have. Scholar William A. Calvo-Quirós goes as far as to state that "we mostly contextualize automobiles as fundamental and 'sacred' objects" (Calvo 2011, p. 135). For Chicana/os then the lowrider is nothing short of a fetish, receiving treatment reserved for relics and religious objects imbued with mystical powers with influence over the self and others. In short, the car has changed many groups, but not many groups can claim having changed the car- Chicana/os can, have and do.

This chapter further postulates the lowrider as a performing entity unto itself that is charged with a type of kinetic signification. By exploring the cruising tradition in East Los Angeles as a starting point, then moving into the ways that lowriders are at times employed to take over public spaces through both motion and stillness thus engaging in an activity that Michel de Certeau would call a *practice of everyday life* that enables and mediates social relations. By tracing the history of the lowrider from the 1950s to the present these highly decorated and manicured vehicles are cast not simply as a means of cultural identity through artistic expression but as a form of resistance to segregation and isolation, aiding in the transformation of the lowrider into a modern-day chariot in a battle for cultural survival. In this way, the lowrider is analyzed as both a dynamic moving site that aids subaltern subjects to circumnavigate class inequalities, and as a canvas of Chicana/o aesthetic expressions including the display of both the sacred and profane.

However, as we focus on lowriders it is necessary to first examine the ways that murals have managed to move from the palace walls of the Mexica temples to the indoor walls of Mexican government buildings, to the silver screen of world cinema all on their way to the bodies of lowrider vehicles. By necessity many important issues involved in low riding are left out of this exploration and this should be read more as an indication of the richness of the topic than an aversion to a given subject, and so the artwork airbrushed on lowrider car hoods or what Charles M. Tatum calls "highly artistic figurative and symbolic paintings" is both our starting and finish line.

Movers and shakers

It was the early 1980s in Watts and the news that had been rumored for some years had finally and officially been confirmed. Our family would have to move out of our home to make room for a freeway that had been designed to rest atop a community that was triply unlucky for being poor, of color and in the way of progress. It may have been coincidental, but this freeway which buried the homes of many people of color would come to be named the "Century Freeway" this freeway and its nomenclature reified in steel and concrete the erasure of bodies of color that had begun many *centuries* before. I was only a child, but I remember what this displacement did to many of my friends at the time. Later I would learn that freeways and the spaces they create underneath them bred crime, vagrancy, drugs and other ills. As Mary Pardo puts it "The freeway construction [...] displaced thousands of residents, compelling some families to move more than once [...] The freeway brought noise and air pollution as they divided neighborhoods without consideration for resident's loyalties to extended family and parish church" (Pardo, 1998, pp. 60–61). Freeways then are not free at all, they bring with them a price tag that more often than not is left to the poor to pay.

If one is looking for a way to divide communities, destroy cultures, and breed isolation freeways are an efficient strategy. Yet as Eric Avila points out "even the deadest spaces created by highway infrastructure sometimes find redemption through local efforts to create a sense of place." People's buried histories sometimes become seeds and no amount of concrete can keep them from pushing through to transform "segments of freeway architecture into sites vested with spiritual meaning and cultural pride" (Avila, 2014, p. 150). One such site located in Southern California is Chicano Park. Located inside a predominantly Mexican American neighborhood known as Barrio Logan in the southeast section of San Diego California, Chicano Park was the result of a community action that saw the annexation of a parcel of land underneath the Coronado bay bridge by a coalition of concerned residents fed up with the ill treatment of the community. According to Chicano Parks official web site:

> The state of California initially agreed to lease 1.8 acres of state land in Barrio Logan for a neighborhood park... The lease would run for a period of twenty years... and the state would prepare the site for public use (Avila, 2014, p. 150).

Unfortunately, the city would later renege on this agreement and send bulldozers to grade the land under the bridge in preparation not for a park, but for the construction of a California Highway Patrol station. When Chicano residents spread the word that city and state officials had deceived them about the development of their park a flood of demonstrators composed of Barrio Logan residents, youth and Chicano activists gathered at the park to prevent the bulldozing from continuing in part by forming a human chain around the bulldozers. The Chicano flag was then raised on a telephone pole, and a twelve-day occupation of the land that would become Chicano Park began. The description of the activities during the occupation is worth quoting in full.

During the occupation of Chicano Park, the three-acre parcel was transformed into a desert garden of plants and grass. Chicano youth and student organizations from Santa Barbara and Los Angeles traveled to Barrio Logan to offer their support. Women prepared meals for the demonstrators, while others donated trees, seeds, and fertilizer. The occupation represented the first time in which residents had come together in unity for themselves and their community (Chicano Park, 2018).

As part of the park's beautification the painting of murals was first conceived by San Diego based Chicano art groups, such as *Los Toltecas en Aztlan* and *El Congresso de Artistas Chicanos en Aztlan* and then organized by a resident of Barrio Logan, Salvador Torres and a fellow artist Victor Ochoa in order to "express [Chicano] identity as Indian/Spanish/European/ American" (Chicano Park, 2018). So in 1973, the bare concrete surfaces of the pylons and walls underneath the bridge began to tell a different story, one that Avila describes as "people of color strive[ing] to reclaim this space through expressive cultural traditions, weaving it back into the fabric of their communities" (Avila, 2014, p. 14). This painting of murals on the concrete piers that hold up a bridge that displaces so much of the community brings with it many theoretically rich elements, this bridge becomes a stationary monument that both facilitates the transit of automobiles and locks community residents out of whole swaths of land, illustrating Avila's assertion that "even the deadest spaces created by highway infrastructure sometimes find redemption through local efforts to create a sense of place, transforming segments of freeway architecture into sites vested with spiritual meaning and cultural pride" (Avila, 2014, p. 14). The murals then are a proclamation that though under the superstructure of a highway interchange the community's literal and figurative mobility will not be arrested.

One of the most featured murals at Chicano Park reads "San Diego Lowrider Council" [Fig. 1]. The letters in old English font along the top are in gold as if to echo the lowrider plaques used to identify a car club affiliation. This mural wraps itself around all four sides of one of the pylons and features a collection of the most popular classic cars in the lowriding scene. Located between an enclosed recreation area featuring handball and basketball courts and a sidewalk, this location assures its prominence among the youth who use the courts. The mural is positioned so that the gate surrounding the area is interrupted by the pylon. One side of the mural also contains a list of some of the prominent San Diego car clubs [Fig. 2]. Two figures appear on the street facing side of the pylon, they are positioned as father and son, but their torsos are obscured by a lowrider and the boy smiles as he holds up a trophy. Here the generational elements of lowriding are made clear as is their kinship elements. The final two sides of the pylon feature six lowriders positioned so as to appear stacked on each other [Fig. 3]. The lowriders are also painted across the corner of the two walls to complete a three-dimensional optical illusion that lends movement to the cars as they wrap themselves around the pylon.

Zooming out from this mural and taking in the site illustrates an entanglement between art, automobility, and transit. The mural seems to hint at the perspective that if this bridge is able to transport cars, it is due at least in part to the Chicana/os underneath them facilitating it through their culture, art, and ingenuity. The mural creates both a place for lowriders and what Chappell would call a lowrider space that "ties the immediate context of a lowrider car to the barrio spaces of Latino urbanity in the United States, both material and imagined" (Chappell, 2012, p. 25). As such the lowrider is an excellent example of a *heterotopia*, a place where multiple spaces of multiple and perhaps contradictory possibilities and significations coexist.

Low riding privileges the hand crafted over the mass produced, getting something from as close to the source as possible makes that thing become much more valuable. A lowrider modified by an owner is seen as much more "authentic" than one modified by an auto shop. This is at the source a sentiment that Rodolfo "Corky" Gonzales expresses in his 1967 epic poem *I Am Joaquin* he writes: "*I must fight, And win this struggle for my sons, and they, must know from me who I am*" (Gonzalez, 2001, p. 28). In other words, if a story is to be told about a people, it is best if they themselves take an opportunity to shape it, independently of mainstream esthetics or preferences. After all, it is they who are the *de facto* "preservers of history" for they hold in them "memory, story, and ritual" (Conquergood, 2013, p. 8). Lowriders then are fragments of a wider cultural practice that pushes against colonially derived culture. What is true for these cars is true for people as well, there are a multiplicity of epistemes, many ways of knowing that cannot be captured without accessing people who participate in or partake of the lowriding life. When thinking about the dynamics of culture and the difficulty inherent in excavating knowledge, a customized vehicle is a good place to start a conversation about subaltern subjects and their memories as counterweights to state sanctioned history (Foicault, p. 7). Lowriders and their artwork often tell stories that only live in the community's memory having long ago been erased from the community's history.

Lowriders can be read as a contemporary manifestation of the walls of the past that held murals going back to *Mexica* times. These vehicles and the murals atop their hoods and on their side panels tell a story whose modern-day roots go back to Mexico. In the 1930s it was famous Soviet director and cinematographer Sergei Eisenstein's relationship with Mexican muralist, David Alfaro Siqueiros that influenced Eisenstein's development of the *Dynamic Square* cinematic theory. Rivera and Siqueiros in particular enjoy significant scholarship given the substantial commissions both had in the United States. Siqueiros's controversial 1932 mural *América Tropical* exists in Los Angeles and has been preserved and given a small visitor center and museum, all this since being whitewashed shortly after its unveiling. William David Estrada details some of the process of *América Tropical* creation as follows "Siqueiros consulted with renowned architect Richard Neutra... as well as with Sumner Spaulding. Estrada was assisted in the forty-seven-day mural project by a collaboration of artists that became known as the Bloc of Mural Painters and may have included Jackson Pollock" (Estrada, 2008, p. 209). This mural is now a symbol for many Chicana/os of the legitimate value of consistent and uncompromised artistic expression in the face of oppression. Many a lowrider has taken literal or figurative copies of these muralist's work and used it to speak of the present-day Chicana/o struggle.

Contrary to widely held belief Siqueiros did not set out to offend or criticize his patrons, it was only, as Estrada put it, shortly before Siqueiros began painting the mural that *La Opinión*—the leading Spanish-language daily—reported that Mexicans in the city were being indiscriminately apprehended at the Plaza and given one-way rail tickets to Mexico. These events had a deep effect on the artist and how could this be otherwise given Siqueiros' zealous Stalinist allegiances (Estrada, 2008, p. 209). He did, after all, conspire to have Trotsky murdered after Trotsky settled in Mexico City (LA Times, 2012). Along with the two aforementioned muralists Rivera and Siqueiros, José Clemente Orozco completes the trinity of Mexico's most influential muralists known as *Los Tres Grandes* or the "the three great ones." It was these three who would most influence the Chicana/o muralists of the 1960s, and whom illustrate just how exactly early Mexican artistic expression has been critical in and to the mobilization of the *movimiento* generally and Chicana/o lowrider art specifically.

The mural, and now, muralism stands as one of the most pronounced resonances between Mexican and Chicana/o cultural expression. Historically, muralism is one of the artforms that enjoys much attention from the Chicana/o scholar community. This attention produces valuable research that provides historiographic information tracing murals back to before Columbus's arrival in the Caribbean. Both the length and breadth of murals in America and specifically in the land that would one day become Mexico point to their paradoxical ability to embody mobility while existing in fixity. It is worth noting that the contributions and influences of the Mexican mural movement extend far beyond the Chicana/o community. Rivera's commissioned work in the United States has had a deep impact on contemporary Chicana/o muralists but also in the Anglo community. George Biddle for example, is credited with being the architect of one of the New Deal's five federal arts projects responsible for hiring unemployed artists to decorate schools, post offices, and other government buildings. What is seldom mentioned however, is that he was a one-time student of Mexican muralist Diego Rivera and that the Mexican post-revolutionary government-sponsored mural program inspired his federal arts project's design (Dunitz).

In a contemporary example discussed by Dylan A. T. Miner, the late 1970s Detroit Michigan mural *CitySpirit* painted by George Vargas and Martín Moreno with logistical help from Carolina Ramón, stands as one of the few remaining Movement-era murals in the Motor City. What is more relevant to this study is that Vargas cites Rivera's *Detroit Industry* fresco cycle executed in 1932 and 1933 at the Detroit Institute of Arts as "one of his most important models." (Miner, 2014, p. 138) Thus leading Miner to conclude that *CitySpirit* "directly links Vargas and Moreno, as well as Detroit [Ch]icanos, to Diego Rivera" (Miner, 2014, p. 138) and by extension to the *Movimiento*. Here then is an illustration of the permeability between and within the indigenous, political and historical elements of murals in the Chicana/o community. Again, murals migrate in through and between space and time on their way to lowrider hoods.

Today, the Chicana/o Movement is admittedly attenuated in comparison to the 1960s and 70s possibly due to the vacuum created by the dearth of sponsorship for the next generation of Chicana/os. However, even given a climate that prides imitation and discourages emulation, some artists and groups have managed to be truly innovative in their artistic expression and to push the boundaries of what Chicana/o performance can be. This pushing, however, oftentimes uncovers uncomfortable historical elements not meant to be excavated, and so it has repercussions. As Shifra Goldman argues "To excavate a hidden history often means to fracture or overturn the existing and exclusionary hegemonic history; it means to replace the well-worn heroes and heroines. . . with new faces, personalities, and agendas" (Goldman, et. al., 2015). It would take a world war to make these new heroes in the Chicana/o community.

The period just before the United States' entry into World War II was a time of massive industrialization along the west coast, making Los Angeles a major center for heavy manufacturing, including the automobile industry. Large companies involved with automobile manufacturing like Chrysler, Ford and General Motors all had assembly plants in the Los Angeles region. This contributed to the solidifying of Southern California as "a region where the car was rapidly becoming central to the lives of working- and middle-class Americans of all national and ethnic backgrounds" (Tatum, 2011, p. 4). One of the ethnic groups who were most public in their embracing of the automobile and its customization were the Chicana/os living in East Los Angeles. Anglo youth had been known for their customizations of cars going back to the 1930s; these youths however focused primarily on modifications for racing, hence birthing the hot rod brand of automobile modifications designed primarily to increase an automobile's power and speed leaving the more aesthetic elements of car modification for others innovate.

Praising the Lowered

The Chicana/o community focused on the automobile as a symbol influenced by both spirituality and aesthetics that was "no longer informed by minimalist notions of elegance and Puritan disdain for decoration" (Bright, 2000, p. 38). This quotation gestures to the pronounced historical relationship between Catholicism and the social movements of the 60s, informed in part by the 1962 Second Vatican Council's call for clergy to shift from a spiritual to an earthlier focus. This new direction would feed the rise of an emphasis on social issues and the tangible ways the Church could help its most oppressed members, this shift would come to be known as Liberation Theology. The Church's intimate involvement in labor and social issues post Vatican II seems to have influenced the Chicana/o nationalist ideology and manifested in both subtle and overt ways, for example the 1969 Chicano Youth Conference in Denver Colorado titled their culminating document *El Plan Espiritual de Azlan* or the **Spiritual** *plan of Azlan* (emphasis mine) in English (Tatum, 2001, pp. 165–166).

Religious fusion has contributed to a particular form of expression involving what scholar Margaret Werry has called "mobile occupation" (Center for Performance Studies, 2018) where individuals inhabit a space not through stillness but prolonged movement in or through a space. The ancient Catholic religious pilgrimages being only one example. But a more relevant example can be found in the way Chicana/os have opted to use the streets and not the historically biased courts of law, or the ivory towers of academia, as the fuel of their political struggle. The Mexican Catholic pilgrimage shows up in Chicana/o culture under a secular name of the march. Likewise, Chicana/o Art grew strong as an alternative to the oftentimes exclusionary mainstream art world. It stood as a form of resistance to and against oppression and as a viable way for Chicana/os to affirm their social identity and worth. Given all these historical examples it can be justifiably argued that Chicana/o artistic expression is consubstantial with that found in Mexican artistic expression.

Perhaps this is why from the first days of the Chicana/o movement vehicles like automobiles and trucks show up not simply as means of transportation but as nodes of spiritual and community building as well as organizing tools. A performance group embodying these uses of the vehicle is *El Teatro Campesino (ETC)*, founded in 1965, it is known for a political style of theatre that uses *actos*, short political plays; *mitos*, plays based on *Mexica* and Mayan history and myths; and *corridos*, Mexican ballads that recount history from the common people's perspective. *ETC* blazed the trail for many Chicana/o theatrical productions today and did so first from atop of flatbed trucks in the fields of Delano during the UFW strike in the 1960s. Some of *ETC* earliest performances incorporated vehicles used for transportation of goods and laborers as part of its performances as a way to honor their farmworker roots and to camouflage themselves from the security and patrols on and around the fields. Chicana feminist scholar Yolanda Broyles-Gonzalez farther illustrates the connection of vehicles, spirituality politics and the movement when she points out that "During the early strike... the back of César Chávez's old station wagon often served as a portable shrine replete with holy images, flowers, and picket signs." It was also César Chávez co-founder of the United Farm Workers (UFW) who in a 1980 interview with *Lowrider* magazine, emphasized the importance of a functional and reliable car to travel from one agricultural field to another (Greenwood, 2011, p. 8). This relationship between the vehicle and the Chicana/o community then included sociopolitical and spiritual elements, specifically drawn from Catholicism. Naturally the conditions of labor can and do exist apart from Catholicism, though for the early Chicana/o movement this was an exception rather than the rule.

Part of the activities striking workers, many of them immigrants engaged in as part of their participation was to keep a 24-hour vigil at Chávez's automobile and makeshift altar and attending the daily mass celebrated at the station wagon shrine (Broyles-Gonzalez, 1994, p. 59). Given this history it is not insignificant that Rubén Ortiz Torres would title his contribution to the first edited collection dedicated to hot rods, lowriders and American car culture, *Cathedrals on Wheels*. Some scholars have implied that this phrase refers to the "many opportunities" that artisans and artists have to "exhibit

their various talents, just as cathedrals afforded many skilled persons multiple and varied opportunities to display their talents" (Tatum, 2011, p. 81)
this interpretation however does not account for the fact that cathedrals
were never completed in any one person's lifetime and that they could not
be individually conceived, designed and completed. Many lowriders can and
are in fact the sole creation of a single individual. It is conceivably the mixture of politics and spirituality that would make these mobile cathedrals
synonymous with the Chicano civil rights movement. As Tatum has put it
"Religious themes and images. . . are popular in Chicana/o muralism and in
lowrider mural art." Biblical quotes and scriptural passages abound on the
inside and outsides of many lowriders at car shows and Saint Christopher
(the patron of bachelors, drivers, travel) cards and figures can be found in or
near many lowriders.

The two Catholic religious figures whose iconographies predominate
are "Jesus in various incarnations. . . and the Virgin of Guadalupe, who
plays a central role in Mexican and Chicana/o religious culture" (Tatum,
2011, p. 101). Of these two the Virgin of Guadalupe is much more present in lowrider mural art. Perchance due to her association with the most
humble and unappreciated of subjects, after all she was said to have first
appeared, near what is now Mexico City, to Juan Diego, a poor Mexican
indio, not a rich land owning *Español.* Scholar Charlene Villaseñor Black
attributes the Virgin's potency partly to the dominance of Mexican culture
for whom the Virgin Mary is sacred and to the Virgin's association with
the oppressed, the downtrodden. As Villaseñor Black puts it "Our Lady of
Guadalupe has a long history of accompanying those who fought against
oppression and for the independence of Latinos, starting with the Mexican
War of Independence against Spain and continuing today" (Desert Sun,
2017). In validation of this claim one need only scan archived photographs
of the Chicana/o movement to see people carrying standards emblazoned
with Our Lady of Guadalupe's image. It is hardly a coincidence that "The
figure of the Virgin was prominent in the iconography associated with César
Chávez and Dolores Huerta-led UFW, which played an important role in
the Chicano movement of the 1960s and 1970s" (Tatum, 2011, p. 107) and
in the lives of many Mexican immigrants. As Jerome Krase and Timothy
Shortell articulate this role "Immigrants generally lack the power to recreate
the valued spaces of their home cultures, but their day-to-day lives are full
of expressive and phatic signs of their ethnic, religious, and class identity"
(Spatial Semiotics, 2011). Accordingly, the automobile is here framed as one
of these signs.

Riding Low and Slow for Show

Cars have a long history of serving as status symbols in American society, scholar Amy L. Best extends this idea as it applies to youth and their cars when she states that "Cars often serve as indicators of social and economic worth as well as key markers of identity." (Best, 2006, p. 4) For Chicana/os cars and specifically lowriders "signify prestige, mechanical expertise, and artistic competency" (Tatum, 2001, p. 173). For this analysis Chappell's view of the car as "a place-identified means of mobility" (Chappell, 2012, p. 25). Is most useful. Undergoing the construction of a lowrider is no casual hobby. It typically involves securing a classic vehicle, preferably from the 60s or 70s perhaps due to their design offering the most surface area to customize and their sturdy steel frame being able to handle the stress of hydraulic induced shocks. Whatever the inspiration for privileging this era of automobile, lowrider owners gradually started to decorate these cars with high gloss multi-colored paint jobs, upholstering them with themed colored crushed velvet interiors, adding hydraulic suspension system, chroming every external metal surface (in some extreme cases even the entire engine) and adding a sound system with amplification powerful enough for *Blasting*, or announcing the vehicles approach from a block away and to rattle windows and turn heads from both sides of a city street with its bass.

Ironically, the early history of lowriding, a most ethnic of phenomena has instances where it has not functioned as a form of resistance, but rather as a way in which to mimic Anglo activities, albeit with a Chicana/o spin. Tatum articulates it thus "Car clubs afforded Mexican American and other ethnically diverse young people the opportunity to be involved in activities that accelerated their social integration into community life and enhanced their leadership skills." The "community" here is code for the predominantly Anglo hot rod clubs, which were "initially inclusive in welcoming individuals from different ethnic and racial groups who shared a common interest in cars with altered suspensions combined with custom paint and other external elements" (Tatum, 2011, pp. 155–156). By the 1950s however car clubs in Los Angeles began to conform to the same racial and ethnic segregation found in southern California society, referring to the admired lowriders as *Taco Wagons*. It is at this time that East Los Angeles would become the center of the then Chicana/o car club scene. These early car clubs were to become the lowrider clubs we know today. In their early days, the clubs functioned as more than simple clubs by providing members with "social, cultural, and economic support as well (Tatum, 2011, p. 156). They built community through local and weekly caravans or convoys, in a type of activity and construction that de Certeau has described as "networks" that are shaped out of fragments of trajectories and alterations of space" (De Certeau, 1984, p. 93). In this way lowrider culture in the Chicana/o community had begun to replace the "individualistic American dream of driving away to escape it all" with the notion "of driving together" (Ortiz, 2000, p. 35) towards a common cause of aesthetic, cultural and spiritual expression. The "why" of this specific form of expression is an important one that has cultural, historical, and geographical elements.

If East Los Angeles was the heart of early low riding Whittier boulevard was the main artery. This famed street has shown up in many films featuring low riding and was immortalized by the *Thee Midniters,* one of the first Chicano rock bands, in their eponymous 1965 song. Whittier has become synonymous with lowriders and cruising in East Los Angeles partially because this is where early lowriders made the choice to first "drive slow, pumping their music and blocking traffic, messing with a social system that is not eager to accept them" (Ortiz, 2000, p. 35). This boulevard was particularly attractive for cruising because of its "glass-fronted stores all along the cruising route reflected the drivers in lowered seats as they carefully and proudly paraded their low-slung cars with their striking paint jobs and other distinctive features" (Penland, 2003, pp. 16–19). Whittier would also be the site of a little-known mass protest in 1968 in which some lowriders, and activists joined forces to protest excessive police presence along Whittier Blvd. and the finding of a 1967 report where the non-Chicano business owners who lived outside of the Chicano barrio called for even more police protection on Whittier Blvd. After violence and looting broke out many people were arrested. This then led to three nights of rioting across East Los Angeles (Penland, 2003, pp. 37–38). This event would lead to the prohibition of cruising on Whittier Blvd that would not be relaxed till the mid-1980s.

The policing of lowriders appears to have been motivated by a strategy to curb protest and control Chicana/o identity. Lowriders however found other avenues (literally and figuratively) to create a place and the lowrider community in East Los Angeles continued on albeit in a less robust way. As a testament to the lowriding communities' emphasis on cultural pride the lowrider clubs extended from the local to the regional and gave birth to the phenomenon of the car show, where first clubs from all over the south west and later from all over the United States could come together and compete as well as take part in a larger low riding community.

Naturally few potentially profitable activities can escape the neoliberal rapacious drive for profit and the lowrider show like so many cultural artifacts and activities has become greatly corporatized. The local car show has its own characteristics and can be as simple as a grouping of cars arranged around a parking lot for a few hours on a Saturday morning to a full day event with food and merchandise vendors. In this less formal circumstance people are invited to move around the parked vehicles and can admire them from a full 360-degree angle. At times mirrors are strategically placed underneath the lowrider so that an audience can see the details underneath a given vehicle. Larger car shows however follow a more formulaic agenda and can draw anywhere from 10,000 to 25,000 people over a two-day period, starting at midmorning on a Saturday and ending late on a Sunday afternoon (Tatum, 2011, p. 173). The modern lowrider car show features a multiday series of events relating to various aspects of lowrider and car culture in general. Some of the most popular outdoor activities at a car show include the car and truck *Hop and Dance* competition where vehicles compete in six events: Single and Double Pump Car Hop, Single Truck Hop, Radical Hop, Street Dance and Radical Dance. During these competitions held primarily outdoors a "switchman" activates and manipulates the hydraulic pumps on the competing vehicle remotely and from a safe distance while a song plays from massive speakers around the arena.

Not insignificantly, motion and a vehicles ability to move is written into the rules for large scale competitions. An inoperable vehicle can be displayed as part of the show but cannot compete for prizes. To assure and enforce this valorization of motion a minimum standard is set for vehicles to demonstrate that they are mobile (because of their value the lowriders in question are transported in covered trailers not driven to the car show) before the show officially opens to the public. A vehicle must be able to start under its own power with an operable battery permanently positioned in it. In addition to other maneuvering requirements, the "engines must be fueled by a fixed fuel tank and transmission... and they must demonstrate their ability to travel 20 feet of **continuous motion** (emphasis mine) ..." (Tatum, 2011, p. 177) for a cultural practice born of both the mural and Chicana/o rights movements this requirement seems to transcend into the realm of symbolic.

One particularly well-known competitor and award-winning truck is known as *Wicked Bed*. It was incorporated into a video instillation titled *Alien Toy (Unidentified Cruising Object)* as part of the *InSITE97*, a triennial public art event in San Diego and Tijuana. The video of *Wicked Bed* features it dancing out its moves, and cuts back and forth from them to images of unidentified flying objects, Mexican dancing marionettes and other assorted images. The movements on the video are the same that helped *Wicked Bed* win the Radical Class category in the *Hop and Dance* competition three years in a row (Chavoya, 2000, p. 43), there is a musium video of an actual competition held in 1997 as part of the *Lowrider Magazine Super Show* in Sacramento California that including footage of *Wicked Bed* in a gallery setting is ironic since the lowrider, with or without murals, grew out of an attempt on the part of Chicana/o artists to use the mural to "bypass the mainstream cultural 'gatekeepers' who dictated what aesthetic and artistic currents and themes were acceptable for consideration to be included in gallery and museum exhibits and collections." This absorption of the lowrider aesthetic into the controlled and mediated environment of a gallery complicates the continuity of Chicana/o tradition of using art to reclaim public places and encourage community participation on the part of individuals who may have received no formal artistic training (Tatum, 2011, p. 97).

Gangsters and Low Lives

Next to the Catholic and biblical iconography displayed in lowriding murals is the decidedly secular representations of *gangsterism* (Tatum, 2011, p. 103). Lowriders that compete in car shows often bear names that signal color as a marker of cultural pride as illustrated by "Brown Pride." The names range in theme, but the most common seem to reference colors and hues exemplified by names such as "Brown Sensation," "Aztec Gold," and "Crimson Envy." Calvo-Quirós has examined the use of color in lowrider car customization and in his unpublished dissertation theorizes a link between a low rider's "use, manipulation, and implementation of color as a visual/design element" and a lowrider's challenge, transgression and resistance to what he calls the "preconceived notions of space, aesthetic hegemony, and social disparity they experience" (Calvo, 2011, p. i). In one example of the way color signifies for and in the Chicana/o community Calvo-Quirós argues that Chicana/o color expression is inseparable from its spatial and historical context and so "by the use of aesthetics and color, a new place for distraction, cultural safety, and auto-academia among members" is created. (Calvo, 2011, p. 107) Lowrider competitions are one of the most recognized events in low riding and it is here that the exchange of aesthetic ideas and trends is made most visible. These shows also carry with them high stakes for the competing car clubs, and "skirmishes" between car club members sometimes occur (Chappell, 2012, p. 174). Bragging rights more than the cash prizes seem to be what car clubs prize most of all. Illustrating the fact that "The effects generated by low rider style [...] are not uniformly or necessarily positive and affirming. Lowrider significance describes the potential of a car to generate not only affinity but also alarm, or to provoke reaction" (Chappell, 2012, p. 20). Sometimes even within the low riding community.

Lowrider participants are keen to differentiate themselves from gang members in their activities and comportment. For example in various car competitions held at large car shows Lowriders make sure to have their automotive elements comply with a variety of policies and rules designed to foster order and even reverence, such rules include prohibiting "dented, damaged, unfinished, or incomplete vehicles from the indoor exhibit space". As well as "strict prohibition against displaying anything in or around a vehicle that the judges could consider obscene, profane, or that could be construed as a weapon [. . .]" (Tatum, 2011, p. 177). These rules seem to indicate that the lowriding community places a high value on dismantling the notion that low riding is a hobby for gangsters and thugs. These rules also illustrate the low riding community's understanding of the power they have to change both the appearance and meaning of their lowriders. As Chappell explains it in his *Neither Gangsters nor Santitos* (little saints) chapter "countering the stereotype of lowriding as a manifestation of gang culture was [and is] a priority for numerous car clubs" (Chappell, 2012, p. 170). This however is becoming an unmanageable task given that the lowrider has become synecdoche for urban gang life in mainstream media representations of Black and Brown everyday life.

Lowrider art, like the murals that inspired it, has from its birth been about seeking out, inviting and controlling an audience's gaze. The portable murals on lowrider hoods trunks and side panels share many elements with the murals found on walls in the streets of many major cities, but they seem to complicate even as they manifest the basic qualities inherent to a mural. Car murals alter not only a vehicle's signification but its functionality as well. For example, a mural found on a wall enjoys a fixity on which people rely to construct its meaning, an image of a crucified Indian fixed upon a wall for example, means differently when put on a portable postcard or a wall calendar. The scale or size of a mural on a wall is also large owing to its purpose of, or objective of, being seen by as many people as possible. In cruising the lowrider operates in much the same way. Though it increases its audience not by staying still as the audience drives by, but by driving by as the audience stays fixed. Bright states that "these cars bring pleasure from performing 'culture' disrupting boundaries and derailing expectations." (Abrams, 2000, p. 41). Indeed, a lowrider mural does not conform to fixity or scale but rather produces its meaning by extending both. Lowrider murals may have been the earliest manifestation of the mural being peeled off the wall and paraded about the city's urban streets, but it is not the only manifestation.

The artwork on the body of a classic car can signify and, in some cases, even narrate a story sometimes even when the design is abstract or devoid of recognizable symbols. By and through its three-dimensional layout the art-work on a lowrider invites and controls the audience's gaze more effectively than artwork on a wall can. The simple fact that an audience is compelled to orbit a vehicle to observe all of the elements of an artwork provides a more episodic consumption of an artwork than the typical omnipresent one. Unlike with a two-dimensional artwork, the artwork on a lowrider cannot be observed in its totality without mobility. An observer must engage kin-esthetically by orbiting around the lowrider or as is the case in some larger venues have the lowrider rotated for them on a rotating platform. Techniques to aid the audience in the consumption of a lowrider's artwork are many and range from the technologically complex platform discussed above to the low-tech technique of placing car length mirrors underneath the car so that the detailing under the vehicle may be witnessed as well. It is not uncommon to see lowriders exhibited with all their doors opened, and their trunk and hood popped. Little is hidden from the viewer when it comes to lowriders. *There ain't no shame in our game* is a phrase often uttered in the lowrider context. Perhaps this is why some of the images emblazoned on the bodies of these vehicles feature not only what Tatum has called "visual imagery for the wider community's civil rights struggles" (Tatum, 2011, p. 97) but more pop cul-turally influenced iconography that can feature cartoon characters such as the Teenage Mutant Ninja Turtles, Bart Simpson, and even the most politically incorrect Speedy Gonzalez.

By far the most visually represented images on lowriders have to do with the female form, often scantily clad and more often than not sugges-tively posed apparently for the audience's scopophilic enjoyment. The con-sequences of this sexualization of the lowrider by associating it with the eroticized female has been examined by Chappell who concludes that "it could be argued that when lowrider mural images draw on sexualized and objectified iconographies of the female body, they also conscript women to the role of pleasure providers for male subjects" (Chappell, 2012, p. 86). Women's role in lowriding has often been reduced to objectification but there are too many undertheorized examples where women have played an active part in cruising, car clubs and lowriding. In only a couple of examples from the 60s and 70s we have a group calling themselves the "Lady Bugs" who built an identity and reputation around the Volkswagen Beetle and another group in San Diego called "Ladies Pride" who was one of the first all-women car clubs. Other groups of women have also embraced this form of cultural expression and have carved out spaces for themselves in what has not only been a historically male dominated activity and practice, but a hostile one towards women (at least the fully clothed ones) as well.

These sexualized representations on cars however, tend to be eclipsed by the actual physical female bodies who pose and interact with audience members on and around the lowriders. Tatum states that it is "common to have women in tight, revealing two-piece outfits walk the floor of car shows, usually followed by a professional photographer" (Tatum, 2011, p. 105). A quintessential event at a large-scale car show involves a wet T-shirt contest. The winner is usually determined by crowd reaction, which incentivizes the contestant's expressive poses and provocative gyrations. Over the last 10 years, the low riding community has opted to deal with the accusation of female objectification by creating contests that objectify the male body. Large car shows now also feature *hard body competitions* in which men display their muscled and sculpted bodies to compete for prizes, interestingly however they are required to keep their clothes on while competing. The resonances with the *hard body* trucks and *muscle* cars that appear in the show room floor are worthy of a deeper analysis.

It is difficult to untangle the sexual objectification of women (and in recent years from the body in general) from lowriding. The fact that lowriders are often called *Pimpmobiles* by enthusiasts and that upgrading and modifying one's vehicle is also known as *pimping out* one's ride supports an argument of consubstantiality between lowriders and objectification of the sexes, but primarily of females. This reading however is incomplete, take for instance Chappell's point that "the connection signaled by the term 'pimped' lies in a common aesthetic of degraded opulence" (Chappell, 2012, p. 86) rather than a direct or actual relationship to the sex trade. Thus, in the case of the seemingly objectionable elements involved in lowrider culture need to be read in a broader context that accounts for the complex chain of signifiers that low riding produces.

The practice of comingling a lowrider's identity with his vehicle. As Chappell argues owners of lowriders are known as "lowriders" themselves, the word becoming an appellation for both man and machine. Chappell goes as far as to claim that "low rider owners become identified not only by their vehicles but as their vehicle" (Chappell, 2012, p. 15). If this is so then it would explain the patriotic feelings expressed by some low rider owners who emphasize the American-ness of their vehicles when confronted with the customization of foreign car models. As Roman, a lowrider from Austin TX. put it "I drive an American classic, not foreign plastic" (Chappell, 2012, p. 75). This low rider aficionado then sees himself as a *man of steel* which gives him a purchase on an all American identity however tenuous it may be. Scholar Brenda Jo Bright extends this idea to cover even the lowrider owner's geographical home, when writing about low rider vehicles and the way that they are "identified with their owners, and by extension, with both his 'home' turf and his cohort" (Bright, 1994, p. 101). It is this identification across geography, identity and cultures that give lowriding its most potent influence.

References

Avila, E. (2014). *The Folklore of the freeway: Race and revolt in the modernist city.* University of Minnesota Press.

Best, A. L. (2006). *Fast cars, cool rides: The accelerating world of youth and their cars.* New York University Press.

Broyles-Gonzalez, Y. (1994). *El teatro campesino: Theater in the Chicano movement.* University of Texas Press.

Chappell, B. (2012). *Lowrider space: Aesthetics and politics of Mexican American custom cars.* University of Texas Press.

Chavoya, C. O. (2000). Ruben Ortiz Torres: Style politics and hydraulic hijinx. In C. B. Jo (Ed.), *Customized: Art inspired by hot rods, low riders and American car culture* (pp. 41–47). Harry N. Abrams, Inc.

Chicano Park. (2018). http://www.chicanoparksandiego.com/index.html accessed on 12/29/18

Flink, J. J. (1975). *The car culture: Mass politics and the adoption of the automobile in Los Angeles, in the car and the city.* Massachusetts Institute of Technology Press.

Los Angeles Times (2012). *The return of 'America tropical.'* Retrieved from http://articles.latimes.com/2012/oct/09/opinion/la-ed-mural-siqueiros-los-angeles-20121009

Lopez-Calvo, I. (2011). *Latino Los Angeles in film and fiction: The cultural production of social anxiety.* The University of Arizona Press.

Pardo, M. S. (1998). *Mexican American women activists: Identity and resistance in two Los Angeles communities.* Temple University Press.

Tatum, C. M. (2001). *Chicano popular culture: que hable el pueblo.* The University of Arizona Press.

Tatum, C. M. (2011). *Lowriders in Chicano culture: From low to slow to show.* Greenwood.

12. Exploring San José's Lowrider Industries

Estella Inda, Kathryn Blackmer Reyes, and
Julia Curry Rodriguez

Introduction

San José, California home to 1.028 million people, is located 40 miles south
of San Francisco and 339 miles north of Los Angeles. Historically San José
is a place where Mexicans, *Californianos*, Mexican Americans, and Chicanos
have contributed to the growth of this pueblo. Indeed, it is a region where 1
in 4 people are foreign-born, but the native population can trace itself back
to the early establishment of the rich multi-racial and multi-national labor
force. Long before San José became known as Silicon Valley with the explo-
sion of the computer industry and the development of the internet, San José
was a rich agricultural community with orchards, fields, and canneries (Pitti,
2018). While symbolically San José was dubbed "the valley of heart's delight"
which provided much of the food-basket, it also provided its labor economic
opportunities to settle down, make communities, and develop a burgeoning
culture that would rise to significant proportions nourished by the relocation
of people from other parts of the United States and international labor force
migration. These people also developed a footprint of rich cultural traditions
that are significant in many ways.

This chapter focuses on one such cultural tradition that of lowrider culture. Specifically, the businesses that grew out of this genre. This economic
outgrowth contributed to lowrider culture and to the economic success of
the Chicano/Mexican-American community of San José. The chapter draws
from "Story & King: Lowrider Culture in San José" which was a jointly
curated exhibit by the San José Public Library's (SJPL) California Room
and San José State University (SJSU) Library's Africana, Asian American,
Chicano, and Native American Studies Center (AAACNA) of the Dr. Martin
Luther King, Jr. Library. The exhibit featured writers, artists, mechanics,

car owners, community members, car club members, and photographers, who provided a glimpse of how San José was central in defining lowrider community.

We examine three local businesses. Sonny Madrid's *Lowrider* magazine, Biney Ruiz's *Five Star Productions*, and Andy Douglas's, *Andy's Hydraulic*. These businesses demonstrate how San José forged its place in lowrider history to make an influential presence that has been overlooked by scholars and art critics in fundamental ways. The fact is that as San José became a national lowrider destination, it did so in large part because of the local lowrider culture and industry of visionary cultural entrepreneurs (Hansen & Cardenas, 1988).

Historical Context of San José

Even as San José thrived as a multi-ethnic community, power in the region rested in the hands of growers and the ancillary businesses that evolved in the region. Despite its diverse demographics, race relations reflected a dominant model of inequality. These relations in San José led to hostile exchanges by the dominant white power and the race/ethnic people in a variety of ways. For the purpose of this essay, two factors were of utmost importance, those are redlining that created segregated neighborhoods and the eventual displacement by gentrification as the city business model changed from agroindustry to techno industry. A predominant Mexican American community would be established through the relocation into what is now known as the East Side, often highlighted by the intersections of Story and King. Segregation and closer quarters, nevertheless created opportunities made by the people themselves which allowed them to thrive and flourish using their cultural and entrepreneurial agency.

The national civil rights movement was present in San José through Chicana/o community activism, tied to the Chicano Movement which demanded greater access to equity and inclusion specifically through equal education, civil rights, wealth, and access to fair wages and economic power. San José became an important area where the Chicano/Mexican American community had important social and political leaders such as Cesar Chavez, Ernesto Galarza, and the Community Service Organization (CSO) which provided unique opportunities by spotlighting the regional inequality, civil unrest including police brutality, disenfranchisement, and low investment in education and the neighborhoods of the segregated city (Méndez-Negrete, 2020). The social climate made evident the growing inequalities experienced by people of color, in particular the dominant Mexican American population.

The Mexican American/Chicano community grew in the East Side of San José, as did the boom of ethnic businesses in these neighborhoods. The community began to define the consumer, commercial, and economic needs and some savvy locals began to strategically satisfy those needs. Among the consumer desires of the East Side residents was the thriving artistic form that comes to be known as Chicana/o art. Some of this expression was found in the growing subculture of lowriders which found a thriving opportunity to meet the cultural consumer needs from the perspective of mechanics, artistic expression, and musical programming.

One cultural indicator of the role of lowriders is *cruzin* as a regular form of leisure, socializing and community-building through public engagement. Historical race relations shed light on another side to this story. While the community thrived in the invention of a homemade leisure culture, the social and political powers forged of strained relations resulting from Jim Crow, racial segregation and inequality evolved into legal ordinances which criminalized the community's activities. The political and economically dominant white community exercised its power and control over Chicanos, in particular the youth, primarily through police action (Flores & Benmayor, 1997). The community assertion of its culture and ingenious mechanical innovations, ushered in harsh regulations making lowriding a criminal act. "No Cruising" ordinances were introduced and enforced through posted signs around downtown San José and on the East Side to curb the public space use of this community-supported cultural form.

Lowrider *Magazine*

San José's *Lowrider* magazine came to be known as the defining publication for lowrider culture. Founded by Sonny Madrid in 1977, it was published in San José for the first five years until it was sold. In its heyday, the magazine helped to make San José a cruising capital attracting people from great distances to participate in the culture and the scene. The magazine featured a car highlighting the mechanical engineering that at the time was unheard of. Specifically, the use of hydraulics to *hop* or *dance the car*. Another feature was the defining artwork of the car. Moreover, the magazine also highlighted the aspect of lowrider culture which came to be seen as family-like celebrations with music and Mexican/Chicano culture at its center including the car club organizing practice.

The growing popularity of lowrider-themed events simultaneously created a vital element of the local economy. At its pinnacle, the cultural form contributed to the economic rise of the lowrider culture as an industry in San José.

Lowrider magazine as a publication was the first of its kind to focus on lowriders. It "was aimed at the heart and soul of the barrio" (Villarreal, 1993). *Lowrider*, was a publication that gained international renown. Yet, its humble beginnings are a man's vision of unity in the City of San José. The magazine provided an authentic look into the lowrider community. It featured articles of inspiration and acceptance written by local community members. The magazine provided images of the people, lowrider events, dedications, artwork, and calls to action addressing political issues facing the community. Madrid and associates created this periodical featuring what came to be known as the heart of the lowrider community. In doing so, they challenged the deficit, stereotypical images of people that experienced discrimination often labeled through criminalized terms such as gang members. The magazine created an appreciation for the people who were also classified as lowriders.

Originally, from Yuma, Arizona Madrid and his family moved to San José in the 1960s. Shortly afterwards he and some of his siblings were drawn and became active in the Chicano Civil Rights Movement. He was involved in the United Farm Workers of America (UFW), United People Arriba, the Community Alert Patrol (CAP), the SJSU Walkout, Fiesta de la Rosas Protest and Tierra Nuestra, among many other causes (Inda, 2019). While attending San José State University, Madrid participated in promoting dances and events on and off campus, leading him to form the event promoting group *Lowrider Associates*. Madrid enjoyed bringing people together, and he wanted to keep Chicanos informed about the injustices that faced their community. He was part of local Chicano/Mexican American publications such as *El Machete, Bronze, La Palabra, Trucha,* and *San Jo Community New*, where he conceived the idea of a Chicano magazine that drew on his love of custom cars with art, satire, fashion, and politics. The idea grew into *Lowrider* magazine, which hit the stands in January of 1977.

At the start of the magazine Madrid and associates attended all the lowrider events to promote their magazine through free distribution in order to create interest. *Homies* creator David Gonzales recalls "I can remember the crew from *Lowrider* cruising into town in a lowered '50 panel Chevy, distributing magazines at parties and along the boulevard from the back of the car" (Gonzales, 2016, p. 25). After the first couple of issues the popularity of the magazine grew beyond Madrid's wildest hopes. "Subscription grew from a few thousand magazines per month to over one hundred thousand" resulting in *Lowrider* facing difficulties keeping up with demand by the third issue (Villarreal, 1993). The magazine's success was in part the representation of the community in such an authentic and positive light. Everyone wanted to be in the know and be a part of such a fundamental project for change. After five years of building the magazine, the continued interest in the magazine's coverage encouraged Sonny Madrid to move it to the international market.

The magazine was supported by subscriptions, announcements, and advertisements related to the lowrider community. The magazine also included articles about the lowrider hairstyle and fashion, different entertainment including music and films, and special features that Madrid felt important in keeping with the unity theme of community. These features are what made *Lowrider* unique, it provided a positive outlook for a segment of the Chicano community. Other features included letters from readers and dedications made to members of the community, giving the community a place to celebrate and acknowledge milestones of pride. "Que Onda" featured the lowrider community. Whereas "Lowriders Pasados" featured images of the lowriders from the 1940s and 1950s. The magazine also published photographs from the lowrider car shows.

By promoting lowriders, the magazine also supported many of the local San José artists and art in the community. Featuring different cars and the custom work gave exposure to the artists. Other featured art forms were flyers by David Holland "Teen Angel" and comic strips done by *Homies* creator David Gonzales (who was also a former SJSU student).

True to his civic-minded commitments Madrid included articles intended as community awareness that addressed is such as gang violence, police brutality, community political issues, and getting out the vote features. *Lowrider* magazine promoted a positive image of lowriding, which also helped the popularity of the magazine to grow. As educator and author, Arturo Villarreal (1993) explains, "No periodical was covering Raza like *Lowrider* did" and people wanted to be a part of that any way they could. "This was the root of what would someday become the biggest selling automobile magazine in the world" (Gonzales, 2016, p. 25).

Andy's Hydraulics

A feature of the lowrider was its physical close the ground look. Initially, that look was accomplished through various methods of weighing down the cars using such things as weights or bags of cement. "Eventually, they would remove the springs or put clamps on the springs of their cars to lower them (Villarreal, 1993)." A second and most popular modification of the car was to make lowriders hop using hydraulics. In San José, Andy Douglas and his shop *Andy's Hydraulics* gained popularity among the lowrider community as one of the innovators of the hydraulics modifications that has become a central feature of these cars. Douglas, is said to be "...the man who was hitting back bumper and flipping cars over as far back as the 1970's" (Mendoza, 2010).

Douglas grew up in East San José, witnessing the lowrider scene and the different ways that cars were being altered. At a young age, his father introduced him to working on cars and restoring them. In 1972, one of Douglas's friends invited him to visit East Los Angeles to see what was happening with the cars in that community's lowrider scene. Andy learned there about hydraulic setups used to raise and lower lowriders. "Aircraft pumps were the norm for the first hydraulic set ups, but Douglas was about to embark on a journey far bigger than he ever imagined (Mendoza, 2010).

Douglas, at age 17, returned home with newly purchased aircraft hydraulics and began to explore by adding them to his restored Impala. But they did not work. After tinkering Douglas worked out that higher voltage was needed to get the hydraulics to work. He began to drive around with this innovation which garnered great interest by others who offered to purchase his car. Like Madrid, Douglas came upon a consumer desirable, and began his business of restoring, building and selling cars. In an interview with *Lowrider* magazine Douglas commented: "All of the first hydraulic work that I did was on the East Side of San José, only a couple of blocks from Story and King, at my parents' house on Gainesville Ave. That's also where *New Style car club* was started" (Mendoza, 2010). The *New Style car club* was founded by Douglas and some of his high school friends in 1973, but it did not officially become a part of the lowrider scene until 1974. It is, however, believed to be one of the first recorded car clubs in San José's lowrider history.

In 1975 Douglas opened up his own shop on 1st Street in San José, which happens to be "a groundbreaking moment in lowrider history" (Mendoza, 2010). *Andy's Hydraulics* would be the first shop of its kind, to meet the needs of lowrider owners in their hydraulic needs at one location. Douglas was constantly going to different suppliers to get what he needed for his work, which led him to create his own pump cylinders, which he called "D&H Red". Douglas's "innovation not only proved to be a more effective design, it also legitimized lowrider customization in the marketplace..." (Mendoza, 2010). This innovation made *Andy's Hydraulics* the foremost car shop in the San José lowrider community and later nationally.

Two years later with the publication of *Lowrider* magazine in 1977, lowriding got its biggest boost ever and the demand for customized hydraulic work would be a boon to *Andy's Hydraulics*. In almost every issue of *Lowrider* magazine featured *Andy's Hydraulics*. Moreover, every lowrider event that included customized cars in the hopping contests featured *Andy's Hydraulics*. *Andy's Hydraulics* experienced great success, especially after moving the headquarters back to the East Side of San José at Story and King. The location marked the expansion of *Andy's Hydraulics* extending throughout Northern California, Los Angeles, Phoenix, and El Paso, with eight locations in all. Douglas made hydraulics available to the masses, making it possible for a completely different type of customization that allowed lowriders to ride low and slow with a little hop. Douglas's mechanical genius applied to lowrider custom work gave him financial success and wealth, provided mechanical innovations, and led to his induction into the *Lowrider* Hall of Fame for Craftsmanship in 2010.

Five Star Productions- Biney Ruiz

According to author, Paige Penland, "In San José where the show scene began, 33 clubs, more than a dozen different lowrider businesses, and *Low Rider* magazine were all holding shows" (Penland, 2003, p. 92). As Mike Pickle of the *Duke's Northern California Car Club* boasted, "Nobody could organize, but people in San José could. It was just a different attitude" (Penland, 2003, p. 61).

A groundbreaking business was *Five Star Productions*, a promotions company, owned and operated by San José resident Biney Ruiz, a single mother of five. She is recognized as one of the first promoters to see the business opportunity that arose from the lowrider community's cultural events. She focused on the different events and the observation that none of them were organized, often leading to disruptions. She filled a niche organizing the first lowrider events held in San José. "Ruiz first organized benefit dances, and soon graduated to full scale lowrider happenings, with several different clubs and live entertainment" (Penland, 2003, p. 61). Biney Ruiz explained that she "started doing events that were called lowrider balls which were concerts and dances combined in 1973" (Villarreal, 1993).

In 1978 she saw another business opportunity finding that many of her events were music driven. In 1979, *Five Star Productions* produced and released the first lowrider record album featuring Mary Wells, "The Incredible Lowrider Ball Live". Using the local fairgrounds in San José, Ruiz organized popular live events featuring singers and bands along with car shows. She recorded many of these shows leading to the production of two LPs and a single. Like Madrid, Ruiz was concerned with the negative stereotypes and stigma that plagued the lowrider community. She organized food drives and toy drive caravans to benefit the community. Biney Ruiz was a one-woman force. She taught herself to be a fast industry- maker, in a male dominant industry. The last show that Ruiz promoted took place in 1989. In the present, she is known as a cathartic actor in the lowrider community.

The Power of Collaboration in San José's Lowrider Business Industry

Biney Ruiz's *Five Star Productions*, like *Andy's Hydraulics*, were part of the lowrider business industry that boomed in San José as the popularity of *Lowrider* magazine grew. The lowrider industry evolved into other businesses including shops that specialized in custom upholstery, painting, and hydraulics. However, ancillary businesses specializing in lowrider fashion, and promotional events are also part of the spinoff of this cultural form. Many of these businesses exited prior to *Lowrider* magazine, but they experienced their biggest boost with the magazine. The magazine served as publicity for these businesses exposing them to larger audiences than word of mouth and local events had in the past.

The multi-million dollar business of hydraulics, launched by *Andy's Hydraulics* included thirteen other hydraulic shops in San José. All of these businesses expanded as technology improved along with the lowrider industry as a whole. With the popularity of the lowrider scene in San José it became common for businesses to collaborate and promote each other, helping to keep the lowrider business industry strong and thriving.

One example of this collaboration is found in *Lowrider* promotion of events that were organized by different promoters and car clubs. *Lowrider* magazine provided promotion for multiple different businesses in their advertisements and by featuring lowriders with information about who owned them. Sometimes they also provided information about who did custom work. While other times *Lowrider* featured groundbreaking events such one that occurred at a Biney Ruiz's program where Andy Douglas and his brother Ralph performed the first ever lowrider flip. Douglas promoted his hydraulics, Ruiz promoted her car shows and hopping contests, and the events were featured in *Lowrider*. These collaborative efforts promoted the three businesses, the individuals, and led to greater entrepreneurial and financial success derived from the lowrider culture. "The business of lowriding proved to be incredibly successful and money spent customization, hydraulics, car shoes, and even Low Rider magazine was being reinvested in the community" and there was nothing like the San José's lowrider business industry to show the power of this investment (Penland, 2003, p. 61).

Cruising Through a No Cruise Zone

Lowrider cars and culture have often been maligned by mainstream culture and forces of social control. However, the people involved in Lowrider culture are innovative, artistic, and creative. They provide and make their inclusion in multiracial society such as the United States. Lowrider culture is part of American culture and it is also a site of the American Dream. San José's Story & King roads became synonymous with the cruising capital because of the imagination of the people of this community. The primary participants were Mexican American/Chicanos who were marginalized as racial/ethnic cultural groups. Yet, by examining the evolution of the culture and its contributions in San José we see that this culture revolved around agency, expression, and access to self-determination. San José's cruise scene became a point of pride for the lowrider community and came to reinforce the city's overall importance to the lowrider industry and community (Robinson, 1986).

As the San José lowrider cultural scene grew so did the negative implications for the lowrider community. This led to greater police presence, negative portrayals of Mexican Americans, but also the opportunity for some members of the Chicano community to showcase their skills as they created opportunities for themselves and their culture. The lowrider community shouldered restrictions on the cultural form of lowriders while actively avoiding the negative impact imposed on them by police, with political and social designation on the people and their culture. San José's lowrider community led to a hugely successful enterprise for many businesses, as illustrated in the three featured businesses in this essay. While the *Lowrider* magazine has left San José, changed its form and is no longer in the hands the original founder, the culture persists and continues to have important cultural impact beyond the city.

Lowrider magazine had a central role in providing the means for businesses, cultural gatherings, but most importantly, for the people it was a space that reflected their community and cultural practices in positive light. Madrid's vision of the magazine led to financial success, but also maintained a central role in creating a space where authentic reflections could be seen and contributed to by the multi-layered and complex participants in this important chapter of San José history. The impact of the lowrider industry includes numerous innovations that ought to be recognized in San José's economic, cultural, and social contributions beyond the Silicon Valley narrative. Lowrider culture remains prideful and multifaceted to this day. Additionally, lowrider culture has a place among the U.S. economic, entrepreneurial, and innovative contributions.

References

Flores, W. V., & Benmayor, R. (Eds.). (1997). *Latino cultural citizenship: Claiming identity, space, and rights*. Beacon Press.

Gonzales, D. (2016). *Homies: A David Gonzales retrospective*. Dynamite.

Hansen, N. M. & Cardenas, G. (1988). *Immigrant and native ethnic enterprises in Mexican American neighborhoods: Differing perceptions of Mexican immigrant workers*. IUP/SSRC New Directions for Latino Public Policy Research.

Inda, E. (2019, January 11). Sonny Madrid: Lowrider legend and more. *San José Public Library* . https://www.sjpl.org/blog/sonny-madrid-lowrider-legend-and-more

Mendoza, B. (2010, July 13). *Andy Douglas – Original: Craftsmanship Honoree*. Lowrider. https://www.lowrider.com/lifestyle/1008-lrmp-andy-douglas-original/

Méndez-Negrete, J. (2020). *Activist Leaders of San José: En Sus Propias Voces*. University of Arizona Press.

Penland, R. P. (2003). *Lowrider: History, pride, culture*. Motorbooks International, an imprint of MBI Publishing Company.

Pitti, S. J. (2018). *The devil in Silicon Valley: Northern California, race, and Mexican Americans*. Princeton University Press.

Robinson, B. (1986, October). Tough cruising penalties voted by San José Council. *San José Mercury News*, 29.

Villarreal, A. (1991). *Culture clash*. West Magazine.

Afterword

Luis Alvarez

In 1965, the East L.A. band Thee Midniters released their first studio single, "Whittier Blvd." An ode to the then-popular and now-iconic cruising spot for Chicana/o lowriders, the song was a smash hit across Los Angeles. It began with lead vocalist Little Willie G (for Garcia) shouting, "Let's take a trip own Whittier Boulevard!," followed by bandmate Ronnie Figueroa's *grito* of "arriba, arriba!" As Chicano deejay and music historian Ruben Molina observed, "That kind of sets it off and says, 'This is Mexicano!' But then, it goes into the surf guitars." Throughout the song, Molina continued, "You'll hear influences from surf music to rhythm and blues to Mexican music. It's basically what the Chicano is: We're a mixture of Mexican heritage but living in America. It kind of signified: We are here. This is who we are" (Del Barco, 2018). Years later, Willie G said much the same about "Whittier Blvd" and its lasting impact on Chicana/o and lowrider culture. "It gave us voice, you know, sort of like a rally cry for us to kind of assemble-right?" (Del Barco, 2018).

The success and longevity of "Whittier Blvd" was not an accident. The song captured the politics, power, and community feel of the lowrider scene. It exemplified the power of lowriders to be seen and heard in a society where young Chicanas/os were often expected to be invisible and silent. Their lowered cars, music, and style were mobile art exhibitions, pillars of community building, and a reclaiming of public streets and space rolled into one. By cruising and jamming together, lowriders showcased their cultural creativity for all to see and hear. Recalling how Thee Midniters crisscrossed L.A. for multiple gigs on a busy weekend night to perform "Whittier Blvd," Willie G emphasized the bands mobility and ingenuity. "We'd start off in San Bernardino, then go out to the San Fernando Valley, then down to Torrance and end up here in East Los Angeles at the Union Hall on a Saturday night.

We could set up Thee Midniters, an eight-piece band, in fifteen minutes and tear it down and be in the van in eight minutes." Reclaiming the streets and city as their own, Thee Midniters, like so many other Chicanas/os, embodied the lowrider sound, politics, and style.

Not unlike the soul, R & B,, rock 'n' roll rhythms of "Whittier Boulevard," or the ubiquitous 12-note hook of War's equally iconic cruising anthem, "Lowrider," the essays in this book evoke the *low y slow* vibe of lowrider culture, making it easy to imagine rolling down the boulevard in a lowered 1949 Chevy or '58 Ford with the stereo bumping! *The Lowrider Studies Reader* delivers powerful *testimonios*, analysis, and insights on the history, multi-dimensionality, and lived experience of lowriders. The chapters herein inspire and innovate. They push scholars to think critically about what lowriders can teach us all about race, ethnicity, identity, community, and culture. They encourage educators to explore how lowrider pedagogy can positively impact the classroom, counseling, and youth mentorship. They also compel anyone who might flip the preceding pages to learn more about lowriders, experience the scene, and open their minds to a wider world of Chicana/o culture and history. From a range of sightlines and perspectives, the authors deliver a sweeping and generative breakdown of lowriders, moving like a musical score from one chapter to the next.

Harkening the composition and improvisation so crucial to lowrider culture, the chapters in this book deliver their own refrains on Chicana/o identity and community. They highlight how lowriders foster a Chicana/o identity that speaks back to power and challenges alienation, discrimination, and societal odds that are often stacked against Chicanas/os. All of the authors herein, including Lea Lani Kinikini and Merlena Wolfgramm and Elizabeth Ramos, reveal a Chicana/o identity and experience that is multiple, transnational, and extends across racial and national borders. They point to the deceptively obvious point that not all Chicana/o folks are the same, that gender, sexuality, class, and generation splinter within Chicana/o communities. They gesture toward the inter-racial and multi-ethnic collaboration in lowrider culture that mirrors social movements and black-brown coalitions, including the tensions and conflict among them. Make no mistake. *The Lowrider Studies Reader* grounds the study of lowriders in community and the voices of people embedded in the scene. The preceding chapters show how lowriders were engaged in art-based community building. This is different and more profound than community-based art making and holds great promise for aggrieved populations to be heard and seen. The authors in this book, moreover, write as members of the community. They are educators, artists, activists, and lowriders themselves, illustrating the deeply human element in the production, consumption, and circulation of lowriders. Emphasizing the social relationships embedded in and around lowrider culture, they offer deep insight into the communal dimensions of lowriders, including its shared value system, epistemology, and ingenious critique of capital. Never uniform, the community vibe of lowriding reminds us that social relations are *always* at the core of art and culture, even when their politics may not always be liberating.

Another of the lessons offered in these pages is that the culture and politics of lowriders are harmonious, always intertwined and never separate. Virtually all of the chapters in this book, including those by Ben Chappell, David Escobar, and Guillermo Aviles-Rodriguez, highlight lowriding as contested cultural and political terrain upon which Chicana/o identity, community, and social movements take shape. They show us how lowriders circulate through channels of pop culture at the same time they create social change and belonging in the face of alienation and discrimination. Like stanzas or verses in a protest song, these chapters illustrate how lowriders were a mobile canvas for the art and politics of the Chicano Movement, Civil Rights, and struggles since. They also remind us that lowriders, like other subcultures, can be hijacked by corporate interests, bought, sold, and exploited for profit. Lowriders are not just reflective of politics, but are constitutive of them. Lowriders remind us that culture and politics are not discreet spheres of life, that political work is inherently cultural and cultural work is often political. As if spontaneously riffing with one another, the authors in this book show how lowriders speak back to power and hold potential for challenging the neglect and marginalization of Chicana/o communities.

With beats and breaks reminiscent of the best cruising jams, *The Lowrider Studies Reader* also underscores the multi-dimensionality of lowrider culture. Chapters by Daniel Osorio, Juan Roman-Medina, and others examine the cars, people, clubs, music, print culture, businesses, film, clothes, politics, and style that make up the scene. Each of these elements- and more- constitute lowrider culture. It is not just one thing and its many ingredients are ever-evolving. More than the sum of their parts, each component comes together with the others to create interlinked social, cultural, and political canvases for Chicanas/os to express themselves and share their stories. While these chapters remind us that lowrider culture often rested on commercialized leisure and was not always radical, they also illustrate how lowriding empowered folks to engage the world around them and try to change it for the better. The extraordinary imagination and creativity at the heart of lowrider culture is a reminder that we'd be lucky if lowriding was a dress rehearsal for what happens in other parts of our political and social lives.

Place and history also figure prominently throughout this book. The lowrider stories shared herein are embedded in local spots at the same time they trace the pulse and flow of lowrider culture across time and space. Essays by John Ulloa, Estella Inda, Kathryn Blackmer Reyes, and Julia Curry Rodriguez, and Martine Morales Ramirez, among the rest, firmly root lowriders as social and cultural fixtures in neighborhoods from East LA, Austin, San Jose, the Salinas Valley, and Hawaii to Japan, Brazil, Saudi Arabia, and beyond. As these authors emphasize, it matters where lowriders are created, cruise, and tell their stories. Lowriders claim space differently depending on the locale. They challenge gentrification, disrupt the school-to-prison pipeline, and build lowrider-centered institutions like newsletters, magazines, production companies, and hydraulic shops. Perhaps most importantly, the lowriders that populate the places and nodes on the global map of lowrider culture each have their own narratives to share. This book contains many of them worth reading and learning from. These places, people, and their stories make lowrider and Chicana/o history. They show the continuity of cultural and political struggle from the emergence of lowriders during World War II through the militancy and radicalism of the Chicano Movement to the present. Although not an exhaustive historical treatment, *The Lowrider Studies Reader* beautifully reveals the cultural imagination and political possibilities that sprouted amid postwar economic and political conditions in Mexican America. It offers an historical arc of lowriders and lowrider studies in which the ingenuity and power of lowriding is clear. And, as editors Guillermo Aviles-Rodriguez, William Calvo-Quiros, Anthony Nocella II, and Elizabeth Ramos underscore in their introduction, there is room for many more narratives and voices to join the chorus.

In true lowrider fashion, the contributions to this book reverberate far and wide. Chapters by Xris Macias, Dionocio Miguel Garcia, and others, for instance, convey the outline of an empowering lowrider pedagogy and methodology that is as applicable in the classroom as it is on the streets. Emphasizing the potency of lowrider and social justice storytelling, they chart lowrider culture as a popular education and social navigational tool that can animate educational and counseling settings. Drawing on the autonomy, pride, and creativity of broader lowrider culture, lowrider pedagogy connects with Chicana/o youth and helps bridge the different social and cultural worlds they inhabit. Like the best deejays, the authors of these chapters mix method, theory, and lived-experience in ways that are applicable to all walks of life. In the stories of lowriders lie the theory. It is not the other way around. This lends the narratives in this book a deep texture, one with multiple perspectives and orientations, an ethnographic feel, and in which the often-contradictory dimensions and challenges of everyday life are front and center.

The chapters in this book are also forward looking. One need not look far or listen long to find the notes and timbres of an abundant future for lowrider studies. New tracks are laid for making sense of the global and local, circulation and place-based, identity and community formation, multiracial and cross-ethnic, and cultural and political aspects of lowrider culture. Read together, the essays function like a "how to" lowrider studies manual for meditating on the historical, current, and future importance of lowriders. All with empathy and social justice at the core. *The Lowrider Studies Reader* paves the way for a future of lowrider studies that radiates in at least three directions, including the cross, intra, and trans. The cross demands we consider the myriad ways lowrider culture and Chicana/o folks engage other racialized communities and struggles. The trans requires we account for how lowriders and Chicana/o experiences traverse regional and national borders. The intra compels us to acknowledge how lowriders and Chicanas/os are diverse and ever-evolving as communities. In the skilled analysis of this book's contributors, the future of lowrider studies is bright. As it moves along these avenues and charts new territory, lowrider studies will animate and engage Chicana/o, Latina/o, and ethnic studies and help remind us all that a more equitable and just world is within reach. Importantly, lowrider studies underscores that, despite the challenges along the way, the journey to achieve such lofty goals is filled with culture, resistance, liberation, and *familia*.

This book is a melody of different voices, stories, and experiences of lowriding. It is about how ordinary folk do extraordinary things as they fight to make their lives and the worlds they live in better. We all have much to learn from lowriders, their cultural expression, and prioritizing of dignity, pride, and conviviality. When commenting on the song "Whittier Blvd" and lowrider culture, Bardo Martinez of the musical group Chicano Batman echoed this sentiment. He described the song and lowrider culture as the essence of Chicana/o culture and a statement to the world that "We own this street. The street is us. And this is- sometimes this is all we got" (Del Barco, 2018). *The Lowrider Studies Reader* takes us to the streets and *corazón* of lowrider culture. Let's enjoy the groove and the ride.

Reference

Del Barco, M. (2018). "The Story of 'Whittier Blvd.,' a Song and Place where Latino Youth Found Each Other." *All things considered; American anthem: Music that challenges, unites, and celebrates.* National Public Radio. Accessed, June 17, 2022, https://www.npr.org/transcripts/671688096.

Contributors' Biographies

Luis Alvarez is Professor and Chair of History at UC San Diego, where he has also served as Director of the Chicanx Latinx Studies Program, Associate Dean of Arts and Humanities, and inaugural Director of the Institute of Arts and Humanities. He is author of *The Power of the Zoot: Youth Culture and Resistance during World War II* (University of California Press) and co-editor of *Another University is Possible* (University Readers Press). His most recent book is Chicanx Utopias: Pop Culture and the Politics of the Possible (University of Texas Press). His work grows from belief that the arts and humanities equip us all with the analysis, imagination, and empathy to build a better world.

William A. Calvo-Quirós, Ph.D., is an Assistant professor of American Culture and Latinx Studies at the University of Michigan. He holds a doctorate in Chicana/o Studies from the University of California Santa Barbara (2015) and a doctorate from the Department of Architecture and Environmental Design at Arizona State University (2011). His book *Undocumented Saints: The Politics of Migrating Devotions* (Oxford University Press, 2022. investigates the relationship between state violence and religiosity along the U.S. – Mexico border region. His other areas of interest also include Lowriders, Chicana/o Mexican American aesthetics, design, and urban planning, Chicana feminist and decolonial methodologies. More about his research/teaching at www.barriology.com

Ben Chappell is an Associate Professor of American Studies at the University of Kansas, and the author of the ethnography *Lowrider Space: Aesthetics and Politics of Mexican American Custom Cars* (University of Texas Press, 2012).

His fieldwork with lowriders blended the anthropological approach to Texas Mexican folklore founded by Américo Paredes with cultural studies. The work was featured in the Lucasfilm short documentary *Anthropology: Looking at the Human Condition,* and has been profiled in outlets such as *The New York Times* online, *Vice, Choice,* Kansas City public radio, and urban anthropology textbooks. As a researcher, he was granted honorary membership in the Knights of Pleasure C.C., Austin, Texas. He has published additional articles on lowriding in collections such as the *Routledge Companion to Latina/o Popular Culture* and the *Oxford Online Bibliography in Latina/o Studies.* He has provided scholarly consultation to the Smithsonian Institution and the Urban Arts Society of Chicago, which hosts the Slow & Low Lowrider Festival in Pilsen. He founded and continues to convene the Ethnography Caucus of the American Studies Association, and has served as a Fulbright Guest Professor of American Studies in Germany. His other research includes an ethnography of Mexican American fastpitch softball between the Midwest and Texas, and an emerging critical university studies project on neoliberal knowledge production.

André Douglas pond cummings is Professor of Law at the University of Arkansas at Little Rock William H. Bowen School of Law where he teaches Business Organizations, Contracts I and II, Corporate Justice, Entertainment Law and Hip Hop & the American Constitution. Professor cummings has written extensively on issues regarding investor protection, racial and social justice, and sports and entertainment law, publishing three books including Hip Hop and the Law and over forty law review articles. cummings has been recognized as Professor of the Year on numerous occasions including the University-wide Distinguished Professor Award by the West Virginia University Foundation. cummings holds a J.D. from Howard University School of Law where he graduated *cum laude.*

David Escobar served as an Administrative Aide to former Fourth District Supervisor Steve Kinsey in Marin County for 15 years. After 21 years of service with the County of Marin, he retired early to take on the position for Center Point as Director of the Re-Entry Programs at San Quentin State Prison. As an adjunct professor, David has taught Indigenous Perspectives at Dominican University and Holy Names University. Escobar has been published in several publications including the Marin County Independent Journal, Nectar Magazine & others. David and his daughter Kila work in their spare time on a 1952 Chrysler lowrider.

Dionicio Garcia (S.S.F) is a lowrider, academic & career counselor, and educator at Skyline College and College of San Mateo. When Dionicio is not in the neighborhood Lowriding with his club brothers, Frisco's Finest Car Club, his scope of practice is predominantly working with first-generation Latinx youth in the *Puente* & *Los Hermanos* programs. In addition, Dionicio has co-developed and implemented a Men of Color program at College of San Mateo called *Brothers Empowering Brothers* focusing on reducing inequity for young men of color. He has also taught courses in *Life and Career Planning* and *College Success* through the lens of *Lowriding*. Dionicio holds a Bachelor's in Hospitality & Tourism Management and a Master's in Counseling, specializing in Career Counseling from San Francisco State University.

Selinda Guerrero, Afro-Latina Feminist, is the Albuquerque Coordinator for Save the Kids, a national all-volunteer organization building a movement to end the school-to-prison pipeline. She leads Millions for Prisoners, the New Mexico chapter, a national movement to abolish prisons and oppressive systems in the U.S. and beyond. Organizer for Justice for Jaquise Lewis ("Albuquerque's Trayvon Martin") continuing our fight for justice. She is a Black Lives Matter organizer with Building Power for Black New Mexico. She is a single mother of six with deep roots in New Mexico. She grew up in a gang environment consisting of violence and drug activity. As a teen mother and eighth grade pushout she became active and motivated to work for change by building networks of community alliances over the last twenty-five years.

Frank Hernandez serves as Dean of the College of Education at TCU. Prior to his work at TCU, Dr. Hernandez served as Associate Dean & The Harold and Annette Simmons Endowed Chair in Educational Policy and Leadership at the Simmons School of Education at Southern Methodist University. Dr. Hernandez' research work has focused on four areas of inquiry: Latinos and school leadership, Latino racial identity development, inclusive leadership for LGBTQ students, and leadership for social justice. He has published extensively on Latino leadership, including two books: *Abriendo Puertas, Cerrando Heridas (Opening Doors, Closing Wounds): Latinas/os Finding Work-Life Balance in Academia* (With Elizabeth Murakami and Gloria Rodriguez) and *Brown-Eyed Leaders of the Sun: A Portrait of Latina/o Educational Leaders* (with Elizabeth Murakami).

Estella Inda is the Research Services and Social Sciences Librarian for the San José State University (SJSU) King Library. Prior to that, Estella worked for the San José Public Library (SJPL) for over 18 years, and has most recently served as a library clerk in the California Room. Since 2018, Estella has facilitated the gathering of material to help fill historical informational gaps found in the library's collections. In December 2018, Estella organized and curated the library's latest major exhibit - "Story and King: San José's Lowrider Culture"- that ran until March 2019. In July 2022, Estella helped organize and curate the library's second largest major exhibit - "East Side Dreams: The Untold Story of East San José". Both exhibits put a spotlight on the different communities that have been historically overlooked. In December 2022, Estella was awarded a commendation from the City of San José for the work she has done for the community.

Lea Lani Kinikini, Ph.D., received her doctorate from University of Auckland, New Zealand, masters from University of Hawai'i, and bachelors from University of Utah. She is a researcher and educational practitioner who has worked internationally in Hawai'i, New Zealand, Oceania and now Salt Lake County. Her research has examined the school to prison to deportation pipeline with a focus on case law and Pacific Islander youth gangs. She has conceptualized how legal fictions are extrapolated both in the public sphere and in the legal realm to produce ranked or 'marked' populations underlined by racial classes. She currently is the Chief Diversity Officer at Salt Lake Community College working on building solutions to over-incarceration and is committed to creating equity through educational justice innovations.

Xris Macias has worked in leadership roles in academia for over 10 years, he has worked primarily with first-generation college students, undocumented students, and other students of mixed status. He now works in local municipal government. He has a master's degree in Education, Culture and Society from the University of Utah, where his research emphasis was on Lowriders being educational tools for marginalized communities. Xris regularly travels to facilitate and lead workshops on the history of Lowriders and chaired the inaugural "International Lowrider Studies Virtual Conference." Aside from research of this artform, he is also a Foreign Language and Area Studies (FLAS) fellow, with the focus area of Latin America, and is Co- Chair of the University of Utah's Chicana/o Scholarship Fund. He enjoys training Capoeira, and riding his bike. He is fluent in Spanish and conversational in Portuguese, and enjoys spending time with his two sons.

Juan Roman Medina originally grew up in Southern California and is a long-time resident of Sonoma County, California. Juan graduated from

Sonoma State University majoring in Chicano Latino Studies where his area of concentration was focused on lowriding culture. Juan is connected in the community through various channels. He is the founder and past President of the Sonoma Lowrider Council, a non-profit organization that embraces generational lowriding and also gives back to the community. For over ten years, Juan has hosted and produced his radio show, The Late Night Oldies with the local radio station KBBF where he plays oldies in both English and Spanish. Juan is an adjunct instructor at Santa Rosa Junior College in the Technology Trade school.

Anthony J. Nocella II, Ph.D., (they/he), lowrider, long-time intersectional total liberation scholar-activist, is an Associate Professor in the Department of Criminal Justice at Salt Lake Community College. He is the editor of the Peace Studies Journal, Transformative Justice Journal, and co-editor of five book series including Critical Animal Studies and Theory with Lexington Books and Hip Hop Studies and Activism with Peter Lang Publishing. He is the National Director of Save the Kids, President of the Salt Lake Chapter of DreamKeeperz Lowrider Club, and Executive Director of the Institute for Critical Animal Studies. He has published over one-hundred book chapters or articles and forty books. He has been interviewed by New York Times, Washington Post, Houston Chronicles, Fresno Bee, Fox, CBS, CNN, C-SPAN, and Los Angeles Times.

Daniel Osorio born and raised in East San Jose, is an award-winning Director/Producer of various films/music videos and is a graduate of Santa Clara University with a B.A. in Communication. "Lowriding in Aztlan", a lowrider film documentary, achieved huge independent success as the film garnered much praise and eventually was formally distributed nationwide by Code Black Films (a division of Lions Gate). Daniel's mission with all of his film projects is to encourage people from diverse, low-income backgrounds to strive for success, inspire creativity and promote education through film entertainment, mentorship programs, and community service.

Martín Morales Ramírez, born and raised in the Salinas Valley, is a survivor of the streets of Greenfield, CA, a small rural town in South Monterey County. The son of campesin@s Guadalupe Morales and Luís Ramírez, Martín's passion for working with students and educators derives from working in the fields as a youth and adult. This experience shaped his outlook on life and drive to support others like him that have the *ganas* to pursue their dreams by seeking a formal education. Martín believes that providing equitable, critical and antiracist educational experiences for students via cour-age's educators is key to making societal change.

Elizabeth G. Ramos is a resident of San Diego County. She has a bachelor's in both Psychology and Accounting and a master's in Clinical-Community Psychology. She is currently working on her Ph.D. in Clinical Psychology. She has worked in the mental health field since 1998. She has worked with indi-viduals of all ages and backgrounds: in group-homes, schools, clinics, com-munity mental health agencies, for the Aging and Independence Services hotline, outpatient forensic programs, inpatient psychiatry, and outpatient psychiatry/psychology services. She has been part of several Latino commu-nity organizations that focus on bridging resources and help identify/meet the needs of local communities.

Kathryn Blackmer Reyes is the Director and Librarian of the *Africana, Asian America, Chicano, and Native American Studies Center* in SJSU King Library. Since 1997 Kathryn has been a librarian that has worked primarily with the Chicana/o/x/Latina/o/x university communities. In 2007 when arriving at SJSU she has overseen the growth, development, and program-ming of this collaborative space and its collections. Kathryn has been work-ing on creating digital collections on the Acequias with Prof. Devon Peña, *El Excéntrico* magazine with Mr. Bert Garcia, WEB DuBois collection from Ghana with Prof. Michael Cheers, personal papers of the late Prof. Jose Villa, and a collection of the U.S. race/ethnic student voices on campus.

Guillermo Aviles-Rodriguez, Ph.D., is an Assistant Professor in the Theatre Arts department at the University of California, San Bernardino. His articles include: "Theatre and Transit: A Transit-Oriented Site-Specific Triptych" in Theatre Forum; "Darning Zoot Suit for the Next Generation" in Aztlan; "Ethics and Site-Based Theatre: A Curated Discussion" in Theatre History Studies; and "Playing Hopscotch on Dangerous Ground: Site-Based, Transit-Oriented Opera in Los Angeles" in the Cambridge Opera Journal. He is also the 2021 co-winner of the Lowrider Studies Scholar-Activist of the Year Award, and a 2021 and 2022 participant in the Mellon School for Theater & Performance Research at Harvard university.

Julia Curry Rodríguez, Ph.D., is Professor of Chicana and Chicano Studies at San José State University. She earned her Ph.D. in Sociology from the University of Texas at Austin. Some of her publications are found in Mothers, Mothering and Motherhood Across Cultural Differences, 2014,

Equity & Excellence in Education, 2012, "the riddle of AMERICA: Essays Exploring North America's Native Expression Spirit," 2012, and Chicana Studies, Volume 1, 2010. Dr. Curry has received many awards including: the 2019 CSU Wang Family Excellence Award for Outstanding Faculty Service, the SJSU *Distinguished Service Award,* 2013–2014, Outstanding Mentor and Leadership Advocate from the Student Advocates for Higher Education, 2010, *Top 10 Educators—Most Influential Latina/os of Silicon Valley,* the Mexican American Community Service Agency (2007), and *Outstanding Female Faculty*-San José State University Associated Students Hall of Excellence (2002). Dr. Curry can be reached at Julia.Curry@sjsu.edu.

John Ulloa is a major voice in the forthcoming documentary "The Great American Lowrider Tradition," and he has been a guest on numerous podcasts, including "Anthro for the Homies." His research examines the global diffusion of lowriding culture from the Mexican-American barrios to various countries outside of the United States including Japan, Brazil, Australia, New Zealand, Guam, Saudi Arabia, France, Germany, Russia, Sweden, Denmark, and Thailand. He is a member of Low Creations Car Club, and he has owned six lowriders, his current work in progress is a 1973 Buick Riviera.

Marlena Wolfgramm is a doctorate student in the Joint Doctoral Program in Education at San Diego State University and Claremont Graduate University. She earned a B.A. in Psychobiology at UC Santa Cruz and M.A. in Education at Mills college. She taught secondary science in Oakland for a decade before becoming a Senior Research Analyst with Dr. Herrera-Villarreal, where she examines the experiences of underrepresented students in STEM which is related to her research on the navigation of Pacific Islanders in STEM. Her interests also include higher education, critical race theory, Oceania and Pacific Islander experiences.

Lowrider Studies

Anthony J. Nocella II, William A. Calvo-Quirós,
and Elizabeth Gaeta Ramos
Series Editors

The new and globally emerging field of lowrider studies co-founded in 2020 by Anthony J. Nocella II, coming out of the lowrider culture, is grounded in Cholo/a, Latinx, and Chicanx culture and studies, while promoting social justice and intersectionality. The lowrider culture was founded in 1940s in California by youth. Taking an interdisciplinary approach to questions of social change, moral progress, ethnicity, race, justice, culture, social problems, economics, politics, and equity, the Lowrider Studies series will connect with a broad range of disciplines such as feminism, globalization, ethnic studies, cultural studies, economics, science, history, environmental studies, media studies, political science, sociology, religion, anthropology, philosophy, and cultural studies.

This book series will prove to be a leading project in the field of lowrider studies and move the field forward in new and creative ways. It is geared around social action, advocacy, and activism, while other book series are more rooted in theory and apolitical analysis.

Against apolitical scholarship, lowrider studies a subfield of Cholo/a, Latinx, and Chicanx argues for an engaged critical praxis that promotes the listening and defending space and place for marginalized and silenced voices to be heard.

To receive more information, please contact:

editorial@peterlang.com

To order books, please contact our Customer Service Department:

peterlang@presswarehouse.com (within the U.S.)
orders@peterlang.com (outside the U.S.)

Visit our website at www.peterlang.com.

www.ingramcontent.com/pod-product-compliance
Lightning Source LLC
Chambersburg PA
CBHW071413290326
41932CB00047B/2814